A SPECIAL KIND OF EVIL
The Colonial Parkway Serial Killings

Blaine L. Pardoe
Victoria R. Hester

WildBluePress.com

Some names and identifying details have been changed to protect the privacy of individuals.

A Special Kind of Evil published by:
WILDBLUE PRESS
P.O. Box 102440
Denver, Colorado 80250

WILDBLUE PRESS is registered at the U.S. Patent and Trademark Offices.
ISBN 978-1-942266-99-0   Trade Paperback
ISBN 978-1-947290-04-4   eBook

Interior Formatting/Book Cover Design by Elijah Toten www.totencreative.com

DEDICATION:

To Cathy, Becky, Robin, David, Keith,
Missy, Annamaria, and Daniel ...

CONTENTS

ACKNOWLEDGEMENTS:

When you read a true crime book you want the traditional end—the trial, the justice. This isn't that kind of book. This is the story of a series of cold cases that remain open to this day. We are going to provide you with the facts and details. We will put you, the reader, in the role of investigators. We will give you the facts we have been able to gather, and hopefully one of you possesses the kernel of knowledge that can bring these cases to closure. As a fellow true crime author and award-winning documentary film producer David Schock told us once, "Somebody out there *always* knows something." We are counting on you to help bring justice to these victims.

As authors we tried to contact as many of the people involved with this case as possible to interview them—including persons of interest or outright suspects. Many were more than willing to help. A few, however were not. We have used their names as matter of record—the reporting of fact. In no way are we implying their guilt or innocence. To date, no one has been charged in any of these murders and all suspects or persons of interest are innocent until proven guilty.

Throughout the book we refer to the killer as the "murderer" and "killer." That does not imply that it was one person acting alone that committed these crimes. This was done to avoid putting "murder(s)" or "killer(s)" in every reference, making for a cumbersome read.

The FBI and Virginia State Police refused our Freedom of Information Act (FOIA) requests to clarify open questions or review even the initial crime scene reports. One would hope they did this because they were ready to move forward on one or more of these cases—especially after thirty years.

This forced us to rely on a wider range of sources.

We leveraged quotes from newspapers of the period. In many cases these were pulled from clipping files from a number of libraries around the country. Often these clipping files were incomplete in terms of identifying the source newspaper, date, or page. Trying to track down all of those sources would have taken longer than the research for the book itself. Our use of these quotes in no amount diminishes the dedicated hard work of the authors that prepared them at the time. We have tried to reference the sources in the text, where appropriate, without turning this into a heavily footnoted textbook. Our longer quotes or extractions we did footnote.

In writing this book we sent out over 125 letters requesting interviews; filed nineteen FOIAs, interviewed dozens of people, transcribed countless hours of conversations, and made over a dozen trips to the Tidewater area for meetings and to walk the crime scenes. We have endeavored to be accurate in our accounts. With the passage of thirty years, memories fade and some mistakes are bound to have been made. We apologize for those in advance.

A number of people assisted us in the research and writing of this book. We would like to thank (in no particular order):

- Jean Armstrong, our ally who did a great deal of research for us behind the scenes. Jean was tireless, often frustrated, encouraging, and always a delight to work with.
- Chief Danny Plott, Colonial Beach Police Department, former investigator for the Virginia State Police—whose help on this project was invaluable. Like most, Danny wants these cases resolved and has never given up. His guidance and memoires were a fantastic source. In a case where many in law enforcement turned us down, Danny treated us like family.
- Irwin "IB" Wells, FBI, who kindly allowed me into his

home for a wonderful afternoon and made me regret the choices I have made in terms of my career. IB was beyond courteous and a wonderful instructor for us to learn how the FBI works.

- Joe "Wolfie" Wolfinger, FBI
- Sheriff James "Doc" Lyons, Northumberland County, former investigator for the Virginia State Police
- Major Ron Montgomery, York-Poquoson Sheriff's Office
- Charlie Phelps, former sheriff, Isle of Wight. One of our last interviews, and one of our more interesting and insightful.
- Mike Mather, former reporter for WTKR
- David Moffitt, former superintendent, Colonial Parkway National Park
- Kym A. Hall, superintendent, Colonial Parkway National Park
- Dwight Woodward, adult services librarian I, Williamsburg Regional Library
- Mary Molineux, research librarian, Earl Gregg Swem Library, College of William and Mary
- Troy Valos, Sargeant Memorial Collection, Slover Memorial Library, Norfolk, Virginia
- Bekki Morris and Wayne Russel, *The Amelia Bulletin Monitor*
- Susan R. Barber, electronic resources coordinator, Paul and Rosemary Trible Library, Christopher Newport University
- Kira Thompson, local history and reference librarian, Poughkeepsie Public Library District
- Don Welsh, head of research, Swem Library, liaison to Philosophy & Religious Studies, William and Mary Libraries, College of William and Mary
- Amy Pfenning, dispatch supervisor, William and Mary Police Department
- Phil Smith, policy analyst, regulatory coordinator, and Freedom of Information officer, Virginia Department of

Game and Inland Fisheries
- Major Susan Galvin, Support Service Bureau, Williamsburg Police Department
- Kyrstin Shackelford, administrative assistant III, Gloucester County Sheriff's Office
- Kimberly Rapien, Gwinnett County (Georgia) Sherriff's Department
- Commander Karen Richman, JAGC, United State Navy NCIS
- Jillian Wagner, information services specialist II, Newport News Public Library
- Captain T. West, Administrative Services Division, York-Poquoson Sheriff's Office
- Sarah Fearing, West Point & King William County reporter, *Tidewater Review*
- Adam Minakowski, special collections and reference librarian, Nimitz Library, United States Naval Academy
- Jennifer Gratto, M.Ed, librarian, Huntington Middle School
- Sarah Mullins, Roanoke County Circuit Court Clerk's Office
- Corey Chuyka, records manager, Roanoke County Police Department
- Lieutenant Dennis Ivey Jr., community and media relations, York-Poquoson Sheriff's Office
- Jim Gerencser, archives and special collections, Dickinson College
- Charis Wilson, PhD, CRM, NPS FOIA officer
- Angenette D. Pase, FOIA coordinator, Hampton Police Department
- Gina Griffeth, administrative assistant, Gibsonville Police Department
- Commander Karen Richman, JAGC, USN, NCIS
- Daniel B. Wilson, Office of Legal Affairs, Virginia State Police
- Deputy Paul W. Nash, Administrative Services Division,

Isle of Wight County Sheriff's Office
- Mike Holtzclaw, *The Daily Press*
- The staff of the Culpeper County Library
- The research staff at the US National Archives
- Ryan Zimbelman for creating our maps
- Kristin Dilley
- Deb Hill
- Bonnie Dodson
- Ginny Dowski Minarik
- Jeanette Santiago
- Joanne Hailey
- Judy Knobling
- Karl Knobling
- Larry McCann
- Joyce Call-Canada
- Doug Call
- Lou Call
- Lynne Jordan
- Michael Knobling
- Mike Mather
- Paula Meehan
- Rosanna Phelps Martin Sedivy
- Tara Cook
- Teri Hailey
- Will Phelps
- Bill Thomas—without whom this book would probably have never happened. Bill tolerated weekly phone calls, constant nagging, and encouraged us every step of the way. Bill made all of the introductions to the family members for us and helped us keep the material relevant. He was a good guiding hand through this year-plus journey.

Three books were very helpful to us as well:
- *The Colonial Parkway* by Frances Watson Clark, Arcadia Publishing

- *Serial Murders, Multi-Disciplinary Perspectives for Investigators*, FBI
- *The Case of the Indian Trader: Billy Malone and the National Park Service Investigation at Hubbell Trading Post*, by Paul Berkowitz, University of New Mexico Press

THE KEY INDIVIDUALS
REFERENCED IN THIS BOOK

A. J. Turner – FBI agent

Annamaria Phelps – victim in the fourth pair of murders

Barbara Call – mother of Keith Call

Bill Thomas – brother of Cathleen Thomas

Bonnie Dodson – mother of Robin Edwards

Brian Pettinger – murder victim in the Tidewater area

Cathleen "Cathy" Thomas – victim in the first pair of murders

Clyde Yee – park ranger

Daniel Lauer – victim in the fourth pair of murders

Danny Plott – special agent, Virginia State Police

Darrell David Rice – suspect in some of the Route 29 Stalker cases and the murders of Julie Williams and Laura "Lollie" Winans

David Moffitt – supervisor of the Colonial Parkway Park

Deb Hill – friend of Cathleen Thomas and sister of Lynne Jordan

Doug Owlsey – doctor and division head of physical anthropology at the Smithsonian's National Museum of Natural History

Fred Atwell – suspect who shared the crime scene photographs with news media

Ginny Dowski Minarik – sister-in-law of Rebecca

Dowski

Henry Lauer – father of Daniel Lauer

Irvin B. Wells III – special agent in charge, FBI, Norfolk Office

J. C. Cross – FBI agent

J. Robert Jasinowski – Virginia State Police

Jack Thomas – brother of Cathleen Thomas

Jacquelin Dowski – mother of Rebecca Dowski

James "Doc" Lyons – Virginia State Police

Jeanette Santiago – sister of Robin Edwards

Jewel Phelps – mother of Annamaria Phelps

Joanne Hailey – mother of Cassandra Hailey

Joe Godsey – rode with Daniel Lauer and Annamaria Phelps the night of their disappearance; possible person of interest in the case

Joe Wolfinger – assistant special agent in charge on the Call-Hailey case for the FBI

John Mabry – FBI agent

John Morse – private investigator

Jolene Schira – friend of Cathleen Thomas

Judy Knobling – mother of David Knobling

Julian Dowski – father of Rebecca Dowski

Julie Williams – murder victim in the Shenandoah National Park

Karen Miller – friend of Cathleen Thomas

Karl Knobling – adoptive father of David Knobling

Larry McCann – Virginia State Police, founder of the Behavior Science Unit

Laura "Lollie" Winans – murder victim in the

Shenandoah National Park

Laura Ann Powell – murder victim in the Tidewater area

Lou Call – aunt of Keith Call

Lynne Jordan – friend of Cathleen Thomas and sister of Deb Hill

Margie Lauer – mother of Daniel Lauer

Michael Knobling – brother of David Knobling

Mike Mather – reporter who broke the story on the crime scene photographs

Patricia Cornwell – author of *All that Remains*

Paula Meehan – sister of Cassandra Hailey

Rebecca "Becky" Dowski – victim in the first pair of murders

Richard Call – father of Keith Call

Richard Thomas – brother of Cathleen Thomas

Robert Dowski – brother of Rebecca Dowski

Robert Edwards – father of Robin Edwards

Robert Meadows – FBI agent

Ron Little – private investigator in the Tidewater area that named himself as a suspect in the Call-Hailey murders

Ron Montgomery – major in the York County Sheriff's Department

Rosanna Phelps Martin Sedivy – sister of Annamaria Phelps

Samual "Sammy" Rieder – suspect in the murder of David Knobling and Robin Edwards

Steve Blackmon – former law enforcement officer in the Tidewater area implicated as a person of interest in the cases

Steven Spingola – private investigator

Tara Cook – David Knobling's girlfriend

Teri Hailey – sister of Cassandra Hailey

Tom Stanley – Virginia State Police

Wallace "Wally" Neprash – chief park ranger

Will Phelps – brother of Annamaria Phelps

William Phelps Sr. – father of Annamaria Phelps

INTRODUCTION:

Jack the Ripper stabbed and disemboweled five victims, throwing London into a state of turmoil for weeks and carving himself out a piece of history that has lasted for over a century. The Son of Sam stabbed, shot, and killed six victims wounding seven, panicking millions in New York City over a scalding hot summer. The "Mad Butcher" Ed Gein killed two women and became the basis for the book and film *Psycho* and the *Texas Chainsaw Massacre* film franchise. The fictional Buffalo Bill from the *Silence of the Lambs* film murdered and skinned five victims before Jodie Foster's wily FBI agent character killed him. His character terrifies viewers to this day.

Yet with the Colonial Parkway Murders, with eight victims, there is no panic, little public uproar, no turmoil, no heroes swooping in at the last minute, and no survivors of the killer. People often say nature always perseveres over time, and that may be the case with these senseless deaths. In these cases it is as if the large pines and oaks and the chaotic waters of the Tidewater region muffle the outcries of terror, seeking to subdue the horrors and smother the outcries of anguish of the surviving family members. It is either nature or the simple fact that people don't want to deal with the concept that anywhere from one to eight murderers killed randomly in their community and got away with it.

The string of crimes dubbed the Colonial Parkway Murders is Virginia's oldest and largest serial killing spree. To this day, the deaths and disappearances remain unsolved … unsolved but not forgotten. With the thirtieth anniversary of the first murder in 2016, the stories of what happened starting in the autumn of 1986 have come back to the surface, like a recurring nightmare that demands some sort of resolution

The names of the victims were joined, by the press and in our own minds, a form of mental organization. Murders that happen in pairs do that with the victims, and in some ways it diminishes who they were. Cathy Thomas and Rebecca Dowski became "Thomas-Dowski" … as did all of the victims: Edwards-Knobling, Call-Hailey, and Lauer-Phelps. It is odd because in the majority of these cases the only thing they shared was the death they both experienced. As authors we have made a conscious effort to tell their stories individually. It is one aspect of control we don't want their killer to have—the forced conjoining of their names.

When you talk to the family members about those they've lost, their conversation almost always drifts to the nights of the crimes. That's what the mainstream media goes to—it is their default set of questions. "Tell us what happened …" For the family members it is the same horror story they have told dozens of times on film or for print. It is almost a safe zone for them when talking about the losses of their loved ones. They've told their story of those sleepless and horrible nights so many times that the emotions are easy to control when retelling it anew. It is something they can almost do by rote.

It's when you ask them questions they don't get asked often about the victims and their memories that the emotions surge to the forefront. These are the stories they don't get to tell often. The fragments of memories, some fading in detail, about their loved ones. There are some laughs, but more often than not there are tears.

Underpinning it all is a burning frustration. How could someone kidnap and murder eight young people so many years ago and get away with it? Many are weary of trying to kindle the fires of hope. They have had so many possible leads dry up and wither, blown to the four winds. The anger is there—some at law enforcement, some untargeted—

because the true target of their exasperation, the killer or killers, remains nameless and faceless.

As you talk to the family members you feel small, insignificant. The problems that you face pale to the ordeal and nightmare they have been dragged through. No words can comfort or offer even a shred of support. As tempting as it is to say, "We'll try and solve this," you know you can't.

That isn't our job. We're here to tell the stories. We're mere authors.

When you talk to the former investigators who worked the cases that make up this string of murders, they all say a variant of the same theme: "I want this case solved." This is followed with their feelings of these cases as the killer that "got away with murder." Few things gnaw at the minds of investigators as much as the thought of a murderer or murderers getting away with such heinous crimes. Even those that have gone into retirement have a burning desire for justice—a justice that has been denied up to this point.

These murders are staggering in their brutality and scope. The full magnitude of the crimes doesn't hit you until you look at the crime scene photos … the sheer horror of these vicious acts. Even the few images that are available are icons of terror. You look at the mortal remains of the six recovered victims and you are hit with the scale of evil that had to have perpetrated the crimes. A part of you is drawn in by the images as you search for some minute detail that the authorities might have overlooked. It is a futile effort, but you are compelled to try because you have spoken with the families and felt their anguish. Try as you might to focus on the background or details, you cannot ignore the dead in the pictures. They have demands that must be answered. They remind you of the awesome responsibility you are taking on. They force you to write the words—to tell the world who they were and that their lives mattered.

Some crimes speak to you as a true crime author. They whisper in the darkness of night in your ear. They come to you as you peruse old newspaper accounts and forgotten police reports. It's the voices of the victims … not tormented but wanting, desiring something … something they are unable to articulate at first. The voices tug at your consciousness, nagging you, compelling action, demanding words to tell their story. They confront your sleep abruptly with dark thoughts, frustrations, evil deeds, and murder. They jolt you awake in a cold sweat. At other times the voices are like a siren's song, luring you in, making you try to go back to that time, that place—where terror and death reigned. The voices force tears and anguish in your private moments. They drive you forward to do the one thing we can do, to tell their story in written words. Cold cases shriek the loudest to you in the night because they remain unsolved.

True crime authors become obsessed with every tiny little detail. We spend every free moment reading and re-reading every article, replaying interviews, immersing ourselves in the cases. The crimes and people involved become a preoccupation, a dark fixation that gnaws at you at inopportune times. The research is not just photographs and reams of words, at its core it is about human beings.

If you don't write true crime books, the compulsion and immersion is hard to comprehend.

As a writer you are coaxed through time and space in those moments you are alone, standing there in mute observation of horrific events, trying to piece them together, desperate to find order in the chaos. Unseen hands guide your own as you sift through the mountains of paper. The distant blurred voices don't just want peace; they want justice. They want the world to know that the sum of their lives was not tied to that moment of their demise. They are much more than victims. They are brothers, sisters, aunts, uncles, dear friends, coworkers, and the children of families that have had them torn away unjustly and viciously.

Such is the case of the Colonial Parkway Murderer's victims.

The word "victim" is misused in these cases. This remains Virginia's oldest unsolved string of serial murders, but the victims were more than those that disappeared or lost their lives. These crimes consumed families and individuals, friends and lovers, and left an indelible mark on the communities where they occurred. The predator who stalked four couples and ended their lives scarred many others beyond those that were killed.

Far too often people are portrayed in cold stark facts in the mainstream media. If you look at these murders the facts alone are seductive. This investigation for us has it all. Eight murders, six bodies, three men and five women, all targeted in pairs. Two of the young victims have yet to be found. The crimes took place in a relatively small region—all connected with the victims' cars. Two of the vehicles abandoned on the historic national park—the Colonial Parkway—which gave the collective crimes the moniker of the Colonial Parkway Murders. To us that didn't seem fair to the victims that were not involved with the parkway at all. It by no means diminishes those victims that were not tied to that stretch of winding concrete between Jamestown and Yorktown, Virginia. Then again, nothing is fair about these crimes and what happened to the victims. For them, time stopped at the moment of their demise—frozen in time.

The cold harsh facts are simple, perhaps the only simple things about this series of murders:

- Cathy Thomas and Rebecca Dowski were murdered in October 1986. Cathy's car was found on the historic Colonial Parkway between Williamsburg and Yorktown, Virginia. Both had been strangled and their throats cut. The car had been pushed off the pull-off into the York River, and someone had doused it with diesel fuel and tried to set it on fire then tried to set it adrift in the river.
- On September 20, 1987, David Knobling's truck was found at the Ragged Island Refuge some twenty-two miles away from point-to-point. He had been on a late-

night rendezvous with young Robin Edwards. The truck door was open and the radio playing. Their bodies were found three days later along the James River. Knobling had been shot in the shoulder, apparently attempting to flee his killer. Both were shot through the back of the head execution style.

- Keith Call and Cassandra Hailey were on a first date on April 9, 1988. They went to a movie then to a local college party and never returned. Call's abandoned car was found on the Colonial Parkway in early April 1988. To date, their remains have not been found.
- Annamaria Phelps and Daniel Lauer were heading back to the apartment that Annamaria shared with Daniel's brother Clinton in Virginia Beach. Lauer's Chevy Nova was found on the westbound rest area of Interstate 64, the opposite direction it should have been heading. Six weeks later their remains were found a mile from where the car was abandoned. This was the last of the murders—Labor Day weekend, 1989.

Then, as mysterious as the crimes started—they stopped. The killer slid into the shadows. That didn't make the fear go away. The communities touched by this waited nervously for the murderer to start again. It was a sword hanging over their heads, a constant threat.

The facts don't tell their stories. The raw data doesn't reveal much. You have to dig deeper. You have to wade through the National Park Service's wall of silence on the matter. You have to track down family members and friends and try and reconstruct the lives of these victims. You have to struggle through decades of people who had forgotten that the crimes remain unsolved. A spider web of myths, rumors, scoundrels, speculation, conjecture, and emotional pain can wear you down if you let it. As authors and researchers, you have to rise above it all.

We did. And now these stories can finally be told. But

before we make the trip to the 1980s, we have to start near the end of it all, with how all of these seemingly disjointed cases are drawn together into a tapestry of terror.

What is most disturbing is the contrast between the horrible crimes that took place and the serene beauty of region that they occurred in. A bit of it is the public nature of where the crimes took place—along a busy interstate highway, next to a heavily-travelled bridge, and along a national park road that has 3.1 million visitors a year. The mix of serene splendor and brutality can be hard for the mind to process.

The Virginia peninsula is in the heart of the Tidewater region. It is a slender strip of lush fertile land bordered by the James River to the south and the York River to the north. The peninsula ends at the state capital, Richmond. Along the James River, the first English colony, Jamestown was founded. Williamsburg, the original capital of the state, is nestled between the two rivers. At Yorktown, near the southern edge of the peninsula, was where George Washington and our French allies forced the British to end the War of Independence. During the Civil War, Maj. Gen. George B. McClellan launched a vast Union Army to the gates of Richmond, only to be repulsed by Robert E. Lee during the Battles of the Seven Days. Those battles prolonged the Civil War for years and cemented the reputation of Lee as one of the great American generals.

The big cities are Williamsburg—home to more pancake restaurants than any city should have and the College of William and Mary. Newport News and Hampton, at the southern tip where the rivers merge into the vast opening of the Chesapeake Bay and the Atlantic Ocean beyond, are a hub of shipping on the East Coast. Newport News is the kind of city where on one block you have pristine, quaint homes and the next street you have seedier rundown homes. Like most small cities, there are contrasts between those that have and those that do not.

With the revitalization of Williamsburg into a tourist destination in the 1930s, one of the biggest commodities that the peninsula exports is history—the history of Virginia and the United States. The Jamestown Settlement, the plantations along the James River, and the quaintness of Yorktown all are enough to make the most jaded historian salivate. The opening of the Busch Gardens amusement park in 1975 brought even more jobs and more tourists to the area.

Running down the core of the peninsula is I-64. This highway cuts through a tunnel of tall trees and is the primary highway for those in the Washington, DC, and Northern Virginia area to reach Norfolk and Virginia Beach across the bay. On any warm summer Friday the narrow two-lane highway southbound is packed with those who are drawn to the beaches beyond the peninsula. On Sunday, the two lanes heading back to the west and north are clogged with those same families who begrudgingly are leaving their vacations behind them and heading home.

The people that live in the Tidewater region are often tied to the military—there are numerous bases in the area—or have been native to this land for decades if not centuries. The peninsula has seen its share of war, strife, life, and glory. Some are watermen—fishermen—many are farmers, and others work in the Newport News shipyards building the US Navy's warships. The people of the peninsula are hardworking and proud.

The roads of the region are lined with tall pines, oaks, and elms—standing like mute sentinels over the winding roads. Sounds are muffled by the overgrowth and the stately trees. Yet it is here, in this almost pastoral setting where these horrible murders took place. At twilight, they cast long dark shadows—and in those shadows there are secrets. There are four places where, if the trees could speak, they would speak of murder, death, and horror.

It is tempting to begin the story there, with the crimes, at the scenes of the tragedies. That would be the wrong approach though. These crimes are complex, held together in a spider web of coincidences, similarities, and speculation. You then want to jump in with the stories of the victims, but that has to be done in the right context. You have to understand the big picture of these crimes first. It is the best way to digest something this complex.

No, you cannot start in the Tidewater or on the shores of the peninsula. To start this journey you have to begin in the most unlikely of places, near the end, in the small community of Orange, Virginia ...

PROLOGUE – BY BLAINE PARDOE

Every book has those "ah ha!" moments as an author where you get revelations about the crime, insights about the killer, that change your perspective. Ours came in Orange, Virginia, on a searing hot, sticky-humid July night. There's hot—then there's Virginia in a heat wave hot. No matter how much you crank up the AC in my Toyota pickup, you can still feel that slickness on your back as the setting sun gets in those last few moments of punishing warmth.

Orange is a far cry from the Tidewater region and is one of those little towns that are off the main track in Virginia—good farming communities, quaint and quiet. We met at the Silk Mill Restaurant, a converted old silk factory from World War II which made parachutes for the war effort. Our choices were limited to the Mill, the Sheetz gas station, or Hardee's—given that the library closed early that night. Fortunately the Silk Mill is awash in Southern charm, deep old wooden floors, booming echoes, and the walls were covered with antiques right off the show *American Pickers*.

A "biker gang" shuffled in before we were seated—the gang being sixteen or so senior-citizen couples whose wives wore pink Harley-Davidson T-shirts and the men wore white beards and sported pot bellies. This was more of a church outing than a biker gang. I doubted that any of the bikes had been driven more than 45 mph in years.

It was an odd place to discuss Virginia's longest standing serial murder case.

We had debated the crimes and their web of connections the entire trip down. We're the only father-daughter duo writing true crime, and we love to challenge each other when working on a book. We make each other better writers, and this is something we share that is unique and exciting and thought-provoking. My mother feels differently, chiding me, "You're getting your daughter involved in *another* cold case? Are you sure that is a good idea?"

"Thanks, Mom. I'm glad you are worried about me too."

"You're fifty-three. She's my granddaughter. It's different."

Indeed it is.

The Colonial Parkway Murders have plenty for the two of us to discuss: eight murders over a four-year period. These victims didn't have enemies—with the exception of three of them, they were teenagers. The majority of them did not have a chance to live out their lives, achieve their dreams, carve out a place in the world.

Victoria was frustrated by the crimes and with good reason. "I just don't see it. I don't see how they are connected. We're missing something. Maybe there's some physical evidence the police have been holding back?"

Her questions were more than valid. In reading the 200-plus articles we had accumulated on the murders, the authorities had flip-flopped numerous times as to whether the cases were related or not. If it was confusing to us, I could not imagine how it was to the victims' families or the communities where the crimes took place. Everyone had a theory, which added to our confusion. Were we investigating four pairs of separate murders—or a serial killer?

"That's why we're here. Larry can help us."

We were meeting with Larry McCann—one of the first people to see the connections to these cases. Larry agreed to meet with us under one condition. "I'll only talk to you if your work helps bring these cases to closure."

It had taken only a little digging on the internet to find Larry. He was impressive. He literally wrote the book *Crime Scene Investigation* as a member of a task force for the Department of Justice. In some respects, I was worried we were in over our heads. Victoria didn't say it out loud either, but I knew she felt the same.

I didn't overpromise him.

"We're storytellers. We want to tell the stories of the victims—their lives, their personalities. We'll tell the stories of the crimes too. We won't solve the case. We will get it out for a broad audience. Our cold case books generate tips which are passed onto the authorities—and I am confident that this book will too."

It was a no-bullshit answer—one that seemed to satisfy Larry.

Larry McCann and his wife, Barbara, come in, and at first glance he is warm and almost grandfatherly. He's struggling with some health issues, walking with some assistance. Since leaving the Virginia State Police he has been working as a violent crimes consultant in the public sector. We learned long ago that there is no such thing as "former officers."

As we take our seats in the back bar area of the Silk Mill, the grandfatherly veneer fades slightly. What emerges is the detective—the investigator. Despite the years he has been away from the crimes, they still dog him—you can see that in his eyes. Larry is still working the case in his mind—you can see it in every fine wrinkle of his face. When he talks about his work, there is a glow about him. It's not pride or ego, it's that dedication that most officers possess. None of them like leaving a case unresolved. For Larry, there are eight that still tug at him.

Larry McCann didn't want to be a police officer.

"When I was in high school in the mid-sixties, I wanted to be a guy that fired those rockets. I was going into astrophysics. I was going to a little college in the Shenandoah called Bridgewater, and it just wasn't quite working out. Barbara and I met there, and we were dating. In my senior year, a recruiter came on campus from the Arlington Police Department in Northern Virginia, he came around and I thought, 'I can do that until I find a real job.'"

His wife, Barbara, flashes a smile of warm memory as her husband talks.

Larry transferred into the Virginia State Police. He graduated at the top of his class and got his choice of assignments. Because his wife wanted to go to dental school, he took a posting in Richmond. Larry worked there for several years and was on the verge of transferring back to the Valley when he was offered an opportunity to report directly to the governor.

After that he transferred to the newly formed Bureau of Criminal Investigations in 1980. A former FBI agent had established the bureau, so it was modeled after the FBI, right down to the forms they used.

"Murder, mayhem, sex, and violence ... and all along the way I kept thinking, 'When am I going to find a real job?' Actually though, it proved to be kind of neat. As such I told my boss I would never turn down any educational opportunities. Then I got an invitation in 1987 to go to the FBI Academy for a year to work with the Behavioral Science Unit."

For a year he shuttled across the state; leaving Sunday night, returning on Wednesday night to see Barbara and their kids, then returning early Thursday morning, only to drag home on Friday evening.

What Larry learned was psychological profiling back when it was in its infancy.

"Now it has a slicker name, criminal investigative analysis."

McCann likes to think of his lifelong learning as gaining tools in his toolbox. Training in crime scene investigations—that was a tool for him to use. Training in any subject simply added another tool for him to use day-to-day. The difference with criminal investigative analysis for Larry was one of perspective. Criminal investigative analysis was an entirely unique toolbox on its own. It had a suite of skills and competencies that were tools in and of themselves. He came to the realization one evening that the Virginia State Police needed its own criminal profiling unit. Larry finally had found the one thing that he wanted to do.

As he speaks about it, his coy smile sweeps across his face—the only hint of his pride he dares show us.

McCann understood how politics worked. So he dropped hints with the FBI first, married to the concept that Virginia needed this kind of unit. He shopped the idea around with other Virginia State Police (VSP) who were at the FBI Academy as well. The FBI called his superiors in the VSP. By the time he made his pitch, all of the proverbial ducks were in a row. The State Police Behavior Science Unit had been born—with Larry at the helm—January 1, 1989.

Larry walks us through some of the techniques they used. After a few minutes we have learned more than I could have imagined about mental health and how that factors into criminal behaviors. Class is in session at the Silk Mill, and we are eager students. In the back of our minds though is the Colonial Parkway Murders. How did all of this fit together? Little did we realize that Larry had planned on taking us on a journey with him, back in time, back to the crime scenes, back to the nights of the murders.

"So Larry, how did you get involved with the Colonial Parkway Murders? Are they really connected?" I finally queue up.

Larry's eyes pull me in as he responds.

"We looked at eighty some cases in the Norfolk area. We are able to say these six, at the time, look *very* similar. And it was the first six. I don't even have their names any more. I do remember that it was the first meeting of the state police and all of the agencies involved in the investigation looking at eighty or so homicides. It was somewhere down the Virginia Beach area. I'm pretty sure the FBI was there … probably the Park Police.

"How weird is that? I don't know what the current investigators are thinking. Back in those days I thought they were related. If you take the eighty cases or so from which we pulled the first three couples, how many of them had the same characteristics? I think most of the rest of them, while they were unsolved, they were pretty cut and dry, or they weren't couples, or they weren't having pretty obvious motives. We looked at the first three sets and again, for our reasoning, these are related."

Larry weaves his thinking for us—drawing us to lean across the table just an inch or two more.

"They were couples, [pairs] alone, no obvious motives. They were in a relatively small geographic area too. That's the big connections. Statistically they stand out."

"You're an expert profiler—what can you tell us about the killers?"

"The person that did this … it was way too much control for one offender. It was *two* offenders. Now realize, this is my theory, this theory has been out there for thirty years and we still haven't solved it. My theory is that it is two people."

I offer a challenge to that.

"You don't hear about couples being murdered often other than Zodiac—I mean how do you keep them from running off in two different directions?"

Larry offers his counterpoint with the eloquence that only a polished professional can.

"But they didn't. There was too much control exhibited at all of the scenes. So you've got two offenders. Now what happens if you've got two alpha males that decide, 'It's Saturday night, instead of sitting here at the Silk Mill—hey what do you want to do Blaine?' 'Well, I wanna do this … what do you want to do Larry?' 'I want to do this, kill all these people.' 'No, no, here's what we're going to do …' So sitting up at the bar the two alpha males arguing about what you are going to do. Nothing happens because they argue. So those are two leaders and they are arguing and nothing happens.

"How about you have two followers and they're sitting at the bar. 'Hey Blaine, what do you want to do? 'I don't know.' 'Hey Larry, what do you want to do?' 'I don't know.'

It goes back and forth and nothing happens. So if you have two leaders or two followers, nothing happens. You have to have a leader and a follower. NOW something can happen. So—a leader and a follower … that's what you have to have to kill two people."

"Are they men?" Victoria probes.

"Oh yes," Larry says with confidence.

"It seems to me that these killers did a lot of planning. If you look at the Thomas-Dowski case for example. There's rope, a knife, diesel fuel."

"Or they got better. 'Next time let's bring a gun.'"

His reference to the second pair of murders, Edwards-Knobling, is clear, both were killed by gunshots to the back of the head, execution style.

Larry turns his attention back to the murder of Catherine Thomas and Rebecca Dowski, the first pair of murders.

"If it was diesel fuel or kerosene [used to try and burn the victim's car], the offender had to have brought that with them. You're not going to leave the scene, go shopping, and come back with fuel—and you're going to come back with gasoline if you come back with anything. That's where the Waterman Theories came from. That this was some kind of fisherman/waterman that had this fuel, a can of this fuel, in his truck—that's where those theories came from. Do you drive around with diesel fuel?"

"No—I think the diesel fuel was a mistake," I respond.

"Yeah, but it was all they had. If they had gasoline, they would have used that, because you know what is going to happen with gasoline. If you pour diesel fuel or kerosene … well, they thought it would ignite but it didn't."

Victoria weighs in, "That tells me this is someone that is not prepared. Maybe not having common sense."

Larry smiles in response.

"They had it with them—that was the key. They had it with them for a different reason than emulating a couple of homicides. They had it with them because that's what they fueled their boat with, that's what they, um, had a kerosene heater at home. They did not bring that fuel to burn anybody. They just had it with them. That's the key to them. There's no [big] trucks allowed on the parkway so it couldn't have been a large truck, even smaller than a tractor trailer. It might have been a pickup truck. They had that fuel, or the other side is that they siphoned the fuel from their diesel pickup truck thinking, 'Okay, the truck burns it; I'll throw a match in it and see what happens here.'"

"Was there any significance to the Cathy Thomas nearly being decapitated by the killers?"

I have to ask the question, but there is a part of me that doesn't want to know.

"She probably fought. That is something that you do from behind. You don't do that from the front. It's much harder to do a subtotal decapitation from the front."

Barbara, Larry's wife, relays to us how he would practice various means of killing victims on her.

"I can't tell you the number of times he's 'killed' me over the years."

I shift to the murders at Ragged Island, of David Knobling and Robin Edwards. They had not been strangled or cut like the first two crimes. These murders were gunshots to the head—though David was also shot in the shoulder. I ask Larry how he thought it had occurred based on his memories of the case.

"Sadly, you want to think she was shot first. So he's trying to get away. Being a gallant man, he should have stayed with her. Once she's dead, 'I've got nothing to lose, I'm out of here!' No one knows if he's a gallant guy or a chicken. Once she's dead, there's no reason for him to be around. So he might have gotten away from the second person, they winged him, he went down, and they finished him."

For Larry—it's a guess, one formulated by the evidence of the shot in his back. The truth is there are a half-dozen scenarios that can be drawn as to David's last actions. As with all of the cases, the experts perform educated guesswork to arrive at plausible scenarios which may or may not be right.

The third crime we don't talk much about—the disappearance and deaths of Keith Call and Cassandra Hailey. Their car was found on the Colonial Parkway just a short distance from where the killer tried to dispose of the bodies of Rebecca Dowski and Cathy Thomas. The car and much of their clothing was found, but not the victims themselves.

The last two murders were of Annamaria Phelps and Daniel Lauer. Their car had been found at a westbound rest area on I-64. Six weeks later hunters located their bodies under an electric blanket only a mile or so from where their car had been found.

"I processed Lauer-Phelps. ... I processed their car. We have nothing that ties them to the eastbound rest area. Their bodies are down at the next exit. Just a mile, maybe two miles, away. Their car is in the westbound area, parked at the far west ramp. I processed that car. That trail was just a little—I don't know what it was—it went up this hill, it wasn't a big deal. They were down there, and the hunters found them. It was over a month before they found their corpses," he says with a hint of remorse

"One thing I used to do that I don't think anyone else does, I would measure from the front edge of the seat the brake pedal. Just so that I would always have something that ... well, I could always put the seat back to where we found it. I remember a case in this series of cases where the seat was moved back—I don't remember which one.[1] All of those measurements I took, nothing ever came of it. We wanted to memorialize where this seat was. I know I did it on the Lauer-Phelps car. If you have a chance to look at the photographs, you'll see I took an exorbitant number of photographs starting with the outside. There's a real process

[1]   This was the case in Cathy Thomas's car. The seat had been adjusted for someone with somewhat longer legs or height.

for taking photos at a crime scene.

"On the driver's window, this window, the driver's, there's a roach clip there with a bunch of feathers that's hanging there. The feathers are hanging on the outside. That's a taunt. That's a taunt to the police. ... They think things through, and that may be why it's only every year because it's so well thought out and everything has to be just right. So the two guys are out there, they're ready to do it, but it's not perfect so they wait and wait, and finally after a year, okay, it's perfect, bingo, we got a couple. The eastbound area, that's where the offenders had to take control of them. They had to drive them to a body dump a mile away."

I had heard that the skulls of the victims were not with the bodies. Larry rebutts that firmly.

"They were all there. I remember that. I remember on the bodies, the skeletal remains, I think there were some cuts. Nicks on them. I remember thinking, 'Wow, these people didn't have any fillings. They must have been well to do.'"

Barbara McCann weighs in, clearly having seen some of the images herself.

"Well, if they didn't have a lot of money, they may have had decay and not had them filled. If the bodies were decomposed, if you had decay, that would be decomposed too."

It's time to turn back to the killer.

"Larry," I push further, "I have found reports that someone was pulling over people, pretending to be a police officer during that period. Could this have been our killer?"

"That would be the way to at least look in the car and see if the right victims are in there. That would be a good way to follow somebody, to see if this possibly could work—stop them, 'Yeah, this works,' and gain control over them. If they're parked, this is a good way to gain control of them quickly. If they're not parked and you're stopping a car, that can be pretty dangerous because who's to say there's not a policeman going the other way and 'I don't recognize that guy,' then you're up the creek. If they're already stopped it is a good way to gain quick control and they're not expecting an assault that way. They think they're going to be talked to or given a ticket or something. They would have their window down, and it would be easy with a knife or gun to gain their control. They put their windows down because they think you're a cop."

Victoria asks the real question, the one that has been nagging us since we began looking into this case: "Why do you think this case has been unsolved so long?"

Clearly Larry has been waiting for this query, most likely because it nags at him as well. "That's a good question. There's just a handful of cases in my experience that I thought, 'You know, we have enough evidence—physical evidence, behavioral evidence—we ought to be able to solve those.' This is one of those series of cases that—well ... we could have. So, what happens? Did they go somewhere else? Did they go to prison? What's the deal here? In VICAP, [Violent Criminal Apprehension Program] I'm sure you know about VICAP, back in those days I searched. Nothing like this occurred anywhere in the world up until the time I retired in '99. There was never anything like this—anywhere.

"So why did they stop? You have a leader and a follower, and the follower is the weaker person and maybe the leader got tired of him and killed him. So now you have a leader, a guy who wanted to do a death—so why didn't the leader get a new follower? Well people that run in these circles, these dangerous circles, they get killed every Saturday night. So maybe the leader got killed. Or he's in jail. He did not move. They either go to prison, get killed, or move. Well, they didn't move because nothing like this ever turned up anywhere. So he's either in prison or dead."

Larry leans back in his seat.

"I'm looking for two people. But nobody has been arrested for thirty years. Maybe I've got people barking up the wrong tree. But that's the thing about profiling—I give you my profile of your unknown offender but I tell you, don't pretend that this is gospel. If you're out and you get somebody who doesn't fit this at all, run with it. This could be totally wrong, usually not, but it could be. So everybody that is given that profile is given that lecture. Here's who I think it is but if you find somebody else through somebody rolling up on them, or some physical evidence, don't worry about the profile—*go with the evidence*. If you don't have any evidence, well then, look at the profile and lay that over your suspect pool and you can lay that against everybody in the world and see what pops out."

THE FIRST

Cathleen Marion Thomas and Rebecca Ann Dowski
Last seen October 9, 1986
Bodies Recovered October 12, 1986

CHAPTER 1

In many respects, Cathy Thomas was the kind of person that you would expect a movie to have been made about her life if it had not been so tragically cut short. Her brief life was one of defiant struggle, groundbreaking pioneering, and an almost idyllic upbringing, but it ended with tragedy. Cathy shattered many accepted norms of 1980s society. By almost any standard, she would have served as a role model for many people had she not been denied her life.

Her father, Frederic Thomas, was a true-blue navy man. He went by Joe to avoid confusion with his father whom he shared a first name with. He was a graduate of the US Naval Academy, class of 1953, and a certified navy diver and explosives ordnance disposal expert, one of the most dangerous roles for a navy officer. Joe Thomas was married to Evelyn McNeice Thomas, a registered nurse. Both of her parents came from Massachusetts mill towns along the Merrimack River: Joe from Lowell and Evelyn from Lawrence. Cathy's parents gave her a strong Irish-Catholic upbringing.

Cathleen Marion Thomas was born on July 21, 1959, in Albuquerque, New Mexico—a seemingly out of the ordinary place for a daughter of a distinguished navy officer to be born. The reality was that her father was stationed there at Los Alamos to study atomic weapons. During the peak of the Cold War such weapons were occasionally lost at sea—three had been lost by the time she was born. The salvage of these dangerous and highly sought after bombs was a reality that the navy was dealing with.

Cathy had three older brothers: Bill, Richard, and Jack. She was the youngest in the family—her parents had been hoping and trying to have a girl and Cathy was their last and gloriously successful attempt.

Her early life was that of a military child, adapting with move and change. Every two years her father would get reassigned. Frederick would sit down the family sometime in the late spring and say, "I've got my new orders." Where many children might cringe at the thought of uprooting their lives, the Thomases embraced the change ... in fact, they seemed to thrive on it. They would go to the library (in those pre-internet days) and research where they were going to move to. For them, it was an adventure, an opportunity.

By the time she reached high school her father retired from the service, returning to Lowell, Massachusetts, and his roots. Her father became a professor and eventual dean of School of Business at the University of Lowell (now the University of Massachusetts at Lowell). He was a deeply respected member of the community, recognized on the street by former students, and his family was part of the positive image that people had of him.

Lowell is often labelled as the birthplace of the American industrial revolution. With ample water power thanks to the Merrimack River, it became a burgeoning hub of the textile industry. The red brick textile mills harkened to an age of growth and national prosperity. By the 1970s, booms and busts over the decades had taken their toll on the community. The old, now abandoned factories were bulldozed in favor of public housing projects or smaller businesses. Unemployment more than anything in the 1970s dominated the attention of the small working-class community. Lowell's population was declining as it quietly shifted more and more to being a footnote in American history. There was a sense of pride in the dinginess of Lowell in that era, a memory of what had once been. Those that remained in the city were resolute and resilient people, defying the spreading urban decay that consumed so many cities of the era.

Some of that can-do attitude came from how they were raised. Life in the Thomas household was almost something that could have been cast in a Frank Capra or George Stevens movie. Cathy, a fiery redhead, easily could have been played by a young Katherine Hepburn in the film of Cathy's life. As her brother Bill fondly recalls, "We, both the kids and parents, were expected to keep up on current affairs—reading the Boston newspapers. The affairs of the day were something we had to be ready to discuss."

Dinner was something that was more than a meal, it was something that the family was expected to prepare for. Topics of the day were actively discussed and debated. Cathy could hold her own—that's for sure. "Cathy had a razor wit," according to her brother, though that did not give her an upper hand in the family discussions. If someone got too big for his or her britches, he or she would be taken down a peg or two by the other members of the family. The message was pretty clear: Don't be arrogant.

The family took advantage of the East Coast, vacationing at Seabrook Beach in New Hampshire. Cathy's father would rent a house so that the family could kick back and relax. The Thomases were a tight clan. Some of that was due to their constant movement in their early years; family remained the one constant. Another was their deep-seated Irish Catholic roots. They were a family that had each other's backs.

Even in a tight-knit family every child is closer to one parent than another. With Cathy, her greatest bond was with her mother. She inherited her auburn red hair from her mother and had brilliant blue eyes, a potent combination. That bond became even more important to her as she started her senior year of high school. Her brothers, who had been so integral in her life were all off to college—her brother Richard had graduated her father's alma mater, the Naval Academy, and was continuing his career in the service. For her that last year of school was a lonely time.

The fiery-haired Thomas was green before green was a thing, but that was a pattern in her life—always one step ahead of the rest of the world. As her brother Bill remembers,

"She was very environmentally conscious. Cathy despised hunting. She owned a shirt that said, 'Support Your Right to Arm Bears.'"

Cathy was a stellar student in high school. She was not boy-obsessed like many of her peers. She did date, and a lot of boys asked Cathy out. According to Bill Thomas, "In some respects she was ambivalent to them asking to go out." Her focus was elsewhere.

She enjoyed sports, not just the competition but pushing herself physically and mentally. Cathy decided to take on the shot put. Most people taking on that sport were large, with strong upper body strength. While she had never thrown a shot before, she was undeterred and practiced it until she became good at it. It was that personal drive that was a cornerstone to her personality.

In late 1975, President Gerald Ford signed a bill which included a mandate providing for the United States' military academies to begin admitting women in the following year. One might think that having a father and a brother who both graduated from the academy that Cathy might have been pressured to apply. That wasn't the case.

"Frankly she surprised the family when she said she wanted to attend the Naval Academy," said her brother Bill. "Richard in particular tried to make it clear that the Naval Academy was not going to be a welcoming place for women. Although he had graduated from Annapolis in 1975 and had gone on to Georgetown Medical School, he knew that the navy was going to be extremely tough for Cathy and her classmates."

Cathy was admitted to the USNA in 1977, the second class to allow female midshipmen.

Plebe summer, where the new inductees begin their military indoctrination, is grueling for most students and especially for the early pioneering women who were the first female students at the academy. Cathy's long red hair was cut short. It was a hot summer, and the upper classmen put them through a level of hazing that would not be tolerated by today's standards, especially the females who were seen as invaders on their historically male-dominated turf. By Cathy's own words: "It was brutal." Verbal abuse tinged with sexual references was not uncommon.

The US Naval Academy was struggling with the forced integration of females. In many respects, it is understandable and forgivable at the time. Only through the prism of time looking back does it seem trite that the revered institution would struggle with integrating women. The pristine campus in Annapolis, Maryland, was steeped in history. Every bench, every table, every chair was either dedicated to a gallant officer or a ship or a graduating class. While it was primarily an engineering school, the soul of the Naval Academy was its history and that history did not include females. The male-centric attitude was so dominant that the graduating class of 1979 had given itself the motto "All Male" to distinguish itself from those classes that would follow.

Midshipman Thomas combatted the hazing and male ego with a strong sense of humor. Clearly those hours around the dinner table at home, being challenged on the topics of the day, had prepared her well for the rigors of academy life.

Cathy tackled the constant emotional uphill battle head-on, a testimony to her navy upbringing. She was often referred to as a "screwed down plebe," someone who studied extensively. Cathy stood out in the hallowed halls of the academy. With red hair and often double-timing it through the halls between classes, she became an easy target for upperclassmen to pick out in a crowd. Being a target never daunted her—it made her stronger and more agile.

Thomas buried herself not just in her studies but in staying in shape. Her plebe year she was recognized at the academy for playing on the woman's basketball team. She played baseball and ran track—the 220, 440, and 100-yard dash. She was of medium height, standing five feet seven inches. As her brother Bill put it, "She was very disciplined, practicing every subject or new challenge over and over until she mastered it." She also took up martial arts where she learned to defend herself.

The academy's curriculum at the time focused on engineering, but Cathy became interested in foreign studies. She took on mastering the Russian language, a skillset that would help her navy career during the Cold War. She received an award for excellence for most improved Russian scholar at the academy, a high distinction. By most accounts, Thomas was fluent in Russian by the time of her graduation. Thomas took on political science as a concentration in her studies, a rarity at the engineering school. Then again, that was a pattern of Cathy Thomas's life—she broke with the norm and made her own path. Her yearbook entry even stated, "She has always been a mid [midshipman] to do her own thing. And she does those things pretty well."

Cathy dated fellow classmen while in school. One went so far as to start talking about her having kids and marrying him. Cathy backed out of that relationship. It wasn't part of the future she had planned.

Her brother Bill remembers her during her academy years as a rigid and dedicated student. "Cathy was an avid reader. She devoured periodicals—probably as a result of her family upbringing. Anything about the news or international affairs got her attention—diplomacy. She had a big music collection, a lot of albums and a good stereo system. She went to concerts and clubs in Washington, DC."

Thomas's last year at the academy affronted her with a newfound sense of freedom. She was able to have a car—a status symbol that gave her the ability to go beyond Annapolis for entertainment. Cathy's brother Jack was attending American University in nearby Washington, DC, and Cathy would leave the academy on the weekends to go and visit him.

At the time, the academy required that when midshipmen left and returned to post they had to be in uniform. Cathy developed a skill for changing out of her uniform at stoplights between Annapolis and the District of Columbia. She would shed her uniform, fold it carefully, and change into her civilian attire during a series of stops, no doubt entertaining or amusing many of the passersby. Her trip back to the academy was a reversal, with her changing back into her uniform. Following the rules while at the same time bending them was a metaphor for Cathy's life.

She developed a reputation as a student that knew how to unwind. The yearbook for her class noted, "Her ability to party hardy was legendary throughout youngster year and second class summer." And while she was known for her ability to unwind, Cathy also was rigid with the new plebes—earning her the title of CT Flamer—a flamer being a hard upperclassman. It demonstrated that Thomas not only could take the ribbing but was fully capable of dishing it out—making herself fit in better with the male midshipmen. That rigidity and verbal prodding of new students was part of the culture of the USNA and is so still today.

Cathy Thomas's graduating class consisted of sixty female officers, but the dropout rate was very high. The female midshipmen were distributed among the companies, and she remained the lone female in her company—the Fifth—to survive the rigor, grades, hazing, and pressures of being a trailblazer at the academy.

It wasn't enough for her to be in the second class to graduate females, Cathy set her eyes on being a surface warfare officer (SWO). The navy had only allowed females to serve at sea in 1978, and then only under orders from a federal judge. Female SWOs were still limited to assignments on support and logistics vessels at the time, not in the man's fighting navy.

Lieutenant Thomas attended the Surface Warfare Officers School in Newport, Rhode Island, and completed the six weeks of training there. Her desire was to become a SWO on a combat vessel, but she was still bumping into an impenetrably thick glass ceiling in the navy. Instead she was posted to *USS L. Y. Spear*. The *Spear* was an attack submarine tender attached to Submarine Squadron Six out of Norfolk, Virginia. The vessel was responsible for support and provisioning for upwards of twelve submarines, a vital support mission during the Cold War. The ship was equipped with shops, material, and the technical and logistical support necessary to repair nuclear submarines at sea. It carried replacement weapons and a fully functioning hospital. She was captained by John Francis Whelan Jr., a fellow USNA graduate also from Massachusetts. Cathy reported to Lt. L. E. Furr, the ship's weapons officer.

While aboard the *USS L. Y. Spear* Cathy began to come to grips with her sexuality. The *Spear* was one of the few navy ships that had a large contingent of females serving aboard it.

One of Cathy's circle of friends, Deb Hill, describes the environment of the 1980s in the navy as one where she was the odd man out.

"From my perspective I was on a ship of 1,200 people, out of that, 400 were women. Out of the division I was in, I was an electronics technician at the time, and in my division of sixty, I was the only girl. So I didn't feel like I had a lot in common with any of the girls. So when I went out, I went out with one of the guys that was in my group," Deb said. "I did know girls that were gay that were on the ship. Some of them I may have felt I had something more in common with. By and large, I felt I had more in common with the guys I worked with than the women serving."

Discretion, secrecy, and outright lying were necessary to protect a homosexual lifestyle in the navy in the 1980s.

"Back then we didn't have the internet and email. I had a secret clearance and a top secret clearance, so with communications you had to be really careful with what you said and what you wrote. Even then we knew if you had letters to somebody—love letters to somebody under your pillow—you could get kicked out for that," said Deb. "You always had to be careful what you said on the phone, what you wrote, what you did, how you acted, who you went out with, all of that. Quite unlike today where they have LGBT birthday cake on the mess deck, celebrate the first kiss between two women; you could have knocked me over with a feather when I saw that picture. My, how times have changed."

During this period as she explored her newfound sexuality, Cathy became tight with a small circle of friends. Jolene Schira and Karen Miller served aboard the *L. Y. Spear* and Deb Hill aboard the *USS Shenandoah*. The three women were also gay. Lynne Jordan, Deb's sister, was also a part of that close-knit group, but she was straight. Jolene and Cathy became a couple, albeit for a short period of time. Jolene moved into the house that Cathy had purchased in Norfolk.

Cathy herself never came out and had a discussion with her family about her sexual preference. According to her brother Bill, "Mom and Dad were there over a weekend visiting. Our parents were going to purchase an appliance as a housewarming gift—they were always getting something practical for those kinds of gifts. She didn't come out and say anything, but her mother noticed the sleeping arrangements and said that the relationship was something 'more than just roomies.'"

Cathy being gay and in the navy was a problem on multiple levels. This was the age before the military's "Don't Ask Don't Tell" policy. Being homosexual was seen as a security risk in the eyes of the navy out of concern that a sailor or officer's lifestyle could be used as a leverage point by a hostile foreign interest. Being gay in the US Navy in 1982 meant that your career hung in a precarious position at all times. Making matters even more challenging were the centuries of male-dominated culture where many officers and sailors resented females being in the service. Probing eyes and prying ears were everywhere.

On top of that, Thomas's lifestyle caused tension within her own family. Cathy's brother Richard had a security clearance and career in the navy. Her homosexuality caused a rift between her oath of honor and integrity in the navy. Moreover, his keeping her sexual preference a secret put his own career in danger. Cathy's trailblazing attitude generated risk and tension on many fronts, and it was only a matter of time before it caught up with her

In the circle of friends, Cathy's role was pivotal. In many respects, she was the control rod in the nuclear reactors of their lives.

"She was the best of us. She was, without a doubt, without arguing about it, without anything else, she was the best of us. I get chills as I say that," said Deb about Cathy. "She had this beautiful red hair that was just beautiful. She was more beautiful inside than she was outside, if that's possible. Just the most beautiful, calm, confident spirit. At the same time she was a breath of fresh air. I quite think she could turn around and be a tornado if she had to. A force to be reckoned with. She was bright; she was well-educated. She was in the second class of women that went to the Naval Academy which is no small feat."

Deb's sister Lynne Jordan remembers how the group celebrated her birthday.

"So for my birthday, the girls all decided that they were going to take me out. My mother had sent me this little red dress; it had a little ruffle going from the top to the bottom. All of us were out there; we weren't being bothered by anybody—it was just all girls—it was a gay bar. We would go inside and we could dance and sing, and outside you could play basketball or throw tennis balls—T-ball, whatever they call it—going back and forth. We ended up staying out," said Lynne. "My mother was afraid we weren't going to get home at a decent hour, but we laughed, danced, sang, talked, sang, and danced. It was such an incredible day that I will always remember it."

The girls stayed at the bar until about two o'clock in the morning, but the party didn't end there.

"Then we went out to get breakfast, and then we ended up getting in ... we ended up getting to bed about 10:00 a.m. So when my mother asked, 'Did you get home at a decent hour?' I said, 'Yes mother, I got home at ten,'" Lynne continued.

"We girls sat up, barrel laughing, not over-indulging. I bet we were having tequila sunrises, I think that was about the only thing we knew how to order. I think Cath may have been a little partial to the Irish whiskey. We weren't serious drinkers; we were just out having fun. There's something about it when a friend is able to make you feel special."

For Thomas the tour of duty aboard the *Spear* was a partial fulfillment of her career ambition to be a SWO, though not on a combat vessel. When her tour was up aboard the *Spear*, Cathy had upwards of 200 sailors reporting to her, many recalling her as one of the best officers they had in their years in the service. For the first time, however, she was unable to find a way around the rules and regulations.

Plain and simple—women were not being posted to combat duties as surface warfare officers. Early in her navy career, Cathy was finding the limitations. The short tours at sea combined with her outstanding performance as an officer—while keeping her sexuality a secret—took a toll on the vibrant Thomas.

Her lifestyle had to have weighed heavy on her, as it did for Deb Hill.

"I always felt like I had a sword over my head. No matter how good I was, I could be the top 1 percent, which I was, but if somebody didn't like you, you could be out the next day. I could be the absolute very best, and I could be out the next day," said Deb. "You can be the most honest, you could be the hardest worker, you could be the brightest—the best, the fastest, you could beat all of the guys' hands down, and still you could be out the next day over an innuendo, just because someone doesn't like you. It's your Achilles' heel; it's the one thing about you that they can take you out [with]. Really back then they didn't have to have proof—just a dishonorable discharge and you're out."

In short, the navy had been forced by law and order from the commander in chief to indoctrinate women into its ranks, but shattering two centuries of tradition was not something that many officers of the US Navy took seriously. While they had to accept females, they could and would make the women's lives a living hell and hopefully drive them out, either through rules and regulations or by attrition. Several females referred to the "witch hunts" that took place against female officers, searches to find reason to drive them out of the service. Chief targets among those were the females that graduated from the academy. Shattering their careers would validate the all-male mentality that some leaders shared; proving that integration of women was a misguided mistake.

Cathy was not quite prepared to give up on the navy though. Her childhood upbringing focused on current affairs and a major in political science did offer her a coveted assignment—that of a protocol officer at the office of the Commander in Chief, Atlantic Fleet in Norfolk, Virginia. Admiral Carlisle A. H. Trost held that post when Cathy was there, and she would have interacted with him often in her position.

Protocol officers were considered some of the highest profile roles at a navy base. They were responsible for coordinating all official visits and inspections, the handling of VIPs, and coordinating high-level command meetings. These positions were almost always given to up-and-coming officers and with good reason. Protocol officers are the face of the US Navy to leaders from around the globe, and it was a position Cathy was well positioned for—even if it was not her first choice of assignment. Being a protocol officer was not easy, and often the job was one where the officers were hand-picked. It was high pressure and required her to think on her feet, perfect for the fiery Thomas. According to one officer that knew her, "Cathy handled the job with grace, shining particularly in coping with last-minute snafus that gave protocol officers gray hairs."

Lieutenant Commander Ken Satterfield summarized her personality and role. "She was extremely professional. Cathy worked with numerous public affairs officers in the area coordinating visits of VIPs from Washington who wanted to visit shore bases and ships at sea in the Atlantic Fleet. She was very personable and professional and made what was a difficult process very easy for all concerned."

Norfolk was a navy city—a port town with all that came with it. In the 1980s it was economically suffering. Efforts to revitalize the city such as closing off of Granby Street to create a pedestrian mall failed miserably. The downtown suffered as well. Norfolk, like any large city, had more than its share of rough neighborhoods and shady establishments— many of which were dedicated to relieving sailors on shore leave of their hard-earned cash.

Despite the prized posting, Cathy still felt stifled and frustrated. She was not about to let that frustration govern her work, as it turned out, a protocol officer was a role she excelled at—her fitness reports listed her as "Outstanding."

That reckoning came in the spring of 1984. Lieutenant Thomas didn't know it but the US Naval Investigative Service (NIS, today known as NCIS) had the Hershee, a known gay bar in Norfolk, under surveillance—looking for members of the navy who might be homosexuals. According to the investigators, Cathy had been seen at the Hershee upwards of ten times prior to April of 1984. On several of those occasions she was accompanied by another crewman from the *L. Y. Spear*. The last time that she had been seen, she had been with a civilian female (presumably Jolene Schira) that she had introduced as her homosexual lover, according to the agents. The conviction of a graduate of the academy and an officer would be a great victory for the male-dominated navy and a plume in the hat of the nine investigators involved on her case.

Covert surveillance of Cathy's life began. Cathy was tailed on April 26, 1984, seen with another woman in her white Honda Civic. A separate investigation was opened up on the person in the car with her, most likely the former crewman from the *Spear*. On May 5, 1984, the lead investigator attempted an impromptu visit/interview with Cathy and a suspected "female subject" at Cathy's residence. Either Cathy wasn't there or ignored the ringing of the doorbell because she did not answer. The presence of two cars in the driveway may very well have led them to believe that Thomas was simply avoiding them.

Undeterred, the navy investigators turned to her postman from the Thomas Corner office, interviewing him about the mail that she received and prior addresses—no doubt trying to see if she was receiving mail that the navy could deem subversive. The investigators tracked down a former shipmate in Ohio for an interview but did not have any luck in connecting with her.

Cathy was not the only target of the investigation, her shipmate from the *L. Y. Spear* was also being scrutinized. On June 19, 1984, the investigators decided to escalate their allegations. Cathy was brought in for a formal inquiry. She was informed of her constitutional rights and declined to give the navy the rights to search her premises. Per regulations, the lead investigator also informed Captain Whelan that Cathy Thomas and one of his existing crewmen were being accused of homosexual activity including sodomy. The entire allegation against Thomas was that she had allegedly been seen going to a gay bar and had told someone there that the individual she was with was her lover. That was the depth of the accusations leveled at her, but in the 1980s, this was enough to scuttle any young officer's career.

For Thomas, this interrogation had to be worse than any trial lawyer scene and her navy career hung in the balance with every word she spoke. The first thing she was forced to do was sign the Military Suspect Acknowledgement and Waiver of Rights. It stated what she was charged with and her acknowledgement that she had the right to remain silent or make no statement at all. It ended with her right to terminate the interview at any time. Her interrogation went for almost two hours, and she relayed the following to the lead investigator. "She had never engaged in homosexual activity. She had never been to the Hershee Bar. She had no knowledge of homosexual activity by her roommate or by her fellow shipmate."

According to her brother Bill, "Cathy ended the interview by saying that she was a navy officer and a graduate of the academy and did not have to be interrogated in such a manner."

She declined further questions and terminated the interview. For the investigators, this had to be frustrating. Without a confession on her part, they had nothing but innuendo and speculation.

The investigation was terminated on August 3 when Captain Whelan contacted them over the phone and requested that the investigation be cancelled. While the details of the conversation were not documented, apparently the captain saw little to be gained out of the trashing of two officers' careers.

For Cathy, the NIS interview must have been a tipping point for her career in the navy. The incompatibility of her lifestyle and the navy, combined with the limitation of her not being a surface warfare officer on a combat ship may have simply been too much.

Deb Hill remembers discussing Cathy's decision to leave the navy.

"One of the last conversations that I had with her I wanted to apply to OCS [Officer's Candidate School]. We were standing out by her white Honda. She was talking about getting out. I just couldn't understand why she was getting out."

Deb pressed Cathy for answers.

"You're a Naval Academy grad. You're the top 1 percent; you're the best. I don't understand."

Cathy's simple reply: "People like you need to stay in, but I have to get out."

That answer didn't sit well at the time with Deb. "I didn't understand that, and I didn't understand that for a very long time."

Lynne Jordan recalls Cathy's decision as well.

"She was ready to get out. I just recall that she felt she was ready, that this opportunity would be better for her. I have that—well, my sister and that whole group of girls were gay, and it was tough on them. There was always some kind of BS going on; whether it was a witch hunt, somebody coming up and saying something negative, somebody trying to allude that somehow that makes you a lesser person, or not fit to be in the military—which, quite frankly, is bullshit. There are just people that have a fear for things they don't know or don't understand," said Lynne. "For her being so brilliant and being an academy grad, and the way she carried herself, unfortunately it doesn't make it an easy place to be. I had some friends that weren't gay, and they had a hard time too! Being on a ship, in that kind of environment, it is hard on women. I hate that it isn't fair, but nobody said it was going to be."

Cathy had been considering leaving the navy for some time. In February of 1986 she was taking a statistics class at Old Dominion University. She sold her house and moved into a house where Karen Miller and Deb Hill lived. She and Joleen broke up around that time—unintended fallout from the NIS investigation. What little is known about that breakup is that there was no bad blood in the relationship; Cathy's group of friends remained cohesive.

Thomas was casting her net wide to look for a new career. She interviewed with a plastics company in New Jersey. She also went to Atlanta and Tampa for a series of job interviews that were promising but still had not fully captured her.

As Deb Hill summarized it: "She wanted, needed something to make her jump out of bed in the morning."

In the meantime, her former lover Jolene had begun working in a stockbroker firm and thought that Cathy might be a good fit. Even better, another of their group, Karen Miller, worked there in an administrative/office manager role. For Thomas it was tempting. She would not be leaving her clique, which had been a good emotional security blanket for her, and at the same time she could launch a new career with almost unlimited potential. It meant being with her friends all of the time and being able to grow to her full potential. Both Karen and Jolene had recently completed their navy obligations as well.

Cathy resigned her navy commission in May of 1986 but retained a commitment in the US Navy Reserve. According to Lieutenant Janet Rostchak, who worked as a command protocol officer and commanded Cathy, "She left loving the navy and with the navy loving her. We regretted that we ever lost her."

She stepped into her new job at Broker's Security Inc. in Virginia Beach, where she worked as a budding stockbroker.

Stockbroker Cathy Thomas was a model employee. As with almost every aspect of her life, Cathy buried herself in her new job—becoming one of the most successful brokers at the firm. She continued taking classes at nearby Old Dominion University as well, preparing for the next stage in her life. After only four months as a broker at the company, President Roger "Buddy" West III said, "She was doing excellent—real well for herself."

Her commissions since joining the firm in June of 1986 were around $4,000 a month—a very good income for a starting broker. "She was a super broker. She stayed on the phone all of the time. She was on her way to the top," West said.

Where most stockbrokers struggled with their board tests, Cathy sailed through them. In the 1980s it could take a broker a year or so to build up a clientele enough to make a living—she was booming. It was more than that, she was a person steeped in deep ethics.

Deb Hill remembers one instance where Cathy went above and beyond to make sure she was behaving ethically. "There was a kid who had some money and wanted to invest on a flip, and it was really, really, really, high risk. Cathy was, 'Ah, I don't think that's a really good idea. It's risky.'"

Cathy took her concerns to his parents. She said, "This is what he wants to do. It's really risky, and I don't feel comfortable with it."

The parents' response was somewhat surprising. "That's his money. That's what he wants to do. He's spending it, and he's learning. So if that's what he wants to do, we understand you think it's risky and you're advising against it."

According to Deb, "The kid wound up making like a million dollars—he made a butt-load of money. Even though she was in the cut-throat competitive brokerage world, she was very honest, equitable, conscientious, looking out for her clients. She came from a conservative background so I can only imagine that she was conservative—I could anticipate she would be recommending long-term, lower risk rather than short-term, high risk things. She developed a reputation quickly for being honest. Her success was very quick."

One of Cathy's former classmates from the Naval Academy, Lieutenant Frank Thorp, who was stationed at Norfolk, met with Cathy at the end of September of 1986 during homecoming. According to an interview he gave with the *Daily Press* newspaper, "She was enjoying herself, seeing all her friends. Cathy's a popular individual, so she had a lot of friends there. She was quite happy with herself."

It appeared that Cathy's shift from her navy responsibilities was settling well with her.

When Lieutenant Thorp thought of Cathy, he summed

up her personality simply. "She was a pioneer, but more than just being a pioneer, she was incredibly enthusiastic and incredibly friendly."

Lynne Jordan remembers her warm, almost sister-like caring. "She had this part of her that almost made you feel that you were on a level playing field. You weren't ... but she made you feel that way. It was a way to make you feel at ease, feel respected, cared about. I got an apartment, a new place to live, so excited that I had a new place to live, I was getting new furniture. She had written a letter to my sister, no email, written letters about coming to see me ... she was so happy about coming to see my new place, how good it looked. Even reading that letter, knowing that she wrote to my sister about me, was like typical Cathy. That was the type of person that she was."

Cathy and her friends were living a lifestyle as if they were in a 1980s sitcom in many respects. Life was somewhat carefree now that the looming shadows over her sexuality in the navy were thought to be a thing of her past. She and Lynne Jordan would go to the beach in their downtime while Deb was at sea.

"I still remember taking a cooler and the big boom box that you had to wrap in a pillowcase so you didn't get sand in it. It looked like you were dragging a suitcase. Singing out loud—not caring if anybody else hears," Lynne said.

"My best memories is [*sic*] when she would come over and see me and just hang out. 'What's going on with you?' I kind of felt like she was looking over me because Sissy was out to sea. It kind of felt like I had someone there. Debbie and I didn't have any family there other than me and her so when she went out to sea, it was really, really, hard. For Cath to come and check on me, make sure I am doing okay, it kind of made me feel at ease. Of course I missed Deb terribly. She [Cathy] was just one of those people that *truly* cared about other people. Back then we didn't have cell phones, we didn't have email and all of that. If you wanted to see somebody you just most likely dropped by."

It was during this period that Cathy Thomas met Rebecca Dowski.

"It was my understanding that Jolene had introduced Becky to Cathy," Deb Hill said. "Some people find that astounding, 'You introduced your ex to somebody?' You know—you're friends. In that circle of friends it was not the 'stab them in the back and they're on your shit list for the rest of your life.' It wasn't that kind of thing."

Jolene was a part-time student at William and Mary, and she and Becky shared a class together.

Cathy Thomas, who had always been an outstanding singular personality was destined to be conjoined with Becky Dowski ... though not in a way that either of them could fully understand or desire.

CHAPTER 2

Rebecca Ann Dowski was born in the state of New York on July 21, 1965, to Julian and Jacqueline Antalek Dowski. Rebecca—Becky to her friends and family—was raised in Poughkeepsie in the Hudson River Valley.

While technically part of the New York metropolitan area, Poughkeepsie was a world away from the big city. For a short period, it was the capital of the state of New York. Vassar College makes it home there, bringing culture to the citizens. One of the city's claims to fame is that the Smith Brother's cough drop factory was built there. Its idyllic countryside, quaint stores, and beautiful views make the city a place where people want to raise families with good values. The heart of business in Dutchess County and Poughkeepsie centered around one thing in the 1960s through the 1980s—IBM.

The Hudson Valley is dotted with IBM factories and facilities, from Kingston to Fishkill to the large "main plant" in Poughkeepsie. It was where the mainframe computers that powered the world in the 1970s and '80s were assembled. Poughkeepsie, despite its outward appearance, was a factory town. In the 1970s and '80s, if you worked for IBM, you had a job for life—such was the bond between the company, its employees, and the community. Becky's father, Julian, was one of a number of rising executives at IBM. It affronted them a very comfortable and seemingly safe lifestyle.

Becky was the youngest of five children. Family was the center of her life. She adored her older siblings, according to her sister in-law Ginny Dowski Minarik.[2] "My first memory of Becky was at a summer camp in the Adirondacks where <u>Bob and I met</u>, actually it was the summer we met. Here

2   Becky's brother Bob and Ginny have since divorced.

comes this little wide-eyed, ten-year-old girl with the biggest brown eyes I have ever seen and the most beautiful smile, and this curly hair. She was looking up to me with wide-eyed wonder, 'You're dating my brother.' She was just full of life—smiles—and just a caring heart. Those were my first impressions of Becky."

She spent every chance she had with her nieces, the daughters of her older sister, Julie. The family had a pool in the back yard—a luxury at the time—and it became a place where she could play the role of older aunt.

Becky was particularly close to her mother. Jacquelin Dowski had a deep love of art and the works of the classic painters—something she imparted on her daughter. Jacquelin shared a love of French cuisine and culture which would play a big role in her daughter's life. Mrs. Dowski was a baker, especially around the holidays, making her own bread and cookies, and her youngest daughter loved the time they spent together baking for the family. The Dowskis' holidays were very family centric. Rather than go out for New Year's Eve, the family gathered together to celebrate.

Ginny Minarik recalls Rebecca's love of family. "She did look up to her big brother Bob. I remember one of the pictures him showing me was in college ... there was quite an age difference there. Bob and I were the same age, and I met her when I was twenty-one. So he was ten or eleven when she was born. He came home from college with his motorcycle. She was sitting on the back of the motorcycle in the driveway with the helmet on. She just wanted to be with her big brother."

Her mother loved craft projects and Becky did too—it was a way for them to bond. She did counted cross-stitch. Becky collected teddy bears too. She loved the outdoors as well. Becky was known for taking long hikes in the area around Poughkeepsie with her family and alone, drinking in the spectacular views of the Hudson Valley. She was fond of going to the movies as soon as new ones were released.

Whatever the latest film was, Becky and her mother made a point of going to it.

Becky's other passion centered on team sports. At five feet seven inches and a muscular 135 pounds, she proved adept at a wide range of sports—basketball and especially softball. Becky did not just play on the team, she pushed herself to be a star player. She worked out regularly to stay in shape.

Dowski family vacations tended to be centered on the extended family. Trips to visit the grandparents in upstate New York were common. Things changed however when Becky's father, Julian, received an opportunity to work in France. It was a move that would change both Becky and the family dynamic forever.

The relocation to Paris initially impacted Becky more than her older siblings who were moving onto college. Becky was high school age, and it meant uprooting her from the stability of Poughkeepsie for a new country, new school, and new lifestyle. She attended the American School in Paris. Her mother's love of French culture allowed Becky to immerse herself in Paris; quickly mastering French was as much a necessity as a means of freedom. Becky joined the intermural baseball team at the American School which took her all across Europe to games in other countries. She was team captain for the softball and basketball squads and earned Athlete of the Year honors before she graduated.

She was affronted with opportunities that many people of her age only dreamed about. As Ginny Minarik put it, "I was just intrigued with how comfortable she was in this new culture—very fluent in French—I saw her from a very different perspective of this emerging lovely young woman. She was very comfortable in navigating herself around the city. She knew French—enough to communicate quite well. She would take the Metro downtown and visit the little cafés along the Seine—like wow, how cool is that? … She really had such an *amazing* experience there."

Becky dated several young men while in France but nothing serious. When she was in Paris it was more about going out with a small group of friends than one-on-one dating. Becky was about small groups of close people—be it in sports or her social life.

While she was in Paris her father announced he was leaving her mother. This put the youngest of the Dowski children in a precarious emotional state. She was in France, far from the majority of her family support system. Worse yet, the divorce was not destined to be amicable.

As her sister-in-law said, "The divorce between Bob's parents was horrifically painful for Becky. It caused a lot of heartache for everybody. She was just torn because she loved her parents and she had had a very comfortable life and things were sort of changing. There were new people in the picture and that piece was difficult. ... It was a very ugly time. It was very uncomfortable, very painful for Beck to be witnessing this while she was in high school. It caused a big rift between her and her dad, which I don't think that Julian and Beck ever reconciled their differences before Becky's death."

Becky's family life was shattered, and she was essentially alone in Paris.

Always a competitive and top-notch student, Becky returned to the United States after two years in Paris to live with her mother in Poughkeepsie. Becky tried to emotionally move forward despite her parent's divorce.

"This was a very bright young woman who had a vision for her future," said Ginny. "She was pursing her dreams and her goals. Family was so important to her. Relationships were important. The relationship that she had with her mother was so tight."

In the autumn of 1983, Becky attended Dickinson College in Carlisle, Pennsylvania. Dickinson was a private liberal arts college with an enrollment of 1,750 students. It was a school that had been founded by a signer of the

Declaration of Independence and had stately old stonework buildings and plush grass common areas. While not an Ivy League school, as a private college it was a combination of expensive, exclusive, and prestigious.

Dickinson was small, a tight-knit family of students—no doubt filling the void that Becky felt disrupted in her home life. At Dickinson, she traveled in a circle of about eight students who formed a core group of close friends. Becky was drawn to fellow students with similar life experiences, especially foreign travel. Several of her classmates remembered that her cadre wasn't as interested in the normal drinking and partying lifestyle of college coeds. For them, a good night on the town was a visit to nice restaurant for some stimulating conversation.

Becky jumped into sports on the women's softball team with a zeal and energy that earned her recognition. At Dickinson, she starred on the school's softball team and was named MVP and Mid-Atlantic All-Conference Team member.

The all-conference honors she earned for softball were a matter of pride for Becky. The yearbook for Dickinson tended to favor the graduating students, but her freshman year they recognized Becky: "Head coach Anne Hurst called her first season at Dickinson a challenge. Facing a very demanding schedule, the Devils' goal to obtain a .500 season was helped by the strong pitching arm of Nancy Oppenheimer and standouts Delores Giachette, Becky Dowski, Sonya Church, Camille Warsnap, and Helenanne Seaman."

During the summers in high school and college, Dowski worked at the YMCA camp program, allowing her to combine her love of the outdoors and that of children. Starting as a camp counselor, she eventually was promoted to teen travel director in the summer of 1986. It was not an easy job, but she stepped up to the role with the energy she always demonstrated. She supervised field trip programs for around a dozen boys and girls between the ages of thirteen and fifteen. Becky set up events to do horseback riding, swimming, and canoeing, and she arranged for trips to museums and other cultural locations in the city and the Poughkeepsie area.

Sherry Daniels, the camp director, said Becky was "a pied-piper-type person with our children. I was never worried about them [the YMCA children] being with her out on the road. She was so responsible and able to handle herself. And the children adored her. I have children of my own. I would say I'd like to see them grow up into a Becky-type person."

Becky was viewed similarly at Dickinson College. Her suitemate Gretchen Ward described her as hardworking and self-directed. "She was very diligent. She always cared about what she was doing. She was always one of the practical jokers on the floor who kept us light-hearted during exams. We all were very close. Our whole freshman floor would go up to Poughkeepsie every summer for Becky's birthday."

Becky was proud of her choice of clothing too. As Ginny Minarik said, "I know she was a clothes horse—she loved Banana Republic, the Gap, those particular stores I remember. She loved a good outfit! She was not particularly a girly-girl, but classic—linen jackets."

After two years at Dickinson College, Becky came to the realization that she wanted more than what a liberal arts education offered her in terms of career options.

"She left to pursue more of a business degree," her sister-in-law said. "I remember her talking to Bob, she was very much interested in the business aspect, going for her master's—MBA—and the financial realm of things. Her brother Bob said Becky choose William and Mary because she wanted 'more focus' in her liberal arts studies.

"That seemed to be where her heart spoke and her desire was, and William and Mary certainly had a very good program."

More than one person said that Becky was looking to get into international business and corporate finance, no doubt leveraging her two years of living in Paris.

The decision to transfer to the College of William and Mary in January of 1986 was one that was destined to be fateful for Miss Dowski—though at the time it was impossible to see that.

The school was the second oldest college in the United States, chartered in 1693. A public school, it was also considered one of the premier East Coast universities. Thomas Jefferson, James Monroe, and John Tyler all were educated in its hallowed halls, along with sixteen members of the Continental Congress and four signers of the Declaration of Independence. It was rated as the number one public school in the United States by the *Washington Post*. The campus was situated in the heart of historic Williamsburg almost always brimming with tourists year round. Every classroom, every dorm room view was oozing with American history.

Becky fit into William and Mary perfectly. Her classmates described her as well adjusted to the new campus. She was "fun loving" and "easy to get along with—nice." In her discussions with family it was clear that she had made the right choice in William and Mary.

For the athletic Dowski, she found she didn't have time for team sports after transferring to William and Mary. She discovered that the expectations and demands of academia took precedence, and she was a person that knew how to prioritize her life. She desired a job in corporate finance and had experience with a number of computer systems and carried a 3.2 GPA during her brief time at the university.

She lived in Chandler Hall, which housed around 130 students at the time. As she had at Dickinson, she became known as a practical joker. As one of her dorm mates would recall for the William and Mary school newspaper, *The Flat Hat*, "Her wit brought relief during tense exam periods."

Becky worked in her free afternoons at a child care center, the Garden of Children, as a teacher's aide, providing care for two-year-olds. Per an interview with the *Daily Press* in October of 1986, Becky was seen as a strong asset by the center's director, Amy Doux. "She was a very dependable, very reliable person—she was a real sweet girl. Everybody here liked her."

As a student, she channeled her competitive nature into her grades. Becky didn't just attend college, she established relationships with students and with professors. When she was taking English Composition in Emily Pease's class, she got a grade lower than she was accustomed to. Rather than complain or provide excuses, she asked, "What can I do to improve?"

Professor Pease said, "She used to appear at my office door, always with that quiet cheerfulness I came to love. She was always generous of her time. She would have given you anything. She babysat my children, and they liked her really well. She had a real knack for entertaining them and taking care of them."

While at William and Mary she did date, but "she just didn't want to commit to anybody. She just didn't want to get too close to anybody, any males, who suggested marriage," said her sister in an interview from the period. The one person that she did date that stood out was Farooq M. Butt.

Farooq and Becky dated for a short period of time, but she broke it off when she was introduced to Cathy. Farooq, being from the Middle East, was angry at having been dumped for another person, let alone a female.

According to Ginny Minarik, "I think, as I recall, she was afraid of him."

It was in the spring of 1986 that their mutual friend Jolene Schira introduced Becky to Cathy Thomas. The pair hit it off quickly though the two only knew each other for a short period of time. They did take a romantic weekend to the barrier islands in North Carolina with another couple. For Becky it had to be intimidating. This was a close cadre of women.

As Deb Hill, who had returned from her Mediterranean

Cruise aboard the *Shenandoah* in late September, recalls, "When your friend has somebody new in their life, I think the rational reaction is you're supportive—if they're happy, you're happy." Clearly she saw the relationship between Becky and Cathy to be positive.

"Becky was going to William and Mary ... I don't know how to put it into words. ... It's not like Cathy was hanging out with some barfly. She was hanging out with a William and Mary student. That kind of equated—it was an equitable match for a Naval Academy grad. You want your smart friends to find somebody that is equally as smart—someone who can contribute intellectually to the relationship. I think everyone was pretty positive about it [the relationship]."

During the early period of their relationship, that early phase of getting to know and understand each other, the problems of the outside world were creeping into the Virginia peninsula. Violent crime was spiking on the tiny William and Mary campus for the first time in its long history. Fears were escalated by the October 3 rape of a student on-campus by two Newport News residents after a fraternity party. It took almost a week for the arrests in the case, and campus unrest was high, as was an increase in patrolling by the tiny campus police force.

CHAPTER 3

October is a month of change and transition in Virginia. The weather seems to lock into a struggle between clinging to the last vestiges of summer while autumn creeps in—usually at night. This battle between cold and warmth is more frequent, more stormy. The wind is a bit colder, the shadows seem a bit longer. In the Tidewater region it comes later than in the rest of the state, with the leaves not reaching peak until the last few days of the month. October 1986 was no exception. A fading green color still feebly held its grip on the trees and foliage, fighting a losing battle. The remnants of a tropical storm had blown through at the end of September, soaking the ground.

The daily intimacies and relationship between Becky and Cathy during the period are not well known. Like everyone, the day-to-day almost mundane details of life are lost after three decades. The bits and pieces that have been put together give no clue as to the violence that was about to come.

Thursday, October 9, 1986, was like any other autumn day. New musical *Phantom of the Opera* premiered in London. A month earlier the *Oprah Winfrey Show* had begun its long run on TV. The moon was in its first quarter but was obscured most of the time with purple clouds, ensuring the night would be dark. The temperature peaked at seventy degrees and that night would only drop to sixty. The winds were stiff as well, and there had been rain, little more than a sprinkle and more at 4:00 p.m.

Despite the ups and downs of the weather, Becky managed to get in some afternoon sports, presumably softball. She wore black athletic shorts and a brilliant red windbreaker over her shirt.

The following day, Friday, October 10, would mark

the start of fall break at William and Mary, and Becky was looking forward to going home. Earlier in the day she packed her car for the trip back to Poughkeepsie either later that night or the next day. She called her mother and told her that on her way home she was planning on seeing some friends in Washington, DC, and possibly Dickinson. Another phone call to her older sister confirmed that Becky was planning on coming home.

Sharon Spitale, her former roommate, said that Becky had made plans to arrive at Dickinson about 8:30 p.m. Friday night. The fall break was for five days and would give Becky some much needed downtime with her mother.

Cathy Thomas came to William and Mary's campus, presumably to spend some time with Becky and mutual friend Karen Miller. Becky and Jolene had a computer project that was due, and Karen and Cathy were there for technical and moral support. Cathy's schedule at the brokerage firm was flexible, but she gave no one in the office any reason to believe that she would not be in to work on Friday. Thomas joined the students in the campus computer lab to assist with the project.

It is hard for many people to remember what computer assignments were like in the 1980s—before the proliferation of desktop computers. Computer labs were cold sterile environments, and students often had to sign up for time on a text-based terminal to do their work. Even printing was a chore and was often done in other rooms or even other buildings. But with the autumn break looming, some students were already beginning to leave the campus for that last trip home before Thanksgiving.

Becky and Jolene's computer project was due on Friday, and her small copse of friends huddled with her in the computer lab in Barrett Hall, nestled in the middle of the old campus area next to Becky's dormitory, Chandler Hall. Dowski's activities were logged by the campus computer network. At around 6:30 p.m., she logged off at Barrett Hall and walked to Morton Hall, about a block away. She logged on there for a few minutes, presumably to use the printer.

Becky and Cathy were last seen near Chandler Hall a short time later. It was the last confirmed sighting of the pair by anyone other than their murderer.

Dowski's car was loaded with clothing, presumably for the trip north. The women left the campus in Thomas's 1980 white Honda Civic 1300 DX, a two-door hatchback. It is believed that the women may have gone to get something to eat. There have been reports that they were seen at a restaurant called the Yorktown Pub, though this has never been verified. The Yorktown Pub is a local bar restaurant and was only 1,250 yards from the start of the Colonial Parkway. It was well away from campus, where two females could have a meal without attracting any unwanted attention.

The next day, Friday, October 10, was cooler—the temperatures barely reached sixty—and the overcast skies continued. Cathy Thomas did not show up for work, and she didn't call the office, which she characteristically did on her days off. Calls were made to her home, but no one picked up. Thomas was known to love long weekends, so her absence was given little concern.

A college student not showing up for classes before the start of a five-day break hardly garnered a moment's notice, but when Becky didn't show up for class, Jolene Schira went looking for her and found her car parked where it had been the night before. Karen Miller was also concerned. Cathy's no-show, combined with Becky's car being on campus, made Karen and Jolene nervous.

Two more days passed, but the disappearance of the two women went unreported. In the age before cell phones and constant connectivity, it was not that remarkable that few people noticed that they were missing. It was the weekend, and Becky's plans were not very specific. Cathy kept a tight circle of friends, but none of them seemed to notice that she was not available.

Sharon Spitale was concerned that her former roommate had not told her of any changes to her plans. "It was really uncharacteristic of Beck not to call. It wouldn't be like Becky at all to do that. We were very close."

Becky's family, however, was used to her periods of silence. Bob Dowski, her brother, told the *Virginia Gazette*, "It was a routine thing for her to go home on weekends and do laundry, just to do what college kids do. The end result was that she wasn't missed when she didn't show up and we weren't alarmed when she wasn't home."

The evening of Sunday, October 12, between 5:30 and 5:45 a jogger on the Colonial Parkway at the Bellfield Plantation pull-off near the kilometer nine marker noticed something amiss. The pull-off was little more than a seven-car parking area, at the time with no real curbs. It was a half-moon configuration, with most vehicles parked there only being ten to fifteen feet from the historic roadway. The pull-off allowed visitors to the park to look out over the York River near the Cheatham Annex, a navy base just upriver.

The jogger would have noticed the broken bushes at the edge of the pull-off first—right before the fifteen-foot drop off to the river below. He moved in closer and saw the rear of the Civic just over the embankment, as if someone had tried to drive the car out of the parking area and into the York River.

The jogger contacted the park rangers immediately.

* * * * *

The Colonial Parkway is part of the National Park Service and as such is federal property. In the late 1920s, Williamsburg was not the historic town that it is today. It was a few old homes and the ruined foundations of others. Rev. Dr. William Goodwin saw the potential for saving those structures and rebuilding Williamsburg as a historic center that people could visit and relive its prominence in early American history. Working for and with John D. Rockefeller Jr., they covertly purchased most of the downtown area and began a renovation that continues on to this day—preserving and rebuilding a colonial town as it once was.

The concept for a roadway to connect Yorktown, Williamsburg, and the Jamestown Settlement came about in the late 1920s. The initial thought was to use a network of the old colonial roadways to create a national park that would allow visitors to travel between the historic sites as if they were on a colonial road—with no views of the modern world. The problem was that the old road networks were not well suited for such a park. The decision was made to have the Colonial Parkway run from Yorktown at the south end, along the beautiful York River, then cut through the heart of Williamsburg (via a tunnel directly under Colonial Williamsburg) then on to the James River and Jamestown. Ironically, the "historic" parkway was a piece of fiction, with major stretches essentially newly laid out and created road.

Much of the roadway was built on historic land. Chief Powhatan's village, where Captain John Smith of Jamestown fame was held prisoner, was right across the York River from where the parkway was constructed. It ran through the possessions of the Chisiack Indians, and Revolutionary and Civil War camps intersected with the parkway's path as well.

Work began in 1931 on the twenty-three-mile stretch of road. It was mostly constructed as part of the Civilian Conservation Corps (CCC) during the Great Depression, providing ample employment for the region. It would take decades for the road to be finished—just in time for Queen Elizabeth II's visit in 1957 for the 350th anniversary of the founding of Jamestown.

The parkway's planners tried to recreate the experience of traveling on a dirt road during the colonial era. Thus the road did not have the traditional roadway markings of a modern road. The intent was simple, provide patrons with a certain freedom to pull over and take in the natural beauty of the area. The Colonial Parkway has the distinction of being the narrowest national park. Eventually the parkway park itself would encompass over 10,000 acres in a narrow band centered on the concrete road.

Trees along the parkway obscure any visible indications of the modern world such as homes and farms. Red bricks were used for many of the bridges and overpasses, to create the illusion that they were centuries old. In 1986 those overpasses were draped with Virginia creeper vines and moss, adding to the ambiance. The bridges on the roadway were almost invisible, with low railings so that nothing gave the indication of a modern road.

The parkway was paved with a special mix of local aggregate (mostly marl) and concrete to give drivers on the parkway a sound and feeling that they were driving on something less than a paved road, with a low rumble as automobiles drove it. Even today cars on the parkway have a distinct low roar as they pass because of the construction of the roadway. The curves were not tight, but long and sweeping, making for a pleasant drive seemingly in a bygone era. The parkway was built to be three unmarked lanes so that drivers would have some leeway as they drank in the beauty and views. The design was to create the illusion of taking a driver back in time.

Access to the parkway was limited. There were seven interchanges and five entrance points to the roadway—with the majority of these being in the Williamsburg area. Even the interchanges were careful to block any views of homes and businesses from the parkway.

The CCC didn't just make a road, they put measures and barriers in place to prevent erosion along the York and James rivers. Replica cannons were made in the shops for tourist locales like Yorktown. By 1936, 14,592 oak, maple, holly, gum, pine, and sycamore trees had been planted along with

16,791 dogwoods—the Virginia state tree. The planting of trees continued for years after that at a rate of sixty trees a day. By the mid- to late-1980s, the trees were fully mature. They created a green corridor around the parkway, making many parts of it seem like a tunnel through a forest. During the daytime, the trees meant that much of the parkway was shaded and cool. At night, it formed an almost eerie, slowly winding corridor of wood and leaves. With no streetlights, no ambient lighting, driving the parkway at night can be a spooky, unnerving commute.

There were two government installations along the Colonial Parkway. The first was the Cheatham Annex—a US Navy base situated along the York River. It was at the site of Penniman, a small town that had a large powder and shell loading factory built by the E.I. Dupont Company in the early 1900s. The facility was well suited for its purpose. The York River was deep enough to allow freighters or other ships passage upriver to the dock facilities. Prior to the Great War the US Navy took ownership of the facility, and while the facility retained the name Penniman, the city itself was erased. During WWI the navy stored sea mines there—dangerous and deadly implements of war.

By WWII the name had been changed to the Cheatham Annex and it encompassed over 3,400 acres of land along the York River as well as an extensive dock for ships to load and unload munitions. The Colonial Parkway ran through the Cheatham Annex itself, providing the best way to reach the facilities. Of course by the start of the Cold War the complex had taken on a more ominous overtone. No longer used for naval mines, the facility was storage for some of the navy's nuclear weapons systems.

The other government facility along the Colonial Parkway was Camp Peary. The 9,000-acre facility was created in 1942 for training purposes—dissolving the towns of Magruder and Bigler's Mill. Camp Peary was dubbed the Armed Forces Experimental Training Activity (AFETA) but to the public it was known as the Central Intelligence Agency's training facility—"The Farm." It is there that the CIA and the DIA clandestine operatives received some of their training. Officially the CIA and the federal government do not acknowledge the purpose of Camp Peary. During the 1980s, with the threats of the red communist Russian Bear looming constantly around the globe, Camp Peary was a busy place where the US and friendly foreign nationals were allegedly trained to fight a mostly clandestine war.

Ghost stories have long been part of the mythos of the parkway. It has been said that near Black Swamp when the fog rolls in at night, you might hear the faint ringing of sleigh bells or hear disembodied voices laughing. Allegedly a couple during the colonial period had been courting along the York River on a snowy night when their buggy had toppled in a bog. The coach had been found, but the couple and their horse were gone—consumed in the darkness and in local folklore.

All along the Colonial Parkway there were half-moon pull-offs and other parking areas that were more secluded. Some picnic areas, like the Ringfield Plantation area (now closed), offered visitors more private parking and during the daytime a place to enjoy a meal with the family and watch the traffic on the York River.

Annually the parkway had over seven million users—many being locals that used the roadway in lieu of I-64. The park averaged just over a thousand traffic offenses per year and approximately fifteen to eighteen drunken driving incidents. The park had between forty-five to fifty vehicle accidents but had not had a vehicle fatality in over a year. Even vandalism was rare—with less than twenty cases annually in that period. It was not a place of rampant crime.

The Colonial Parkway had seen kings, queens, prime ministers, and presidents from around the world along its rumbling route. The National Park Service had a lot to be proud of with this skinny park. It was quiet and pastoral, a bit of pseudo-colonial life, created to shuffle tourists between the three major attractions along its route. In that perspective, the parkway was a stunning success.

The parkway had a reputation at nighttime. When the tourists left for the evening an entirely different culture emerged at the Colonial Parkway. The ranger patrols after hours were erratic and inconsistent at best, and local law enforcement didn't patrol the roadway because they lacked the jurisdiction.

There were even stories about the rangers themselves being part of the problem after hours. Certain park rangers were law enforcement officers, albeit limited in scope. Per David Moffitt, a former park superintendent, during the 1980s, law enforcement rangers underwent extensive training at the federal law enforcement center in Brunswick, Georgia. The program at the time was six weeks in length. The types of crimes the rangers dealt with were rarely on the scale of what they would face with the Colonial Parkway Murders. No matter how extensive the training, they were ill-prepared for what was about to confront them.

The exact how and why Cathy Thomas's Honda Civic ended up nose down along the embankment of the York River remains unknown, only speculation remains. But it was there nevertheless ...

* * * * *

The first park rangers who arrived on the scene were Jim Redford and Byrd Ewell. To them the car must have looked as if it had been part of an auto accident—that it had been driven off the parking area and crashed only a few feet from the York River. The vehicle was perpendicular to the parkway, as if it had been driven straight at the York River. Only the thick brush and the steep angle of the embankment had prevented the Honda from splashing into the river and possibly floating away or sinking in deep water. It is likely their first thoughts were around drinking and driving. The parkway was known as a place to party at night. If this was that kind of incident, it was one of the worst they had ever seen.

They didn't treat the accident lightly. They crawled out toward the Honda and saw that there were bodies in the car. One of them, we don't know who, shattered the back window of the hatchback, most likely to try and see if one of the victims was alive. Fragments of glass and autumn leaves littered the interior as the rangers vainly attempted to determine if the victims were alive.

They should have known instantly something was amiss. The heady aroma of diesel fuel would have greeted them the moment they shattered the glass. Strange that it would have come from the interior of the vehicle. The other thing that was painfully clear was that the bodies were not poised in positions that one would have expected if they had driven over the embankment. No one was in the front two seats. One body was in the back seat. One was in the far back of the hatchback.

The tan interior of the Honda had bloody splotches in it. As they looked at the two victims, it was clear that this was no drinking and driving incident. The young women's throats had been cut. They climbed into the car enough to check both women for any sign of life, despite the fact it was painfully evident that both were cool to the touch and had been dead for some time. The rangers, still unsure of what they were dealing with, contacted emergency services.

CHAPTER 4

The radio message that came in to John Mabry at the FBI from the park rangers sounded almost routine: "We think it's a traffic fatality, but we're not sure. A visitor spotted a car down an embankment next to the Colonial Parkway, near kilometer marker nine. It looks like two bodies inside."

Calls from the national park were relatively uncommon. The National Park Service had jurisdiction over its parks, as did the FBI. For most of the minor crimes, the park service handled the investigations because of their simplicity and expediency. Irvin Wells of the FBI recalls the involvement of the bureau in the unique case.

"The bureau doesn't work a lot of murders. Now the reason we were on this case was that it was on a government property. We get involved on government reservations, Indian reservations, particularly where bureau agents work murders routinely. Normally though that's not our forte. That doesn't mean we can't investigate it. Just that this was a unique case in that the Dowski-Thomas case was on government property so that gave us the jurisdiction in it," said Wells.

By the time the FBI's unmarked car arrived, additional park rangers had converged at the turnoff: Herman Hardy, Clyde Yee, and Ken Johnson. The rangers and emergency services team had cut a path alongside the car, supposedly to check on the victims and ensure that the vehicle did not continue its tumble into the York River. As they stood in the area around the vehicle, the FBI's first thoughts had to be that the crime scene was contaminated.

Special Agents John Mabry and J. C. Cross were the first on the scene for the FBI. They lost their footing going down the freshly cut path alongside the vehicle. Armed with flashlights they peered in at the victims.

"This is no accident," John Mabry said. [3]

"You're not kidding," Cross responded.

A quick assessment had to be made. Was it best to leave the car where it was or to extract it for further investigation? Given the number of hands that had already touched the vehicle, the call was easy for Mabry to make. "We can't get into the car from here. Why don't we just tow it up the road and see what we've got?"

A local towing company was called in and slowly pulled the vehicle back up over the embankment. Donning gloves, the two FBI agents began to check to see who the victims were. Two purses were found under the seats. One had the wallet in it, belonging to Rebecca Dowski, according to her William and Mary student ID card. The other purse had the wallet out, as if the driver had taken it out for a reason. That one had the driver's license for Cathy Thomas. The FBI radioed headquarters in Norfolk. Their next of kin would have to be notified. The agents also called in for assistance.

Mabry took note of what wasn't missing. Both of the girls' wallets had money in them. Robbery was not the motive. The stench of diesel fuel clung to everything in the interior of the Honda.

As twilight set in they checked the area. There were tire prints a short distance up from the turnoff on the grass that seemed to match those of the Honda. Had the car been there before it had been pushed over the side? Near where the car had gone over were a number of burned matches. Combined with the diesel fuel in the interior of the vehicle and on the victims, it appeared that whoever had committed this crime had tried to set the vehicle on fire. The problem was that diesel fuel has a higher ignition point than gasoline and was difficult, if not impossible, to set on fire using matches. Whoever the killer was, he had tried several times

3   Dialogue taken from: Schneider, Greg. "Agent stalks dark path of serial killer," *Virginia Pilot*, May 12, 1991, pages A5-A9

to ignite the car and the girls, then, out of frustration and options, had apparently then pushed the car over the steep embankment hoping to get it into the York River. Only the bramble prevented the vehicle from floating out in the river and sinking—or drifting out to sea.

From the identification found in the Honda, they were able to ascertain that it was the car's owner, Cathy Thomas, who was in the rear hatch area of the Honda. Rebecca Dowski was in the back seat, her foot wedged between the door and the front seat and her head against the passenger seat. While there were blood stains in the Honda, there was nowhere near enough blood to indicate that they had been killed in the vehicle. A search of the area around the turnout did not reveal any pools of dried blood. It was clear they had been killed elsewhere.

The Virginia state medical examiner arrived at the scene as lights were set up to assist the investigators with their grim task. As respectfully as possible given the circumstances, the victims were removed from the vehicle as photographs were taken. Cathy was removed from the rear hatch and Becky through the driver's door. In the open, under the lights, it was clear just how savage these crimes had been. Both women had their throats slashed. There were ligature marks on their necks—an indication of strangulation. Cathy Thomas had a deep one-inch long knife wound on her lower left thumb. Rebecca Dowski had some cuts on her left thigh.

The car seat was back—much further than it should have been for either woman. This was an indication that the killer had been behind the wheel, most likely in the attempt to drive the car over the embankment. The setting on the seat was measured and logged.

Special Agent Mabry contacted headquarters via the radio. "As dark as it is out here and with all the dirt and glass and leaves and blood in the car, we're not going to be able to do much with it."

The response was clear. "Send the car up to Washington.

Store it tonight, then we'll get it on a flatbed tomorrow and ship it up so they can go over it in the lab."

Nathan Williams brought his tow track out from Grafton, carefully loaded the vehicle, and took it to a garage for storing overnight.

The autopsies of the two women required their identification, a process that took days. Richard Thomas, Cathy's brother and a navy doctor came in from Hawaii to identify her body. Richard was toughened by his service in the navy. He had worked on helicopter crash victims and had seen grizzly sights, but nothing had prepared him for seeing his sister. Her body was covered with a sheet up to her neck. She had been cleaned, but even with the covering, the viciousness of her attack was clear. Richard's comment to his brother Bill was grim. "Nobody needs to see that."

Ginny Dowski Minarik recalls how she had been informed of Becky's death.

"Then that horrible call that I received from Bob's sister Julie … I will never forget. It was a warm fall day, and I'm a nurse. We were getting ready to work in the emergency room. Running home from Toys"R"Us with an armful of diapers because we had a son at that point that was about a year and a half to two years old. And then sliding to the floor as I picked up the phone and Julie shared that Becky had been killed. As she went on to describe the circumstances you just melted," Ginny said.

"I frantically placed a call to Bob who came home from work. Immediately he was on the phone with the FBI and making arrangements to go to Williamsburg to identify her. Then the nightmare began. It's horrible."

Bob Dowski's experience in identifying his sister's body was more difficult to process. Where Richard Thomas was a navy doctor and used to human injuries, Bob Dowski was a business executive who was forced to identify the brutalized remains of his beloved sister in the most cold, clinical, and horrifying circumstances. Nothing could have prepared him for the task before him.

"It is that wound that never, never has healed," Ginny said. "I remember when Bob was traveling to Williamsburg to meet with the FBI; I was home with the two children, scared. I thought that bubble of safety that you felt surrounded you was no longer there. You could not understand why … why did this happen to Becky? Are we safe? It's irrational—but that is how I felt. I was scared for us because you just didn't know what the deal was."

The contents of the Honda offered little to investigators. Tipping a car rear-end-up tends to dump the contents all over the place, not where they might normally be found. Cathy Thomas was known for keeping her car interior pristine and orderly—a fragment of her navy training.

On the front passenger floor was a flyer for the Holy Alamo Christian Church and a cassette tape for "Torch," Carley Simon's album. The keys to the Honda were found on the driver's side floor. The radio was dislodged and partially pulled out from the dashboard. A McDonalds's game card piece with the picture of Jeff Bostic of the Washington Red Skins was face down on the dashboard. On the rear of the driver's side floor, under where Becky was discovered, was a blue blazer still on the hanger. Under the jacket was a barrel-style gym bag that was black with red straps. Under the bag was a small blue cardboard carton of unknown origins. On the rear seat, midway between the back and front seats were shorts that were stained with blood.

In the trunk where Cathy's body had been placed, there was a poster and map. In the fragments of the rear window that had been shattered by the park rangers was a US Naval Academy Alumni Association sticker which had fallen on the driver's side floor. Blood, seepage from their injuries, stained the rear seat and the hatchback area.

Cathy was found to have strands of human hair in one

of her hands, as if she had torn it from her assailant.[4] The car itself was filled with a number of hairs and fibers, all of which had to be meticulously preserved. The FBI carefully processed the vehicle, and then to ensure they would maintain all of the possible evidence, the car's interior and carpeting was removed and stored for possible future analysis.

The autopsies revealed new evidence and clues as well. Both women had undigested meat in their stomachs—an indication that they had eaten hamburger or similar food prior to their deaths. The time of death was nearly impossible to establish—all the medical examiner could confirm was that they had been dead for at least twenty-four hours before the examination.

Entangled in the subtle waves of Cathy's auburn hair, just above her left ear, was a small piece of plastic roping— line. The piece was just over one inch in length and had been somehow cut off during her struggle with her killer. How that small segment of rope was cut was perplexing—except if it had been removed when the rope was cut from their necks.

There were ligature marks, deep and visible, around the necks of the two women. Both women showed signs of bruising, evidence of being strongly manhandled while they were still alive. On Thomas's right buttocks was an eerie handprint-shaped bruise. Neither woman showed any signs of sexual molestation, ruling out rape as a motive. Rape tests and swabs were administered simply as a matter of protocol. There was no indication that their hands were tied in the crime scene photographs that were released many years later, but one newspaper's accounts indicated that their

---

4   The mysterious hair has both been confirmed and disputed by the FBI over the years, depending on who was the agent charged with the case. At times the FBI has denied that the hair was recovered, while at other times they have told family members it was found. This hair is mentioned in Thomas's autopsy report. It is likely that subsequent agents have tried to suppress the information from the killer.

hands were, in some manner, bound.

The severity of the slashing of their throats was grim, especially with Cathy Thomas. She had suffered a subtotal decapitation—with the blade nearly severing her head. The slash on Becky was deep as well but not nearly as much as Thomas. Despite the new information gleaned, Special Agent James Watters said the autopsies revealed "very little. … They were unexceptional in providing new clues."

The death certificates for both women listed respiratory arrest due to ligature strangulation. In other words the cutting of their throats had been unnecessary to everyone but the murderer. What they could tell about the blade was that it was extremely sharp and had to have some length to it given the wounds on the victims. Strangulation had been the means of death, but this murderer had carried it further to his own sadistic satisfaction with the cutting of their throats. Both women had a description of the injury on their death certificates as: "Strangled and throat cut by unknown assailant."

It was that "unknown assailant" that became the focus of the FBI. They contacted the William and Mary Campus Police force who began to try and piece together every little detail of Becky's life.

Mark Johnson headed up most of the student inquiries for the tiny on-campus police force. Becky's dorm room was sealed off, and a hired security guard checked the room every few hours. The university put in new card readers for access to the dorm rooms and hired an additional nine officers for patrolling the campus. New phones were installed in public areas and in hallways on the serene campus, all directly tied to the campus police. As the last place that the girls had been seen alive, the student body was shaken by Becky's and Cathy's deaths.

Piecing together the murders was daunting. First and foremost was the missing block of time from when the women were last seen on Thursday, October 9 in the evening and when the car was found on Sunday, October 12 at sunset. Had the car been there the entire time? How could it have gone unnoticed for so long if it had been there? And if it hadn't been there, where had the victims and the car been since the time they had been last seen?

The fact they had food in their stomach that had not been digested led investigators away from the thought that the women had been held hostage somewhere over the course of the weekend. The thinking was that they had been murdered the night they had disappeared or in the early morning hours of Friday the tenth of October, but the sequence of events was a mystery. Did the murderer bring the car to the parkway after the women's deaths to try and dispose the bodies, or did he kill them in the vicinity and try and destroy the car and their remains immediately? There was no evidence that pointed to either scenario. This case came to the agents complete with a big basket of frustration and heartache.

Searches were made of the Colonial Parkway and the thick brush on both sides of the roadway. The FBI was hoping to find the murder weapon—the knife used in the grisly attack—tossed out by the killer. The FBI search spanned from the Cheatham Annex all the way down to the parkway entrance at Yorktown covering over two miles. It was slow, plodding work that yielded nothing of value.

The navy was engaged, and the logs were pulled by the US Naval Investigative Service for the Cheatham Annex to see if there was any suspicious activity at the base during the time of the murders. Other than a few minor spill incidents and the unloading of a ship, the base itself had been quiet.

They tried to piece together the murder as a sequence of events, but significant parts of that puzzle were missing. The assumption had been that Becky and Cathy went the parkway to be alone, talk, or be intimate with each other. The fact that Cathy Thomas had her wallet out suggested that someone—an authority figure or someone posing as an authority figure—had approached the vehicle and asked for her driver's license. Was it possible that a gun was involved to gain control of the situation?

At some point the victims were extracted from Cathy's Honda and a piece of plastic rope was looped tightly around both of their necks. It may have been that Cathy was reaching up to pull at that rope around her neck, or she fought her assailant outright, resulting in the cut to her hand.

A battle was inevitable between the women and their captor. These were not weak cowering females. Cathy Thomas had been athletic her entire life and had been trained in martial arts. She was more than adept at defending herself.

Becky Dowski was no cowering victim either. Her former roommate at Dickinson, Sharon Spitale, summed it up best in an interview with the *Daily Press* on October 19: "I can't imagine someone being able to overcome her without a struggle."

Dowksi was five feet seven inches weighing in at 135 pounds, known for her strength and tenacity. Becky was feisty and very athletic, having competed in sports that demanded strong muscles.

Despite their resilience and strength they were cowed or overpowered by their assailant. The rope around their necks was used to strangle them—hopefully quickly. Then their throats were slit in an act that screamed of overkill. In that cutting of their throats, a small fragment of the rope was left in Cathy's hair. The killer put them in the Honda and took the car to the turnoff where it was found. The bodies and the vehicle were soaked in diesel fuel, and the murderer tried to light the car on fire. Failing at that, he tried to push the vehicle into the York River. Then the killer disappeared into the night.

All of these actions took considerable time—during which anyone may have driven by and seen something. Every moment that the killer spent with that vehicle and the victims would have put him at risk of being spotted. Even if he had driven the vehicle to the parkway, tried to set it on fire, and then pushed it over the embankment, it was not a quick series of tasks.

The pieces missing in this puzzle were many. Where did the murder take place? Was it at the turnout where the car was found? The turnouts themselves were far from private … cars rumbling down the parkway did so only fifteen feet away, often with headlights flashing as they made the slow turns. That meant one of the other more private parking or picnic areas may have been used. Searches revealed nothing in terms of a location. It was entirely possible that the two women were killed elsewhere and their bodies and car were merely disposed of on the parkway. Given that Cathy Thomas had, in the past, gone to the Colonial Parkway for intimate moments—the thinking was against a remote killing, but it still could not be ruled out.

The Colonial Parkway took on a different culture and patronage after sunset. Many locals used it as nothing more than a roadway, other than I-64, to drive north/south in the area. During the daytime, it was mostly traveled by tourists. At night a different group emerged and called the parkway their own domain. For local teenagers, it was a place to go and make out. There were rumors and hints over the years that it was a favorite locale for the homosexual community to come and connect. Partying was commonplace—drinking and driving in 1986 was not nearly as illegal or frowned upon as it is today. There were Peeping Toms that crept up on cars to watch couples during moments of intimacy. The turnoffs and picnic areas were used for drug deals. Many locals avoided the stretch of road at night just because of its reputation. The parkway became a different place at night—a bit of the Wild West.

According to David Moffitt, supervisor of the park during that period, patrols were sparse and inconsistent after hours.

"I can speculate that there were probably two patrol rangers on duty until midnight and possibly one or even none after midnight or 1:00 a.m. I cannot be totally sure about the 'none' as I think we had a twenty-four-hour dispatcher available, and if there were no rangers on duty there probably would be no need for a dispatcher. The parkway not being heavily used at night or early morning might be the reason for limited patrol.

"Basically the patrol ranger, after dusk, was expected to patrol the entire length of the parkway and to assist any motorist with mechanical problems, investigate any vehicles parked in unauthorized areas, and to enforce all traffic laws, i.e. speeding, driving under the influence. When there were two or more rangers on duty, the patrols would have been broken down to one ranger patrolling from Williamsburg to Jamestown Island and the other from Williamsburg to Yorktown."

The lack of consistent patrolling at night may have contributed heavily to the murderer spending so much time with the vehicle before Cathy's car was discovered by the jogger on Sunday morning.

As it was, the diesel fuel posed another problem. It ruined and contaminated the evidence on the women and in the car interior. If the killer left fingerprints, chances are they had been lost. Any prints on the back window of the Honda had been destroyed due to the zealousness of the park rangers in shattering the rear window.

The agents turned to the viciousness of the crime as a possible link to the killer. This was not a simple murder, this was brutal. Whoever committed this crime executed the women in an overkill-mode. The cutting of their throats was not necessary, and if he had been successful in destroying the car and the victim's remains, it would have carried the crime to a new level of cruelty.

Cathy's wounds were the most extensive. Was it because she had resisted, or was this personal in some way? Perhaps a jilted lover or a love triangle? The FBI agents turned their attention to the lifestyle that the women led, peering into Cathy's tight circle of friends, but the agents' understanding of gay lifestyles was alien to their own cultural mindset. The FBI in the 1980s was predominately male; the FBI had not allowed women into the academy at Quantico until 1972, and then only two. The male agents awkwardly attempted to penetrate a culture they could not fully comprehend at the time—a tight-knit supportive circle of lesbians where Cathy Thomas had been the lynchpin. The FBI zeroed in on Jolene Schira, Karen Miller, and Deb Hill.

While the theory of a love triangle was far-fetched in that group of friends, to the FBI it was not just plausible but explained a great deal. The fact Jolene had introduced Cathy and Becky seemed to be lost on the FBI. They showed up to interview people at the Hershee Bar, the men in black suits standing out considerably in that secretive community. Given the viciousness of the crime, they believed it had to be someone that was intimate with the victims.

The FBI was less-than-subtle in their accusations that the women may have been responsible for the murders. Accusations flew fast and furious. While on the surface the logic of the agents made sense—that perhaps one of the women, in a fit of jealous rage, might have killed Cathy and Becky—it did not fit the personalities of the women, nor their relationship. Still, the stiff-shirted men of the bureau drilled the women extensively, looking for any crack, no matter how insignificant, that might help them close the case quickly. In putting so much pressure on Schira and Miller early-on in the investigation, and without the calming influence of Cathy Thomas to hold the group together, the once tight clique began to fracture. Deb Hill recalls those times bitterly.

"When the FBI knocked at the door, I opened the door. … I talked to them. I answered their questions. I went down to their office in Norfolk because I felt compelled and honor-bound that that was my friend, that I was going to do whatever I could," said Deb.

"Karen and Jolene, understandably, were in a retreat,

protection mode, [and] that caused a schism in our relationship that we have *never* repaired. I will say in no uncertain terms, that's how they felt. They never forgave me for cooperating with the FBI. I don't know if they've forgiven. They felt I was aiding and abetting the FBI.

"I didn't see it that way. I felt like my loyalty was to Cathy, and if somebody was working the case, especially the FBI, I was going to give them absolutely everything I could.

"The FBI ... in the early eighties, they were pretty [much] pre-Stonewall [in their thinking]. They just weren't sophisticated in their behavioral abilities [like] the agents are today. ... Joe [Wolfinger], he was a gentleman with me, he didn't push me around, he didn't threaten me. He asked me some questions about, were we violent back then—that's not the right words—did we argue? 'No!' I said, 'Karen never raises the tone of her voice.' If I raise my voice it's like World War Three, like I committed the cardinal sin. He went and talked to my sister, and she said, 'They're just not like that. They don't talk loud. They're not boisterous. They're not reckless.' We just weren't like that."

The lines were formed though, and the group came apart. For all of their attempts to lay the crime at the feet of the women, it proved to be nothing more than a theory that lacked even a shred of evidence. One of the women suffered a mental breakdown as a result of the stress of the investigation. The group disintegrated and remains apart even to this day.

The FBI slowly shifted to Becky's acquaintances as someone with a possible motive. The suspicion fell on her jilted boyfriend, Farooq M. Butt. Being Muslim, coming from a culture in the United Arab Emirates that was intolerant of homosexuality, and his possession of a temper, Mr. Butt was high on the list of persons of interest. He underwent scrutiny but had an alibi that he was in Washington, DC, the weekend of the murders. While only two hours away, it was enough to scratch him off the list from the FBI's perspective.

* * * * *

Robert Dowksi spent time on the campus of William and Mary doing what he could to keep up the pressure on the FBI. The Dowski clan was struggling not just with the death of their beloved Becky but with the shocking news of her relationship with Cathy Thomas.

"We had no idea that she was struggling with her identity. We had no idea that she had been dating Cathy—that came as a total shock," said Ginny Minarik. "It was so much new information, and you had no idea as to who in the heck would do this—why would they do this? She was so bright, so caring, just this great gifted young woman whose life was snuffed out long before it should have been."

Becky's death was not the first murder of a student at the College of William and Mary. Part-time student Audrey Jean-Weiler had been murdered by Michael Marnell Smith near the James River in 1975. Smith had been a member of a tight-knit religious community that lived along the James River not far from the Colonial Parkway, albeit at the opposite end from where Cathy and Becky were found.

As Ms. Weiler had strolled along the James River to do some sunbathing, Smith had jumped her, forced her to strip, raped her, strangled her with his bare hands, dragged her to the beach, held her head under water, stabbed her three times, and left her corpse floating in the river. His justification for the murder—it was the devil that had done it. Smith had no role in what unfolded with the bodies found on the Colonial Parkway though; six weeks earlier he had been put to death by electrocution. In a strange twist, both deaths took place on the same isolated stretch of road.

Becky had achieved a first in the history of William and Mary, the murder of a full-time student, clearly not an honor anyone would have desired.

Mark Owsiejco, a seasoned stockbroker that worked with Cathy Thomas suddenly found himself taking on her client load. He remembered his colleague fondly. "She was a pleasure to work with, to tell you the truth, because she took her work seriously and did a good job. Many times she was probably one of the last people to leave the office." Owsiejco remembered taking messages for Cathy from Becky but beyond that had little to offer investigators.

A memorial service was held for Becky on campus at the Sir Christopher Wren building, and a scholarship fund was established in her name at the Poughkeepsie YWCA. Sixty students attended the memorial.

The campus newspaper, *The Flat Hat*, eulogized her with the following: "John Donne once wrote our lives are like chapters in the same book, and when someone dies, a chapter is not torn out, but rather translated into a different language. Rebecca Ann Dowski's chapter will continue to influence those who knew her, and those who loved her. Her death, most certain, diminishes the rest of us as well."

Julie Travis, her sister, said, "She was a wonderful girl. She was very smart, had a head on her shoulders. She was not at all a druggie. If anything she was an all-American girl. She doesn't deserve to die at the side of the road the way she did."

The family held a private ceremony at the First Presbyterian Church in Patterson, New York, far from the prying eyes of the media and spectators. Becky's remains were quietly cremated, and her ashes spread in the Hudson Valley where she had been raised.

Memorial services for Cathy were held at a navy chapel in Norfolk and at the United States Naval Academy. Cathy was also cremated, her ashes scattered at sea by a US Navy ship off of Norfolk at her family's request.

*****

The FBI was struggling after a few short weeks of investigation. The story about the pair's murder in the quaint Williamsburg/Yorktown area in a national park made newspapers in Washington, DC, New York, and Chicago. The media wanted answers, and those answers were not forthcoming. Some of this was the standard FBI policy about not releasing information related to open cases. Some of it was that the FBI didn't have much to report. Their early hopes for resolving the murders quickly faded as the leaves began to turn brown and tumble down onto the parkway.

The law enforcement net was cast wide. FBI Special Agent Jim Waters told the press, "Every police department you can think of is busy fielding phone calls."

Captain Ron Montgomery of the York County Sheriff's Department said, "Most of these calls are citizens trying to be helpful."

Larry Vardell, the chief of the Williamsburg Police Department was quick to weigh in. "There doesn't seem to be [a] stalker involved with this." How he arrived at that conclusion only a few days after the discovery of the bodies was a mystery in and of itself.

In reality, it would be seventeen days after the bodies of Thomas and Dowski were discovered before the Williamsburg and James City County police were given any details about the incident and asked to check to see if they had any contact from the victims after the time of their last appearance. The search of the York River along the shoreline for any evidence did not take place until sixteen days after the discovery of the Honda. The embankment where the car was found could only be searched by water, and that was done by the York County Sheriff's Department and Fire Department divers on October 28. The FBI did not seem to be in hurry, which only frustrated the family members more.

Other law enforcement agencies were being drawn into the investigation but found working with the bureau to be a one-way street in terms of information flow.

"The FBI isn't maintaining contact," Mike Yost of the Williamsburg Police Department told the *Virginia Gazette* newspaper on October 22, 1986. "I don't want to give the impression that there's bad blood between us, and I don't know if this is normal procedure for them or if they aren't maintaining contact because there's nothing to relate. And we don't know what's rumor or truth, so we don't know if the calls we're getting have been helpful to them."

Sheriff P. S. Williams of the York County Sheriff's Department seemed to concur. "We had two men helping the FBI the day after the bodies were found but we haven't had any contact with them since then, except that we turn our leads over to them."

The FBI remained a wall of silence. Jack Wagner of the bureau was queried about the autopsy reports. "I'm not sure I'd release the reports if they were in. We're still too deep into the investigation."

York County's Sheriff Williams offered his own opinion. "I think this is an isolated incident. My personal opinion is that the murder happened somewhere else and the car was brought there. But I want to stress that this is my opinion only."

National Park Services spokesperson Ann Meyers offered caution. "We don't encourage people to be out on the parkway after dark. The parkway is 23 miles long, and there are few exits. And it's sometimes hard for a ranger to get to you right away if there's a problem. It's neither more or less safe than any other area, but federal property is susceptible to crime too."

Sheriff Williams quickly added, "I wouldn't advise parking along the parkway."

One has to keep in mind that the FBI historically had not utilized other law enforcement to do its work in terms of interviewing sources of information. As Irvin Wells of the FBI put it, "It's not that we wouldn't. We would have done it. We have a system in the bureau. We have a way we write up interviews and what we do. If a sheriff's deputy went out, with who knows what kind of skills, and conducted an interview and gave it to us it wouldn't be like an FBI agent who knows. I don't mean to sound elitist, don't take me wrong."

Robert Dowski remained in Williamsburg for long painful days, struggling with the loss of his sister and trying everything he could to generate tips and leads. "There is no clear motive in the case. The wallets were found on the victims. They had money. Beyond that, not a lot is known. Where were they going—I don't know."

In another interview with the *Daily Press,* the fact that there was no sign of a fight was disturbing. "That's one of the puzzling aspects of the case. The facts of the case suggest there weren't any signs of a struggle, at least inside of the car," said Robert.

The problem that the FBI was facing was that the leads were not advancing the narrative of the case. The initial focus on Cathy's circle of friends had led the women to simply retreat, rather than help, their accusers. These were two young women that did not have enemies—no one that would have inflicted this kind of pain on Becky and Cathy. The thinking began to shift from looking at someone that was intimate with one or both of the women, to a killer with no previous connection. At the time, the logic seemed sound.

As a result, the FBI pivoted to their Behavioral Science Unit at nearby Quantico, Virginia. In 1986, behavioral science as a tool for law enforcement was relatively new in its infancy, but a review of the evidence and circumstances could provide the agents in the field with a profile of a possible killer. This led the bureau to arrive at a new theory—dubbed, the Waterman Theory.

Irvin "IB" Wells of the FBI remembers how it all came

together.

"Here's what we thought. In Thomas's hair, there was a piece of line. I use the word 'line' as opposed to 'rope.' *Nautical* line, okay? There were line or rope marks around their necks, apparently to subdue them at that time. I imagine Thomas fought back like hell. Also the diesel was poured over the bodies and the car … interior. Diesel fuel, as you know, you know more than I do, burns very hot, but it is hard to ignite. And it didn't ignite. Their throats … I think Thomas's, her head was almost severed.

"So, here's what we came to learn. … Most of the boats run on diesel. They don't buy diesel at the marinas because it costs more. They buy diesel at gas stations where it is less. Thus most of the watermen drive pickup trucks with a diesel can in the back. The cuts [on the victims] was so sharp few knives would do that, but the knives fishermen use are made to cut fish that way. We had nautical line in Thomas's hair. We had the diesel poured over the bodies inside the car, which didn't ignite. We had throats slit—probably with a knife like what watermen might use—and I guess that's it."

All this information was sent to the Behavioral Science Unit at Quantico.

"They said [it was] clearly two [men]. One guy didn't take charge of these girls. One would be dominant over the other. They would be macho. Based on the information you gave us, they were probably waterman. And they would have a typical macho vehicle."

The thinking at the time, per the Behavioral Science Unit, was that the killer did not come prepared to commit the crime.

"Our assumption was they *used the tools they had*. They didn't bring the diesel, they *had* it in the back of the truck because they were watermen. They didn't bring the lines because they *had* it. They didn't bring the knives because they *had* the knives. They were all tools and implements of convenience.

"I don't remember what Behavior Sciences said … but could it be, could it *be*, that two watermen came upon these two women and were so infuriated they killed them?"

Thus armed, the FBI began to survey the fishermen working in the area in hopes of spotting a pair of individuals that fit the profile. There were some, but none seemed to stand out. Watermen, as a group, tended to work in small groups or alone. They tended to be independent operators who sold their catch to whoever happened to be buying. Most were hardworking. All were strong men; that was the nature of their work. They lived paycheck to paycheck on the whim of whatever Mother Nature gave them in terms of their catch. They were a culture in and of themselves, often closed to the outside world. The bureau tried to penetrate that small universe, and while they had some people that looked more suspect than others—nothing immediately came out of the Waterman Theory, at least not for another two years.

Concerns and fear turned to the park itself. There were allegations that some of the park rangers may be the killers. Attention focused on two rangers, one of which was Clyde Yee—as one of the first responders, he seemed to be a viable person of interest. That theory, however, did not hold water. Yee was cleared by polygraph, though he would continue to find himself a part of the Colonial Parkway Murders over the years, as well as other murders and crimes.[5]

Murders in the area were fairly rare events. There were seven murders in York County that year, all of which were solved relatively quickly. There were no murders in Williamsburg in both 1985 and 1986. Only two murders in 1985 remained unsolved, those of Cathy Thomas and

---

5   Yee's activities were documented in length in the book by Paul Berkowitz: *The Case of the Indian Trader: Billy Malone and the National Park Service Investigation at Hubbell Trading Post.* Yee was also one of the investigators that was early on the scene of a double-murder of two females in the Shenandoah National Park, covered elsewhere in this book.

Rebecca Dowski. Try as they may, the FBI and local authorities found their leads drying up. They had theories with no solid evidence and a profile that had, initially, led them nowhere. The case went cold ... and would remain in that state for another two years.

People remembered the crimes though. Parents warned their children to stay away from the Colonial Parkway at night. It took on the form of ghost stories, a local legend of sorts. The fact that this heinous crime remained unsolved seemed to be acceptable to everyone but the investigators and the families of the victims.

Years later Robert Meadows of the FBI reviewed the case files for the crime and commented to the press, "It's almost like they went willingly to their deaths," despite the evidence of the struggle that took place with both women. His words pointed to the need for more—more information, more evidence, more *anything*.

Chief Park Ranger Wallace "Wally" Neprash said the park service was treating the murders as "an isolated incident." Those words were going to come back at him in the coming months ...

THE SECOND

David Knobling and Robin Edwards
Disappeared on the early morning hours of September 20, 1987
Remains recovered on September 23, 1987

CHAPTER 5

Underneath his truck, on the cold concrete garage floor, David Knobling found peace. Tinkering with model cars—and later full-size vehicles—he grew up watching his adoptive father race at local racetracks. Being elbows deep under the hood, David enjoyed working with his hands and being able to enjoy his hard work. Nowadays, Michael Knobling can't listen to Lee Brice's "I Drive Your Truck" without getting emotional thinking about his older brother. The song harkens to a man driving his truck with the windows down, tearing up a field, merging human and vehicle. "It just fits because I wanted his truck. Just because I loved that truck and just because of him," said Michael.

David Lee Knobling was born on January 31, 1967, to Judy and Justin Ward. As a baby, David never knew his father—Judy took David and left her husband after she witnessed signs of abuse. She met a German man, Karl Knobling, when David was only eighteen months old.

Karl Knobling was a hardworking mix of Southern good old boy and rigid German ... a heartwarming combination. Karl came to America in 1956 from Munich and grew up in Mississippi. During his time in the Army, he ended up spending four years in Germany.

"I saw more of Germany in those years than I did when I lived there. I was in transportation and drove trucks all over Germany. I saw the wall go up and saw the wall come down," Karl said of the Berlin Wall.

Judy Knobling was born in Martinsville, Virginia, and grew up in Hampton Roads. She was the kind of person that believed you didn't have to have anyone support you, you provided your own way in life. Judy lived that ideal by working from the age of seventeen until the time that David was born. She found her true calling working in a small law firm in the 1970s.

When David was four, Judy and Karl got married. Karl Knobling legally adopted David. Shortly after they got married, the couple welcomed David's little brother, Michael.

"While married to Karl, I sold my motorcycle in order to get money to attend the College of Hampton Roads, specializing in legal studies," said Judy. "I began working as a receptionist and later secretary at Patten & Wornom in the Denbigh section of Newport News."

She went on to a successful legal career as a certified legal assistant, including managing the asbestos department of the firm. "I tried to instill this sense of hard work and accomplishment in my boys."

Growing up, Michael and David shared their father's love for cars and racing.

"I got into racing. I started out doing drag racing then moved to tracks. David started out on my pit crew," Karl said.

The boys loved spending time with their father, watching him race in the demolition derbies and working in the garage together. Both boys loved cars and proclaimed themselves "gearheads." Karl's gift to both boys was to infuse motor oil into their bloodstreams.

"My dad used to race cars at Langley Speedway. Just local trucks, nothing major. David raced in Enduro racing a couple of times. It's pretty much a demolition derby on an oval track," Michael recalls while sitting in his own workshop and garage today. Enduro racing was rough, tumble, dangerous, and exhilarating—and David enjoyed it.

The Knobling family lived in Newport News, Virginia, at the mouth of the James River in the Chesapeake Bay. During the Civil War the town didn't exist, it was a series of plantations and fishing villages that were eventually merged and combined to become a city. At one end of the city was

Fort Monroe, America's only fort with a moat, witness to the clash of the ironclads *USS Monitor* and *CSS Virginia* during the Civil War.

There were rough sections of town, such as Warwick, and wealthy neighborhoods, often only separated by a single street or block. The community was and remains a merging of races and widely diverse incomes. It was a community that had a blend of military personnel—retired and still in-service, as well as those that worked at the nearby shipyards. It was in the Newport News shipyards that WWII was forged and put to sea and even in the 1980s was still putting new ships out to face the Soviet threat. Newport News in the 1980s had a gritty element to it, and its people were generally hardworking and hard-playing folk.

Family vacations were spent in the Outer Banks off the coast of North Carolina, including Nags Head and Kill Devil's Hill. The Knoblings visited Buckroe Beach in Virginia where the boys enjoyed fishing off of the pier.

"One memory I have is of Christmas. We were all there all around the tree, with the boys putting toys together. It's hard to remember that stuff now," said Karl.

Judy and Karl separated when David was eleven and Michael was seven. Both boys went to live with their mother in a small apartment and visited Karl from time to time.

Michael Knobling looks back at his childhood fondly.

"Bless my mother. She raised us, and [we] were both hellions. We fought all of the time. I would get him in trouble so easily. My mom would be sitting on the other side of the wall, and I would call 'Mom, David hit me!' I used to get him in trouble all the time. But he got me back for sure," Michael said. "I don't see why my mom isn't gray-haired and dead by now just off the stress we caused her. She left her husband, got an apartment, and was working full time with two boys. In high school, she and the dean were on a first name basis—skipping, fighting, the typical teenage stuff."

David's mother struggled as a single mother to raise her

two boys.

"After we got separated, I was a single mom again. We were living in a dinky apartment. I was working all the time it felt like, and I would often have to leave the boys together at home. Being brothers, they fought constantly," Judy said. "I would get calls at work from them, saying how the other did this or did that, and I just couldn't take it anymore. I looked into military schools and decided to send him [David] to Hargrave in Chatham. It was close to Martinsville, and I had relatives that lived up there."

Hargrave is a private American college preparatory boarding school with a solid reputation.

"At first, he hated it. He would call and say 'They made us march in the rain for four hours!' or 'They have all these stupid rules.' This went on for a couple months until all the sudden, he got it. He started following the rules and actually loved the structure the military school gave him. He got promotions, to sergeant or whatnot, and I think that also helped him enjoy it more," Judy said.

"We would load up the car and go and visit him, but only a couple of times a year since it was so far and I was working full time and Michael was in school. I was so tickled that his cousin attended a formal dance with him at the school. He was one of the few guys to bring a date, and, of course, she was very pretty. There's a picture of him, with a grin …"

After a year at that school, David moved to Frederick Military Academy in Portsmouth, Virginia. Karl was not helping with school for his second year, and Judy was determined to make sure David got a good education.

"We really liked the fact that it was so much closer to home. He would attend school during the week and come home weekends. Michael and I drove over every Friday to pick him up and come Sunday evening, we would take him back to school. It gave us a chance to get to know each other. Unfortunately, Frederick Military Academy closed down the following year and David wasn't able to continue."

He went to Warwick High School his senior year but didn't graduate.

"On his own, he got his GED without anyone even telling him to," said Mrs. Knobling.

That David would go back and complete his education on his own accord speaks volumes of his character. David was a good student when he applied himself. He liked to read and play football with his friends.

"He was always a cool dude to me. He had huge biceps. I hated him for it; I was so jealous. He had everything I wanted. He got the girlfriend before me and the car before me," laughed his brother, Michael.

When he got old enough to drive, Judy took her oldest son to look at trucks. She told David that she would co-sign a truck for him, but he fell in love with every truck on the lot. Unable to make a reasonable decision, David didn't get a truck that day. One day, he drove a brand new 1986 black Ford Ranger home to his mother's surprise.

"He had gotten it on his own. He could talk his way into anything," she said.

The truck helped the Knobling brothers bond. Michael helped David install a new radio, rigging the wires so the radio would play without the truck being on. Both boys loved that truck to death.

Judie recalls that her eldest son "loved people. He liked talking to people. It didn't matter how old they were. He just liked getting to know people. He was a loner in a way."

The oldest Knobling son knew a lot of people and got along with everyone but he had a pretty small group of friends. His brother remembers David's broad circle of friends.

"David and I were always different. I was the short chubby guy, and he was tall, skinny, and muscular," said Michael. "He had a fantastic personality. I didn't know until after his death, but he kept in touch with everybody. Friends that we had in a neighborhood we lived in. I found out that David would go back to the neighborhood and visit the parents of the friends we hung out with. He did that a lot. I've talked to a lot of my friends and they say he would just come by and say hi to their parents."

When he was about sixteen years old, David learned the identity of his real father. David still referred to Karl as his father but wanted to know more about his real father, Justin Ward. Karl and Michael knew that David had gone to meet his birth father at least once, but no one in the family knew that David had created a relationship with Ward.

"I knew nothing about David visiting his real father. He never once told me. Justin actually came to his funeral. Come to find out, David had not just visited him once but he actually hung out with his family often. David had a good relationship with Justin's other kids; it was crazy to know we didn't know that about him," said Judy.

David was a true child at heart.

"He was the oldest grandchild in the family. We always did a huge Easter egg hunt every year for all the kids. The year he was eighteen, all of the younger kids were older, too. We didn't plan an egg hunt that Easter. He organized the egg hunt on a whim; he convinced everyone that there just had to be an egg hunt. It didn't matter if everyone was older then," said Mrs. Knobling.

Mrs. Knobling remembers a special Mother's Day: "One year, David dragged Michael and loaded up the car with flowers. Not just a bouquet, but a ton of flowers. They actually planted them all for me, but it was all David's idea."

As he got older, he became more of his own man, his father Karl said.

"We argued, especially when he was spending so much time with his mom. I only saw him one or two days a week. We got along pretty good. Michael tagged along with him everywhere."

Holidays were always a big affair.

"We always had the two holidays thing going on. We

went to my dad's house on Christmas Eve. And of course we'd spend Christmas with Mom and that side of the family. Mom always spoiled us. We always got what we wanted. She spoiled us rotten. We spent a lot of time with my grandparents, aunts, and uncles. Christmases were big back then, a big family affair," said Michael.

Another fond memory for Michael involved the local Yorktown drive-in.

"He [David] was driving and told me I could bring as many of my friends as I wanted, but we had to all ride in the trunk. We had a big Oldsmobile Delta 88, so I think we got six or seven people in that trunk," Michael said.

David enjoyed building model cars, listening to rock and metal music, and drawing. He loved to draw dragons and monsters; he seemed to be really talented with his art. Michael and David both loved watching the movie *Grease*. His favorite bands included Pink Floyd, Kansas, Rush, AC/DC, Marshall Tucker, and some Charlie Daniels.

"I remember us going on a vacation; I don't remember where we were going. We were both sitting in the back seat singing 'The Devil Went Down to Georgia.' I can remember it like it was yesterday. Me and him, there singing it. I don't know nothing else, but I remember that stuff. If I hear that song today, I still flash right back to it," Michael said.

Michael remembers his older brother always hanging around a group of friends. The teenagers were always going over to someone's house or out to the movies or to dinner. He met his girlfriend, Tara Cook, when he was leaving his brother's birthday. The couple started dating, and on December 30, 1985, David told Tara he loved her for the first time. The couple had a three-year gap in their ages, with Dave being nineteen in 1987 and Tara being sixteen. If they had been thirty and twenty-seven, the difference in ages would have meant nothing. Being nineteen and sixteen raised some eyebrows.

"David and I had our ups and downs. We were not perfect.

We broke up and got back together on several occasions," Tara said. "We dated other people during the few weeks we would be apart. Normal teenage drama. He loved the ladies and didn't like being alone. If he and I broke up, he was on the move to find someone else. We always found our way back to each other. We loved each other."

He was always very kind.

"He was the type of person that you knew had your back. He did not just say he was your friend … he acted like your friend. He put in the time to be a friend to everyone. He was goofy. He had a silly sense of humor and wasn't afraid to show it. He had a quick temper, but it didn't last long. He forgave easily. He wore his heart on his sleeve. He was outgoing and loved spending time with his friends. He loved group outings and get-togethers," Tara said. "He loved cars and even tried his hand at dirt track racing in Saluda. One race I went to he placed third. In the little over two years I knew him he owned three different cars. A beat up Pontiac, a Mercury Capri [the only 'Mustang' he could afford], and his Ford truck."

Tara remembers how David's smile lit the room.

"In a gathering, he was usually at the center of attention or trying to be. Either by funny jokes or silly actions. It was hard not to like him. He was just so outgoing, gregarious, and active. He was easy to talk to and loved to talk even more. I swear he could talk forever and you would think he was the expert on everything. We jokingly called him a 'know it all' because he had an opinion on everything. Even if he was wrong, he would swear he was right and try to defend his position. He was stubborn; once he made up his mind about something it could be pretty damn hard to change it. We were both young and stubborn and boy would we argue. He smoked cigarettes, he drank alcohol, and he smoked pot," Tara said.

"He did not live a perfect life but he did live. He was genuine, kind, funny, and loving."

Tara Cook can recall the exact amount of time she knew David Knobling: Two years, two months, and twenty days. She still refers to him as the love of her life.

The start of September 1987 was proving to be life-changing for David. Tara told him that she was pregnant with his child. David and Tara informed both of their respective families of the pregnancy, and the couple started to discuss marriage.

"I told him that he should marry her ... it was a different time then. Not like in the sixties, but not like today either. I thought he should marry her, and if it didn't work out in the future, that was fine," Mrs. Knobling explained.

The previously on-and-off couple decided to truly commit once they learned of the pregnancy. According to Tara, David was preparing to sell his beloved Ford Ranger in favor of something with a back seat so that he could transport their child when he or she was born.

With parenting responsibilities looming, David looked to changing his career. He had worked for his father doing landscaping for a few years but had gotten a job at a water purification company. He took his new job as a salesperson at World Health Corporation seriously, even doing presentations for his family and friends to practice. Three weeks into his new job and he got his first paycheck on September 19, 1987.

"It was a big paycheck, too. Eight hundred dollars was a lot of money back then for a paycheck," said his mother. David wouldn't get the chance to cash that check.

David Knobling, a soon-to-be first-time father in a committed relationship, was caught in a twist of fate that brought him to rendezvous with his destiny in an unlikely place. His cousin Jason was going out with a young girl, Robin Edwards. David agreed to be the driver on the outing. He invited his brother Michael to join him.

The weather report called for rain, but they all piled into his truck, the excess riders taking to the back of the Ranger. It was a simple gesture of his time, agreeing to take his cousin on a date. It would prove to be fateful.

CHAPTER 6

In our youth, a popular fantasy we share is the thought of running away from home. At one point or another, we all have contemplated packing up and starting over. Whether it's the desire to get away or the lure of the unknown adventure, most of us never fulfill that fantasy. Fears, self-doubt, and even a cold hard hint of reality discourage us from even trying. These thoughts smother the thoughts of living on our own and taking big risks just for the sake of trying. The mundane routine of our lives overpowers that burning desire for pure independence. Not so with Robin Edwards.

Her whole life was about running away both physically and metaphorically. It wasn't that she was running away from home—it was more that she was running to something. The excitement, the independence, the adventure, or even just being there for a friend was enough to make Robin want to run. In reality, one could say Robin was running away from her childhood, putting it in the rearview mirror. She was chomping at the bit to be an adult in almost every aspect of her life. Her physical age was not where her head was; in her mind, she was more mature. While Robin may have been physically fourteen at the time of her death, she was many years older in terms of life experience.

The world for runaways is a dark place. It isn't filled with the elements of excitement and happiness, but instead a seedy, dangerous place with people who seek to take advantage of you. Robin climbed out of her bedroom window one night too many, and her fantasy life she had so dearly embraced came to a screeching halt.

On August 3, 1973, Robin Edwards was born in Lexington Park, Maryland, to Bonita "Bonnie" and Robert "Bob" Edwards. She was named after Bob's mother, Robin

Margaret Edwards. Robin had one older sister, Jeanette, at the time she was born. Bonnie fell in love with Bob when she only fifteen. "Only by the grace of God did I not marry him then," she said fondly of their courtship.

The couple was off and on for about six years, and every six months or so Bob would write to her and ask her to marry him. Bonnie always had the same response: "I would tell him to go to hell."

Despite her resistance to Bob's written proposal, fate was destined to intervene. In 1969, Bonnie headed down to help her sister in Coco Beach, Florida. She was recovering from thyroid surgery, and Bonnie helped with her four children. The ever-persistent Bob called Bonnie to ask her to marry him once again, though it was far from the romantic down-on-one-knee proposal she had hoped for. "He sounded like he had been drinking. I told him to call me back when he wasn't drunk the next day. I don't want a drunk proposal."

Bonnie was starting to soften her feelings, despite Bob's failed attempts. "He called me back that next day but his buddy had to hold him up; he was that drunk. I told him to come to Florida."

The navy sailor flew from Norfolk to Florida, and the couple hit it off. In person, Bob clearly made the connection she had been hoping for. The pair of lovebirds drove to Harrisburg, Pennsylvania, where Bob's mother lived, and got married right in her living room. It was an intimate family affair with his aunt, cousins, mother, and the landlady all in attendance as witnesses for their wedding.

Jeanette was two when her mother married Bob, and the family packed up and moved to Norfolk. Only a month into the marriage, Bob was sent out to sea for seven and a half months. The first two years of their marriage, they were only physically together for five months. From Norfolk, the family moved to southern Maryland where Robin was later born.

Robin proved to be a feisty child, even as a baby. "When

I couldn't get her to settle down and sleep, I would take her outside. She wanted to hear the bugs. I would walk her around the yard, and she would go right to sleep," Bonnie said.

In 1975, just twenty-two months after Robin was born, the third Edwards daughter, Pam, was born while the family lived in Puerto Rico. The Edwards family lived in the Fort Alan Base along with other military families. Everyone at the base didn't know Robin by her first name, but instead by the nickname Boo-Boo.

"From the time she was walking she was very independent. She would go anywhere that she wanted to go. There was a swing set near the apartment; she would scale the poles and hang from her knees on the top of the swing set. She was fearless. If she wanted something from the top of the fridge, she would scale the cabinets to get onto the counter to get those cookies. You could lock the gates, but she would just climb over. She would always find the most handsome young fellow to bring her home. She would walk up to them and say 'My name is Boo-Boo, and I am losted.' She was a darn flirt!" Bonnie said. "She never knew a stranger."

Jeanette Santiago, Robin's older sister, recalls being the responsible sister. Jeanette would often search the base on her bicycle looking for her adventurous younger sister. Robin was always nonchalant, she was always "just going on a walk!"

When Robin started taking dance classes, she began to wear her leotard daily. Jeanette told Robin and Pam to at least put shorts on over their leotards while they played outside. Robin responded in true Robin-fashion, by marching to the end of the driveway and pulling her leotard up even farther.

Robin, at just six years old, decided she was going to run away. She stuffed a bag with underwear and socks as she headed for the door. Jeanette decided to call her little sister's bluff. "That's all you're going to wear? You're going to need shirts and pants! Let me help you pack."

Robin, not realizing what running away truly meant, started to get upset and cry. That day she didn't run away, but it was a premonition of what was to come with her.

The Edwards family settled in Norfolk after a few years in Puerto Rico. Bob retired from the navy in 1978 and took a job in security. The Edwardses seemed to fit right into the Newport News area. The area, on the north shore of the James River, was home to many military and working class families. Joint Base Langley-Eustis employed thousands, making the economy in Newport News very military-based. The James River provided a harbor and boating area to Newport News.

They spent their family vacations in Pennsylvania to visit Bob's mother or at Luray Caverns. "The kids loved staying on the campground. There was so much to do and they had a ball," Bonnie said

Robin spent her time babysitting the neighbor's two sons and riding her bike. She loved to swim and enjoyed drawing. She wanted to grow up and be an artist. Def Leppard and Michael Jackson topped her favorite music. She loved the Michael Jackson song, "Bad." Her favorite movie was *Dirty Dancing,* and she enjoyed watching *M*A*S*H* with her dad.

She loved wrestling; Hulk Hogan was her favorite wrestler.

"One year for Christmas, we got her a Stretch Armstrong Hulk Hogan. To keep her from guessing or peeking as to what it was, I put it in a can so she couldn't find out," said Bonnie.

Robin was the kind of child you had to stay one step ahead of.

She was always her daddy's little girl. In Bob's eyes, Robin could do no wrong and he spoiled her. She started smoking at age twelve, a habit she learned from Bob.

Robin was rambunctious and seemed to get wilder as she matured. She got in trouble at school for wearing shorts that were too revealing. Bob was called down to school to bring her "suitable attire." He walked into the school and came across a student wearing a miniskirt and top far more revealing that what Robin was wearing. Bob vehemently defended Robin, telling her principal to not waste his time bringing her clothing when she was dressed more conservatively than other students.

"Robin was extremely bright, but too much so. She needed to be kept interested and constantly challenged in order to do well. We weren't a perfect family but there was a lot of love, teasing, and kidding around," Bonnie told the *Daily Press.*

During a parent-teacher conference, her teacher said Robin was a troublemaker and a ringleader but she was the most polite trouble maker the teacher had seen.

On one occasion she had set off on her bike to go to the circus that was in Newport News. "She was going to run off with the circus," Bonnie Edwards said. She had plans to marry someone with the circus and go on the road with them. The Edwards went down and rounded up their wayward daughter.

Jeanette confronted her sister about being sexually active when she was twelve or thirteen. "I'm young enough, by the time I get AIDS, they'll have a cure for it. I'm not worried," Robin told her.

Robin told her sister she didn't need to learn how to cook or wash dishes because she didn't plan on ever having to. "She thought that wasn't going to be her life. She wanted to be taken care of," said Jeanette.

Jeanette recalls how Robin was wild in her ways and always seemed to push the envelope. She had gotten a little white kitten and came up with a name for him.

"He was pure white, and she wanted to call him Cocaine," Jeanette said. "I told her no, of course, and she tried to settle for the name Coke. Again, no."

Robin's response: "I guess I'll just call him Classic then."

"So we ended up naming the kitten Classic." The family laughs at the story even today.

Robin was quirky and funny, and she knew just what to say to get her family and friends to think *"Did she really just say that?"*

"Robin loved animals. She would lay Classic upside down on her lap and stroke his paws. He would go right to sleep. Robin would say to me, 'Mom, just call me the cat whisperer.' She was horse crazy. We found out later that she would skip school with her friends and they would go visit this one horse. I didn't know she was skipping or that she ever visited that horse, but I found out after she died from the horse's owner," said Mrs. Edwards.

Skipping school was easy for her with two hardworking parents who were not able to monitor her every move.

"She had the maturity of an 18-year-old but she was still 10 or 11 in other ways. She felt like she was ready to be on her own and she really wasn't. She had the idea she could take care of herself. She was very independent, confident, and very trusting of other people. She wasn't afraid of any situation," Bonnie told the *Daily Press*.

Robin's older sister, Jeanette, believed Robin was doing drugs at a young age. One day, Robin asked her mother to take her to the hospital to visit a friend. "I took her up to see him. She called him Mouse. She looked terrified when she saw him. He had kidney damage. She later said to me, 'Mom, I didn't know drugs could do that to you.'"

It was burst of stark realization.

Jeanette moved out of the family home when she was seventeen and into her own apartment. Jeanette had her own daughter, Rachel, while she was in high school. Robin stayed close with her sister, often bringing Classic along for weekends at her apartment.

"Rachel always wanted to be with Robin, but that wasn't cool when you're trying to be cool," Jeanette said. Jeanette got married and had another baby shortly after moving out.

Bonnie faced a crossroads with parenting her girls: "When Jeanette needed the help the most with the two little ones, I had to figure out who needed me the most."

Robin first disappeared in May 1987. Her close friend Donna Miller told Robin that she wanted to run away after she got mad at her parents.

"She emptied her piggy bank, took her pillow, blanket, extra clothes, and cans of food. Donna didn't take much of anything. … Robin wasn't the one who wanted to run away, but she was the one who prepared," Mrs. Edwards said.

Robin was gone for a total of eight days with Donna. The girls had met a waitress at a diner, and the sympathetic waitress let the girls stay at her trailer by the James River Bridge. Robin went as far as to dye her naturally dirty blonde hair coal black. Mrs. Edwards drove around Newport News looking for her daughter. When driving through a trailer park, she thought she spotted Robin, but her hair had been dyed.

Later, Robin told her mother, "I knew you'd come looking for me, but I knew you'd never know it was me if I dyed my hair black."

The Edwardses pleaded for their daughter to come home.

"We did an interview on the news station and asked that she come home. We talked to the paper, and they ran an article. Robin saw the article in the paper and the news, and they decided they better go home. It was probably a moment of realization that, 'Our parents really *do* care about us.'

"When she ran away, she hung out with one guy, who was an adult and should've known better. His last name was Gross. He had no business messing around with a thirteen-year-old. That's what started some of the arguments, because I didn't approve. She wasn't allowed to see him if I knew about it," Mrs. Edwards said.

"She had older friends that had apartments. She told me once that they told her she could stay there with them as long as she would sleep with them and their friends," Jeanette said. Even for the rebellious Robin, that kind of relationship didn't have appeal.

Robin was only thirteen but seemed much more mature than other girls her age. Whether it was her quirky confidence or her aspiration to be older than she really was, Robin's attitude and personality seemed to change after she ran away with Donna. One night, after an argument with her mother, Robin pulled a knife on her. Mrs. Edwards sought help by having Robin taken to a juvenile detention center.

"She was a different person after she ran away. She was hate-filled, always angry at Mom. She would sharpen her fingernails so that if Mom ever grabbed her, she could scratch her," Jeanette remembers of Robin's personality change.

Due to Robin's good behavior in the detention center, she was bumped down to a less secure unit, but in July 1987, a judge ordered a physiological evaluation on the young teenager. After the ruling, Robin ran away from the detention center. For twelve hours overnight she wandered around Newport News. Her feet covered in blisters, she walked up to a Hampton police car parked outside of a 7-Eleven convenience store. "I'm Robin Edwards, and I ran away from secure detention. Can you take me back?" she asked the police officer. The officer, somewhat stunned, complied.

Robin was diagnosed with severe depression and ADHD after a psychiatric evaluation. She was sent to Charter Colonial Institute in Newport News and started on medication for her depression. She spent a total of six weeks at the behavioral center and started to take Zoloft daily.

"When she came home, she was a different person," said Jeanette. "Pammie did something that would normally piss her off, but Robin said, 'Relax. Let's just calm down.'

"We were all shocked. Robin just looked at us and said 'It's really okay. It's not that serious.'

"I think it was a combination of the program and the medication."

Robin returned home just in time to start middle school.

In September 1987, Robin started eighth grade at Huntington Middle School.

"On the first day of school, she was upset with me because I couldn't get her new school clothes before school started. She said 'Well, I'm going to wear what I damn well please then.' She looked like a pilgrim. She had on a black long sleeve top and a black maxi skirt with black tennis shoes and black socks. I told her I would get her new clothes that weekend, and I kept that promise," Bonnie said.

During Robin's final year at school, she started taking French class.

"She fell in love with French. She fell in love with the culture. She decided she wanted to become an exchange student in France," Bonnie said. "I told her that if she wanted to do something like that, she would have to bring her grades up. I told her she had to show them that she would be a good representative of the school and the country. She told me, 'I can do that, Mom.'"

Whether it was the interest in French, the medication, or the therapy, Robin had changed.

"She was doing her homework more regularly. She was honestly trying," said Bonnie.

Robin had just turned fourteen and seemed to have completely changed her attitude. The free spirited and snarky eighth-grader started to show her more serious side by volunteering to work with the Newport News Public Schools in a peer counseling program. She wanted to help troubled youth and seemed to be taking her school studies more seriously.

Seemingly gone was the rebel and runaway of her youth. Robin seemed in control of her emotions, at least to her family.

She accepted a date with a boy at her school. It wasn't intended to have any risks associated with it … just a trip to the movies then home.

CHAPTER 7

Their meeting was a fluke, one of those random events that occurs in life. What began as a chance encounter turned into three decades of frustrating loss and heartache.

David Knobling's and Robin Edwards's paths didn't cross until the night of September 19, 1987. Robin Edwards, an eighth-grader, had plans to go on a date with David Knobling's younger cousin Jason. The plan (as the Edwardses understood it) for the night had originally been for David Knobling's mother, Judy, to drive both Jason and Robin to the movies.

"She got a migraine and asked David to drive them instead," said Robin's older sister, Jeanette.

Judy Knobling recalls the evening vividly, though a little differently.

"The plan was for Jason to take her to the movies on his moped. However it was drizzling so David volunteered to drive them, and Michael just went along. I can remember that it was just misting and David asking if he should wear shoes or sandals. It was very warm out though for this time of year, and I told him that the sandals looked comfortable," Judy said.

"I was very proud of him to offer to take them. He was bummed out with the news of the baby as he and Tara were on the outs again and he knew she had been dating a friend of his. I was glad he got this off his mind for a while because we were both talked out from discussing the issue earlier in the day."

Jeanette knew David Knobling from his time in school. "He was a bit of nerd, the way I remember him." If anything that familiarity would have eased any concerns that the family might have had that night.

David had just started a new job and thought he would show the passengers where he would be working. David drove the young couple, along with his brother Michael, to the movie theater in his trusty Ford Ranger, but the movie they wanted to see, *Dragnet*, had already sold out for the night.

"We didn't go to a movie; we went to an arcade. Jason and Robin hung out the entire time while David and I hung out," said Michael. "It was raining that night, so we let Robin ride up front in David's truck—it only sat two people. Me and Jason rode in the back of the truck, and they rode in the front. Other than that, her and Jason hung out the entire time. I guess they planned to get back together again, it had to come when they were in the truck alone."

By Michael Knobling's recollection, David and Robin were only alone that evening for the twenty minutes or so they were in the cab of the truck. In that incredibly short period of time, the two made arrangements to rendezvous later that night, unbeknownst to their riders in the back of the rain-pelted truck bed.

Robin had a curfew that Saturday night of eleven o'clock and was home by 11:15 in order to call her mother at work to let her know that she was home. Robin watched television with her younger sister, Pam, until 12:30 a.m. or so.

Michael Knobling's memories of the night are still crisp. "We went and dropped Robin off, dropped Jason off, then me and David went back home," he said.

Judy Knobling ordered pizza for her sons, and they watched television for a while.

"Around midnight or so, David said he was going out for a while. He was twenty years old. He had lived on his own—in his own apartment at one time—and he came and went as he wanted. Neither Michael nor I asked where he was going," Judy said.

His kid brother was the last person to see David.

"I can remember him saying he was going somewhere,"

said Michael. Michael bummed a Marlboro Red off his older brother before David headed out into the dark, rainy Saturday night. "I was the only one who got to say bye to him. I sat there smoking a cigarette as he drove off, and that was the last time I ever saw him."

Michael didn't think of asking where David was going.

Robin's disappearance was not discovered until the next morning. Mr. Edwards had awakened around five Sunday morning before leaving for work and checked on the two girls. Pam lay asleep in her bed, but Robin's bed was empty. He called his wife at work to ask if she knew where Robin was.

"Evidently she's gone again," Mrs. Edwards said. With Robin's recent history of running away, it wasn't too farfetched to believe that she had snuck out again, possibly running away.

Mr. Edwards called his oldest daughter, Jeanette, to see if Robin was at her apartment. Jeanette remembers the night before as chaotic in her life.

"I was so exhausted from being up that entire night. My husband had gone out and came home so intoxicated that he couldn't even stand straight. He jumped through a window instead of coming in through the door. He wasn't coherent at one point, so we were at the hospital the entire night. He had alcohol poisoning, and we didn't get home until 3:00 a.m. from Riverside Hospital," Jeanette said.

Robin's rebellious side had caused a minor rift between her and her older sister.

"Robin and I weren't on speaking terms the night she disappeared. A few months prior, Robin had rode her bike all the way to Yorktown to meet some guy then rode her bike back to my house. I had to tell Mom about it, and Robin was so mad at me. She was still mad at me and wasn't talking to me still."

Robin had apparently sneaked her way out of the house sometime after 12:30 a.m., climbing through the window, and going down the street to join up with David. Unlike her previous runaways, it appeared that she hadn't taken anything with her this time, hinting that this was not a long-term departure but perhaps just her stepping out for the night after curfew.

After Mrs. Edwards had gotten home from work around 7:00 a.m., she immediately went down to the police station to file a missing persons report.

"They wouldn't let me put in a police report because she hadn't been missing long enough. There wasn't anyone in juvenile or anyone available on the weekends to take information," she said.

In the mid-1980s police were not as concerned about children running away—it was a different time where fears of killers and molesters were things only rumored about and certainly not in Newport News.

For Bonnie Edwards though, she was living every parent's nightmare: A quasi-street-savvy fourteen-year-old girl sneaking out of her house in the middle of the night. Robin's recent history of running away didn't make the ordeal any less stressful for Bonnie Edwards. All she knew was that in the middle of the night, Robin left her home and had gone into the darkness and had not come home.

At the Knobling household, David's presence was not cause for immediate alarm. As his mother recalls, "It was normal for him to come home late, especially on a Saturday night. Since we slept in that Sunday like we always do, we didn't realize he wasn't home until almost noon. As the day went by and I still hadn't heard from David, I became very concerned. Not hearing from him was very unusual. By late afternoon, I was calling everyone I could think of to try and track him down, but no one had seen or heard from him."

As the day wore on, concern started to mount. In two households in Newport News, only a mere few miles apart, each passing hour ratcheted up the tension and concern. At this point neither family knew how intertwined their lives were about to become. In fact, neither knew of the connection between the two missing offspring.

* * * * *

David's black 1986 Ford Ranger sat in the parking lot at Ragged Island, a state wildlife refuge in the rural Isle of Wight area the next morning. Ragged Island sits on the south side of the James River Bridge, just twenty miles south of the Colonial Parkway. The area was well known as dangerous to locals and well known to local police as a drug deal and crime area. Ragged Island is poorly lit at night with the deep marshy swamps leading into the James River.

The truck sat unlocked with both doors open. Almost eerily, the radio was playing when deputies walked up to inspect the abandoned vehicle. With the rains, the open doors with the radio on seemed strangely out of place.

Situated in a swampy lowland, the 1,537 acre refuge was thick with smartweed, marshmallow, black needlerush, wax myrtle, and loblolly pines that cover an almost impassible bog. From the lonely unlit parking area there were only two ways to the water. One was along a roadway that ran parallel to Route 17, depositing visitors at the base of the James River Bridge. Even with the proximity of the over four-mile-long bridge a few feet away, the pathway was obscured by a thick row of trees and cyclone fences.

The other path to the James River was a wooden boardwalk through the depths of the swampland. It has changed since 1987, with much of the tree growth thinned now, but even then it was a snaking path. Stepping off it puts you in the impassable swamps. The path slithered through the trees for nearly a mile through the bog to a sandy strip of beach along the James. The beach was sometimes inaccessible due to the tides, and with the rains that came that weekend, the tides were exceptionally high.

When you visit Ragged Island Refuge today it appears eerily similar as to how it did then, though the tree growth was much thicker and denser in 1987. Another difference now is that across the river the land has been somewhat more developed. The sparse downriver apartments, homes, and other development that is there provides some small amount of ambient light.

Ragged Island had a reputation for drug deals and seedy encounters that prevails even to this day. "There was a Newport News officer we dealt with about homosexuality there [Ragged Island] that was concerned. There was a lot going on there at that place. It was isolated; at the end of the bridge, traffic was slow at ten-eleven o'clock at night," former Isle of Wight Sheriff Charlie Phelps said, "When you came off the bridge, about the next building you saw, which isn't there now, was the Virginia Department of Highways and Transportation building at the intersection of 17 and 258. You didn't see Bojangles and shopping centers and all that stuff. It was a popular place, especially for those from the peninsula to come, because they could come across the bridge, drop right off there, run around, go right back when they finished with their business."

The discovery of David's truck was the first indication that something was amiss.

"The black 1986 Ford Ranger was found early Monday in the parking lot of the game preserve at the south end of the James River Bridge by a county sheriff's deputy on routine patrol. The keys were in the ignition, the radio was playing, and a door was open," said Deputy Joey Willard. What caught his attention, the deputy said, "There were two pairs of underwear and two pairs of shoes in the truck, along with Knobling's wallet," the *Daily Press* reported.

Witnesses at Ragged Island reported seeing the empty vehicle as early as 5:30 that morning. The keys were turned to the Accessories setting, presumably to play the radio.

Unaware of the potential crime scene, police called Judy Knobling early Monday morning regarding her son's truck being discovered at Ragged Island. The abandoned vehicle was a red flag to the Knobling family, who knew David would never leave his truck unlocked let alone with the doors wide open.

"I called into work, and my boss came over to take me to Ragged Island. We looked around there for a while but didn't see any sign of him. I could only go to work for a half day that day, but after a few hours, I was too upset to work. I went back to Ragged Island that evening," said Mrs. Knobling.

David was no stranger to the Ragged Island Refuge. According to David's girlfriend, Tara Cook, he had been to Ragged Island and was familiar with the area, although it was not the normal area that they parked. They favored a church that backed up to I-64 for their intimate moments.

Judy Knobling reached out to her ex-husband.

"I also called Karl and told him what happened. He came right over. The police wanted me to move the truck. I explained that something was wrong, this is evidence, but they insisted that there was no sign of foul play. I pointed out that he was missing and his wallet was on the dashboard. They wouldn't listen," said Judy. "At their insistence, a day or so later, I asked Karl to take the truck to his house as I had nowhere to put it and it was very upsetting looking at it because I knew something was wrong."

Karl Knobling was not the kind of man to sit back and let others search for his son without his involvement. The burly man decided to take the search for his son into his own hands.

"Judy called and told me that police found his truck out at Ragged Island. I went out there and met with the Isle of Wight Sherriff's Department. They were all standing there talking, a circle of jerks. I wanted to look around—check out the beach. I walked down and checked out part of it, but the tide was high. I went home and got my waders—went into the swamp," said Karl. "You know, I wasn't sure if he was out there, injured or something. There were some cops there, a couple of them, but they were not even looking. They said they searched the beach with a helicopter, but the entire time I was there I didn't see a helicopter."

Despite the arrival of the Knobling clan at the sight and their concern, the Isle of Wight Sheriff's Department seemed to take a lackadaisical approach to looking for David. This is odd given that missing persons reports for both David Knobling and Robin Edwards were filed independently with Newport News Police that Monday, September 21, 1987. Despite the fact that David was missing, they felt the best course of action was to tow his truck from the parking area.

"The police screwed up the investigation. They brought his truck out to me. Then, when they realized it might be a crime scene, they came back and took fingerprints. When they left, I found the fingerprint cards out there in my front yard," said Mr. Knobling.

A white pair of women's Keds shoes with writing all over them was found in David's truck. Being women's shoes, the authorities began to piece together that David and Robin had met each other the night before. Moreover, they began to connect that the two both might be missing together.

Bonnie Edwards recalls when the authorities were able to confirm Robin's presence in David's truck. "The police came to the house with a picture of Robin's shoes. I identified them as hers ... white tennis shoes that she drew all over. She put a Band-Aid over a spot she didn't like. That's when I found out she had been at Ragged Island," said Bonnie.

Two missing youths and an abandoned vehicle should have triggered an in-depth search, but the effort was lackluster at best.

Sheriff B. F. Dixon of Isle of Wight County reported to the *Daily Press* on Tuesday. "There are no signs to point to foul play but the circumstances are suspicious. Something's just not right."

It was a gross understatement. Authorities still harbored the illusion that Robin, who had runaway before, had runaway again. This time with David Knobling. Why the two would abandon his beloved Ford Ranger, doors open, no one was willing to speculate.

Newport News police, state police, and state game commission assisted in the feeble search of Ragged Island for the couple on Tuesday evening. They tended to focus on the areas that were easily accessible, which left the vast majority of Ragged Island as largely ignored. The weather didn't make searching any easier for authorities, the rain had been heavy and constant since Saturday night.

"The rain is what killed us. It rained for three or four days straight," said Michael.

With no sign of David or Robin, the search continued Wednesday morning at Ragged Island. The Edwards family held out hope that Robin had just run away again.

"We taped an interview with Andy Fox about her being missing. It was supposed to show on the six o'clock news on that Wednesday night," said Mrs. Edwards.

The Edwards family complied with police, staying away from Ragged Island as the police conducted their own search. Each passing hour the tension mounted. This was not like the previous disappearances of Robin—and was totally out of character for David. They stayed glued to the television, thinking they would be seeing the segment they had filmed on Robin running away.

Judy Knobling, her parents, and Michael were at Ragged Island as well for several hours on Wednesday. The terrain was so limiting it made searching difficult if not impossible.

A man hunt with the use of K-9s was organized for that Wednesday at Ragged Island. The Virginia State Police flew a plane along the shore, looking for any signs of the pair but with no luck. Karl Knobling returned to Ragged Island that morning to continue his own search for his son.

"About a quarter of a mile down the beach is a little inlet. I was going to go there, but the tide was up and I couldn't get there. So I was waiting. A guy showed up and parked his car. He got out and went jogging down the beach. He went off and a few minutes later he came back running—I mean really running. He peeled out with a cloud of dust, and I figured I would get my butt in gear and go down there where the pine trees start. The deputies stopped me. They said it was now a crime scene, you can't go down there. I told them I was gonna go down there—my son is missing. They said I had to wait for all of the police departments to show up. It took three hours. Nobody was looking at all, they were just standing there waiting. They were going down there finally, and I told them I was going, too. They said I couldn't. ... They didn't want me disturbing a crime scene. Finally they said I could, and a deputy said he'd accompany me," Karl bitterly said.

The man seen running on the beach was Louis Ford of Virginia Beach. The potential crime scene was so poorly managed by the Isle of Wight Sheriff's Department that Louis Ford showed up to go for a run at Ragged Island and no one even bothered to stop him. Shortly before 4:00 p.m., he noticed a pile of clothing near a tall embankment along the James River and walked closer. As he neared, he noticed the pile of clothing was actually a girl's body. It was clear that her remains had been washed up on the shore by the tide; she laid face down on the beach. Without touching anything, Ford ran to find police.

"They found a body of a female. They stopped us there. So I started out with the deputy going another twenty-five to thirty yards down the beach. I found him [David], tangled up under the roots of those pine trees. He was all bloated, but I knew right away that it was him," said Karl Knobling.

Both David and Robin had been shot. David had a wound in his shoulder and a devastating wound in the back of his head. Robin had been shot once in the back of the head in the same manner, execution style.

Mrs. Knobling, unaware of the discovery of her son's body, sat at home watching the 6:00 p.m. news with her youngest son.

"They show a picture of him, his body and everything. I remember looking back at my mom and watching the blood just completely drain out of her body. I mean, she turned ghost white. Screaming screams I never want to hear again in my life," said Michael, almost shuddering at the memory.

The Edwards family crowded around the television, waiting for the interview they had taped earlier that day with Andy Fox.

"My heart was ripped out of my chest. The news anchor said she was shot in the back of the head, execution style," said Mrs. Edwards.

That was the way both the Edwards and Knobling families had found out that their children had been killed, on the 6:00 p.m. news replete with grizzly images of their loved ones.

"That was the worst part—finding out that way. It was horrific," said Bonnie Edwards.

Tara Cook, the mother-to-be of David's child, found out in the same cold media-fed manner.

"I had the television on the news station. ... I remember the phone ringing, it was my mom telling my grandmother that something was getting ready to be aired. ... She had seen a clip, and she wanted to make sure that someone was with me," Tara said. "I will never forget the words. 'It has been confirmed that David Knobling of the first block of Sanlun Lakes Drive has been found dead.' My entire world shifted on its axis. Pain like I had never felt before. I was only sixteen, so I guess it was more magnified by the fact that I was so young and teenagers' lives are already so dramatic."

What had been a case of possible runaways had turned into a double homicide. Worse, the police had already badly lost control of their crime scene.

CHAPTER 8

The long jagged roots of the pine trees hung along an embankment almost like icicles hanging from cave ceilings. The bodies of Robin Edwards and David Knobling had washed up on Ragged Island's sandy beaches. The tide had been high the past few days from the amount of heavy rain that pounded the Newport News area.

Robin, dressed in just a blouse and pants, had washed up on the shore. She appeared bloated due to the decomposition of her body and exposure to the elements for three days. Her dyed auburn hair was disheveled with an apparent gunshot wound to the back of her head. David lay only fifty feet away from Robin, tangled in the roots of the embankment. He was found wearing only a pair of pants, with a bullet wound to the back of his head and to his shoulder.

The high tide was still in full effect, even causing a four-wheel-drive police vehicle to become stuck when attempting to remove both bodies from the scene.

Danny Plott of the Virginia State Police, a member of the Colonial Parkway Murders task force, remembers the Ragged Island murders vividly. Plott was born in a little place known as Maggie Valley, North Carolina. He spent thirty-four years with the state police, retiring as a division commander in Hampton Roads. Danny had been working narcotics at the time of the Ragged Island case and was a special agent, the equivalent of detective, by the time he was on the task force. His insights into Ragged Island provided a good roadmap for what the state police were thinking about the case.

The cause of death for both Robin and David was a homicidal gunshot wound of the head, causing an immediate demise. Based on the injuries that David Knobling sustained,

Plott's theory is that David attempted to escape the murderer by climbing up an embankment but was shot in the shoulder which would have caused him to slow or even fall down from the embankment. David was then shot execution-style in the back of the head, causing an instant death.

Plott recalls a detail regarding Robin's body. "It was clear she had been either sodomized or had anal sex. We believe she was raped," he said. "Unfortunately, because of the three days between the time it happened and being washed up from the James River, the DNA was contaminated."

The medical examiner released that Robin had sex before she was killed and a surviving sperm sample was extracted from Robin's remains.

"The DNA has been tested twice. Nothing came back from the DNA, not that I know of," said Danny Plott.

Of courses in 1987, DNA tests were much cruder than they are today.

Plott's thinking that David tried to escape is a theory. Judy Knobling, who knew David best, has her own.

"A chicken? Really? He could have been fighting with his own killer. Knowing David as I did, I doubt very much he was a chicken. Far from it. What he was, however, was very protective of women. Frankly, I can see him getting shot trying to assist Robin more than running away. That sounds more like him. He was fearless."

The day after the bodies were recovered, Isle of Wight's Sheriff Dixon was interviewed by the *Daily Press*: "Right now we're just doing old-fashioned police work; looking for a gun or a cartridge and talking to as many people as possible. I think we're making progress. Right now we don't have a motive, a type or size of the gun, and are not able to pinpoint where the murders occurred."

Police used metal detectors to search the Ragged Island beach for possible shell casings, but none were ever recovered. Searchers less than an arm's length apart searched the waters of the river by touch of foot, hoping to find a tossed handgun, but they had no luck

The bodies themselves did yield physical evidence in the form of bullets. A bullet was recovered from David Knobling's head wound; the shoulder wound had an entry and exit wound and that round was never recovered. A partial bullet was recovered from Robin's wound.

"Back then .44 calibers were not big. We speculated that it was .38 caliber recovered from Knobling from what I can remember," said Plott. Without the recovery of a weapon or shell casings, it remained possible that a revolver was used in the murders.

Another clue as to their whereabouts came from David's autopsy. There was evidence of beans in his stomach that were undigested. Since he had had pizza with his family earlier in the night, the theory was that he had gone out to Wendy's for chili or to Taco Bell. It is one of the very few clues as to where David and Robin were after they left her house.

Sheriff Dixon reported to the *Daily Press* just two days after the bodies were recovered that the murders of Robin and David had been the most baffling of his career: "We believe the killer sought solitude and a place that couldn't been seen from the bridge. We believe Robin and David were surprised by their assailant and killed at the end of the half-mile walkway over the marsh that ends at the James River."

Ragged Island's elevated walkway was surrounded by marsh and pitch-black at night. The only lighting at the wildlife preserve came from the James River Bridge and in the parking lot. Given witnesses in the area that saw David's truck, it was presumed that the murders occurred sometime after 12:30 a.m. but before 5:30 a.m., leaving the area without light. Both David and Robin's shoes were found in the truck along with both of their underwear and Robin's bra. It seems farfetched to believe that Robin and David, who were both found mostly clothed, would willingly remove underwear and shoes to leave inside of the truck to follow a dark walkway toward the beach area of the James River in the middle of a rainy night.

"I know my son and his truck. He'd never leave his truck like that. He'd lock his truck up in my backyard," Karl Knobling reported to the *Daily Press*.

Yet David's truck was found not only unlocked but with the driver side door opened and the radio playing with the keys in the ignition.

Michael Knobling is sternly convinced that David's Ford Ranger was staged by the murderer.

"There is no doubt about it. The keys in the ignition—the ignition was set on Accessories, so the radio could be on. Well, I helped David wire the stereo up in that truck. In order for the radio to be on, you just turned it on. We had wired it straight to battery. There's no reason in the world to have that truck on Accessories to have the radio on. Someone else did it. You could take the keys out and it would still have the radio on, the way we had wired it—it wasn't tied to the ignition at all," Michael said.

"And of course, with the door wide open and all that— there's no way. David used to lock the truck if we walked into a 7-Eleven store. It was his pride and joy. He had a good Pioneer stereo system with a box in the back. Back then, that stuff was expensive—hundreds of dollars. He didn't walk ten feet from that truck without it being locked, windows locked—everything. So when they said the door was open, in the rain, right then I knew he had been forced out of his truck or it was set up."

Judy Knobling has additional insight into the staging of David's truck.

"We were all aware that David *always* parked his truck with the front facing out. He would not leave it parked the way it was found, and once I saw it, I was concerned that it wasn't him that had parked it that way. The items in the truck were so carefully placed, not tossed off haphazardly."

A local task force was formed to take over the Ragged

Island case. Virginia State Police along with Newport News Police Department and Isle of Wight County Sheriff's Office offered a $3,000 reward for information leading to arrest. All tips could be given anonymously. An additional $1,000 reward was offered by the Peninsula Crime Lab.

Sheriff Dixon gave a public update on the case in early October: "Rain may have washed away blood from the kill spot. Tidal action would have immediately taken them to shore. They may have been pulled by hand several feet into the water—the water is only a few feet deep. The only gut feeling I have is that I have two dead people and I don't know who killed them."

To the grief stricken families it seemed as if authorities were already at the end of their proverbial ropes.

It was released to the media that David Knobling had received "death threats" just days prior to his murder by someone he apparently knew. The Knobling family does not recall these apparent death threats, but police did pursue them. Regardless if the death threats were a rumor or if they were true, the police reported "no suspects" on the matter. David Knobling's funeral guestbook was also studied without result.

A little over two months into the investigation, and Sheriff Dixon had little to update the public on. He would soon retire. Clearly this was not the way he had intended to end his career in law enforcement.

Another article in the *Daily Press* was borderline embarrassing for the Isle of Wight Sheriff's Department: "We still don't know why they were killed. There's been speculation but no facts. Someone didn't want them out alive. That's the only thing I know. The task force hasn't met recently because there is no new evidence in the case. We've never been able to establish where the murders took place. We're not even sure the murder occurred in Isle of Wight. The bodies and the truck were found there so naturally that puts the burden on us."

Kathy Knobling, who had recently married Karl Knobling before David's death, was also quoted in the *Daily Press* article: "The police wasted too much time by not acting on the missing persons reports sooner and by not investigating the truck which police first noticed on Monday evening. They photographed the truck but let Karl drive it home before waiting several days before searching for fingerprints."

Without a motive, murder weapon, exact murder location, witnesses, or even a general direction the case seemed to go cold rather quickly. In February 1988, the Knobling family posted 250 posters around the area with a reward up to $5,000 for information about the murders. Karl had one plastered in the back window of his truck.

"I don't care if I have to go wherever to put them up. Leads are slow and I'm hoping this helps. They lost so much in the length of time it took for them to find the bodies," Mr. Knobling was quoted in the *Richmond Times-Dispatch*.

A few theories have been raised on what may have happened to Robin and David. One theory involves Robin and David walking down the beach and somehow meeting their killer on the beach area. This theory seems unlikely due to the bad weather and the fact that both pairs of shoes (along with only undergarments) were found inside of the unlocked truck.

According to Danny Plott, Ragged Island was a lovers' lane type of place, and the Virginia State Police worked their own theory on how they believe the murders occurred on September 20, 1987.

"I'm pretty sure what David had in mind and I know what Robin had in mind because she was very sexually active. She didn't pick and choose really well, but that ties into her murder," Plott said.

"We think they probably decided they wanted some marijuana and made plans to see each other later that night. David dropped her off and took his little brother and cousin home. He came back to pick her up. They weren't seen anywhere else by anyone, so we assume they went to Ragged Island.

"Robin Edwards had gotten approached at a party sometime before her murder by a black drug dealer in the Newport News area. His last name was Washington. There are several witnesses to this—he made it known that he wanted Robin to go with him and she wouldn't. It really pissed him off, mainly because Robin wasn't one to turn anybody down. If I remember right, he punched a hole in the wall at the party. He's a very violent guy, and it was known that the only kind of sex he liked was anal. He didn't care if it was a man, a boy, or a girl.

"We think a call was made to this guy. They probably called him that night to meet at Ragged Island to meet up to buy marijuana. Washington brought a boy with him. We think this boy was a witness.

"They walked on the walkway that went down to the water to get out of the parking lot. We think he pulled out the gun and said, 'You ain't gonna turn me down again,' to Robin.

"The other guy, who's a witness, we don't believe took an active part but was there. However it went down, he forced himself on Robin anally. He shot Robin in the back of the head—I would say first. And then when Knobling took off he took off after him and shot him in the shoulder and then in the head.

"We tracked down the witness. He was very, very hesitant to talk. He was scared to death of Washington. In fact, he had been raped by him at one time and Washington had been charged. The guy had been so scared for his life that he backed out of the charges. Larry Johnson, a Virginia State Police officer, was making inroads with the witness. He was finally starting to get him to talk to him. Shortly thereafter this guy and another guy were drinking at a bar that Washington was at. They supposedly left the bar that night and fell asleep on some railroad tracks. The witness was killed; the other guy lost an arm and a leg.

"Larry got this Washington guy to come in and talk. He had the proverbial set-up: the files on the desk and a picture of Robin Edwards. He basically said to him 'We've solved this. We'll give you a chance to tell your side of the story. Tell us where you were that night.'

"Washington looked right at him, smiled, stood up and said, 'You ain't got shit,' and walked out.

"And he was right. We didn't have shit.

"After reading Larry's investigations, I believe Ragged Island was a separate crime [from the other Colonial Parkway Murders]."

According to this theory of a drug deal and rape of Robin, the state police do not believe that David's truck was staged by the murderer.

"We think that the drug dealer walked up to the truck and either demanded they get out of the truck and may have even pulled a gun on them there." Danny Plott said

The assailant may have demanded that both Robin and David remove their shoes prior to leaving the truck in order to gain more control. The sandy area of Ragged Island was riddled with rocks as well as shells which wouldn't be ideal for walking on without shoes, especially in the dark. David and Robin's bare feet would have been badly cut up—but that wasn't the case with their remains.

With the drug dealer theory, the murders may have not been planned. It was quite possible that Washington had just planned to rape Robin and either she resisted, started yelling, or David attempted to intervene. It is nearly impossible to say whether David or Robin was shot first, but it is believed that Robin was killed first which would have caused David to flee.

The Virginia State Police believed that David had been trying to climb up the embankment to get away from his assailant and was shot in the shoulder first, thus accounting for the upward angle of the wound. In other words, despite the tides, the assumption was he was shot near where his body was found. If that was the case, the round that passed through his shoulder should have been buried in the embankment as it exited. Despite the use of metal detectors, no bullet was ever recovered.

The state police focus was on two possible reasons for Robin and David to connect. In their minds, it was either for sex or for drugs. Given where the bodies were found, a locale known for drugs and sex, that's understandable. Branching out from there, a myriad of theories and scenarios are possible.

David's father, Karl, offers another theory of the murders: "Ships come in there across the bridge and bring in drugs. Small boats go out there and load up. David may have seen something he wasn't supposed to see."

Judy Knobling believes this is as valid a theory as any. It is possible that they interrupted a drug drop by boat at the end of the walkway near the bridge. They could have been ordered into the boat, then forced to get out in the area where they were found.

The other problem with the state police theory is that David's vehicle was clearly staged for theft. Why would a drug dealer/rapist take the time to set up the vehicle? Also, marching them out to the beach area, nearly a mile distant, was filled with risk. There was no way to be sure who might be down at the beach when you arrived. Further, there's no evidence that they were ever at the beach. No blankets, no flashlights, and thanks to the rain, no footprints.

Years later, FBI Agent Robert Meadows, while on the Colonial Parkway Murders task force, posed one of the most probing questions with the theory that they were killed on the beach a mile from the vehicle: "Why did Knobling wait so long to resist? God, it must have been dark out there. Why would he march a mile out into nowhere before trying to get away?" It made no more sense then than it does today.

The Virginian-Pilot interviewed Larry Johnson, who was a Virginia State Police investigator on the task force that would be later-formed to look into the murders. "Johnson had built a tidy scenario for what happened to David Knobling and Robin Edwards at Ragged Island: 'It's easy—somebody killed them over in Newport News, drove out on the James River Bridge and threw the bodies over the side then left the truck at Ragged Island. The bodies washed ashore later.'"

The problem with that theory was that the bodies had not been in the water long enough to back that up—that and stopping on the James River Bridge, even in the dead of night, was a risky, often deadly proposition. Thus, the state police settled on their most probable theory—David and Robin were killed where they were found or close to it.

Working another theory, Virginia State Police also investigated and kept a Newport News police officer under surveillance. "We thought he might have been involved. He never went to Ragged Island. In fact, I never surveilled him doing anything other than coming home and going to work," said Plott.

David Knobling's family all believe that David would have complied with an authority figure. "Anyone with authority, he would have shown respect to. I still think to this day that somebody with a badge is the one who did it," said Michael Knobling.

Assuming the Robin and David met at around midnight or 1:00 a.m. on September 20, there were significant observations that came in. One was that a group of ten teenagers were at Ragged Island to party at around 2:00 a.m., and there was no sign of David's truck. Another was a tip called in by Samuel Rieder who said that he had seen the pair at Ragged Island that night. That left a gap of at least two hours when, if the sources were correct, when David and Robin were somewhere else other than the refuge.

But as it would turn out, one of those sources, Samuel

Rieder, came with some potential strings attached that made him a person of interest

* * * * *

The Virginia State Police were not the only investigators digging into the deaths of Robin and David. At the Isle of Wight's Sheriff's Department, the new sheriff, Charlie Phelps, found the case dropped onto his desk—both metaphorically and physically. He had been in the middle of a heated sheriff's campaign when the murders had taken place in September of 1987. Four months later on January 1, 1988, the case became his.

Sheriff Phelps came at the case with his experience solely centered on Isle of Wight County. He was raising his own four children and had already been a parental figure for his younger brother and sister. He was a family man who set his roots deeply in Isle of Wight once he got a job there.

Today, Sheriff Phelps remembers his forty-four years in law enforcement fondly.

"People always said, 'We never thought you'd end up being a law enforcement officer.' One used to say to me, 'I always knew you'd have a number behind your name, but I didn't think it'd be in law-enforcement.' He was just carrying on with me. I always made the statement, 'I couldn't beat 'em so I had to join 'em.'"

He had joined the Smithfield Police Department while waiting for an opportunity to surface in the Hampton PD.

"I was waiting to get into one of the local departments here in the Tidewater area. A friend of mine, he was with the department. He told me that his daddy was chief of police in Smithfield. He told me, 'Go and see Daddy; Daddy needs somebody right now. Then when Hampton calls you, you can come on.' It was the Hampton Police Department I was trying to get on. So I did. I went onto Smithfield. Twenty years later I left there to be sheriff. It worked out pretty good you know. Hampton did call me, and I refused to go. I stayed with Smithfield and didn't regret it."

Having won the election, he found himself now facing a double-murder in his jurisdiction that was still unresolved.

"It just kind of fell into my lap. They said, 'Hey, *you* have this problem.'"

The task didn't daunt Phelps, even given the fact he had just stepped into the job. Having lived in Isle of Wight for decades, he knew the families and the people there. He had the experience of being local and began to look for locals. And like any good law enforcement officer, he had some names in mind, people of interest, who were worth considering for the crimes. In this case it was a person that was named "Sammy."[6] But how he connected the dots to Sammy was by working another crime.

Samuel Rieder put himself on the sheriff's radar by calling in his tip that he had seen Robin and David at Ragged Island. He was a twenty-eight-year-old dishwasher who had just finished time for forging a sixty-dollar check. He claimed he had stopped at Ragged Island to sit and think on his way home from a date in Newport News. Rieder claimed he had driven down the sandy/gravel roadway out of the parking area down to the James River edge to park.

While there he recognized the black Ford Ranger. "That truck's not easy to forget. It had a certain look to it. I wish mine looked as good as his did."

His initial claim was that he saw David and Robin get out of their truck and walk down the nature trail, leaving the door of the truck open and the radio playing … something that David Knobling would never have done.

Samuel "Sammy" Rieder then claimed, "Around 1:30

6   While Sheriff Phelps does know the suspect's full name, he was reluctant to provide it. Through the authors' own research, we were able to confirm from other sources that it was, indeed, Samuel Rieder.

a.m. or quarter to two, I heard two shots. They had to be coming somewhere from the marshland, way in the back. All I heard was the shots, and I decided it was time to leave and I left. Nothing like that had ever happened down there before."

Rieder drew attention because each time Sheriff Charlie Phelps talked to him, his story changed. Sammy claimed in one account that he had helped Knobling get his truck out of the soft sand at Ragged Island. In another account he remembered Knobling being there with a group of friends. For Charlie Phelps, that was enough to put him high on the list of persons of interest. Reider's jumbled versions of events might have been written off if not for another crime and a witness that claimed Reider had more involvement.

As Phelps remembers: "We were working another case. That case was a robbery—a larceny of firearms. The person that reported it to us ... had a boarder who was living with them. And they suspected this boarder of stealing the weapons. We sent out a Be On The Lookout [BOLO alert] for him. He was arrested in Jacksonville, Florida. Myself and an agent from the state police, and I can't remember what agent it was, we flew down. The son of the lady that reported the weapons missing, the son was on our radar as a possible suspect in the double-homicide.

"So we said 'Whoa, what's going on here?'

"So I got one of the agents from the state police, and I flew down to Jacksonville, Florida, where he was in jail. We got a detainer on him because we charged him with the larceny of the weapons. We had a detainer on him to bring him back to Virginia."

The gun thief proved to be the key to tying Rieder back to the crime.

"We went down and met with him. He admitted to us that he had stolen one gun. He didn't say anything about the other three or four that were stolen. He just admitted to stealing one. Even down to selling that weapon in Gulfport,

Mississippi, to a pawn shop."

Then the conversation started to shift to Rieder.

"He got talking to us about this particular woman that had reported these weapons; he got talking about her son. That maybe he took the weapons. Well, we knew who her son was, and we were kind of interested in him. He was a person of interest.

"We started hooking things up with what he was telling us. We came back to Virginia; we picked up the young man that we suspected, that we thought knew something."

Law enforcement is both science and art. The art part often is knowing your community, knowing the key players (good and bad) and following your gut instincts. In this category, Sheriff Phelps was well equipped. He decided to confront his witness to see what he knew and what he didn't.

"We—the state police—ended up running a polygraph test on him for us. He [Sammy] failed the polygraph test. I can't say he failed it all of the way. We could never pin him right down on the actual murders. But, what we did do, through his own statement, was place him at the scene.

"In this regard ... Knobling's truck, he left the truck door open and the music running. He had this young girl. From what I understand, of course I never got to the crime scene— this is the thing that bothers me—from what I understand he and the Edwards girl, Robin Edwards, were in the bushes. This guy that we suspected of maybe being involved in the murders, he was at Ragged Island."

Sammy, by his own declaration, happened to be at the scene of the crime near the time it occurred.

"He was drinking beer, by his own admission. The truck doors were open on this truck. He went over there, to where the truck was, and even so much as to admit that he stole money out of the wallet of the pickup."

Phelps tried to probe deeper. Was there a conversation or a clash between Sammy and David?

"I said, 'Okay ... did you have a confrontation? Did

you have a run-in with the guy that owned the truck and the wallet?'

"He says, 'No. I got scared. I heard the bushes rattling so I jumped in my truck and left.'

"That's when I tried to pin him down. 'No you didn't! You ended up shooting these people.'

"He never would admit it. We couldn't prove it any different with the polygraph. The polygraph was inconclusive. I didn't have any witnesses, as far as him taking the money was concerned. So I didn't charge him with anything. I didn't charge him with a thing. I was going to keep working it."

A friend of Rieder's said that Sammy had told him on Sunday that two people had been shot at Ragged Island, but Robin and David's bodies had not yet been discovered for three more days.

The determined sheriff's investigation showed that Sammy Rieder was a troubled young man. The gun-theft suspect interviewed with Phelps extensively, sharing information on the man whose house he had lived in.

"He [Sammy] always argued with his mother. [He] was upset; his daddy died and his insurance money was not distributed among all the children, so on and so forth. That was some of the anger he was explaining to me that he saw by living in the house."

The gun-theft suspect offered even more tantalizing details to Sheriff Phelps.

"I asked the guy from Jacksonville that I interviewed, 'Do you think that if he was confronted by an individual while he was stealing his money, do you think he would fight him? Or resist him? Or would he run? What would he do?'

"He said, 'If he weren't three times his size, he'd fight him.'

"The guy that we interviewed in Florida, we brought him back to Virginia, and I personally conducted an interview with him when he got back here. We had a lengthy interview. *Lengthy.* He told me things about this guy, this suspect that I had, supposedly, the day that the bodies were found, he was going to go across the James River Bridge and when he got to Ragged Island, he saw the police, so he stopped out of curiosity. He went over and talked with them and supposedly gotten some details about it from some law enforcement officer.

"It was just so many things that were so coincidental. It was just circumstantial. Why would you stop at Ragged Island—'cause you see a bunch of law enforcement officers there?"

There were a lot of things about Sammy that simply didn't add up.

The sheriff's scenario of what may have gone down at the Ragged Island parking area the night of the murders was surprisingly simple.

"So what I picture there is, even based on my suspect's statement that he took the money, my belief is that Knobling came out of the bushes, heard him in his truck, caught him in his truck, and somewhere along the line there was a weapon used.

"Here's the thing. If you look at David Knobling's wounds, he was shot in the shoulder and in the back of the head. Robin Edwards was shot in the head. My suspicion has always been there that he shot Robin first, and that Knobling was coming after him and he ended up shooting him. It could have been the other way. Knobling could have been coming out of the bushes. This guy could have pulled the trigger on Knobling, hit him in the shoulder. Robin Edwards comes out of the bushes; he kills her. He kills him, 'cause he's wounded. Right there in the parking lot.

"It was, what, 200 yards to the water from the parking lot."

The killer would have then dragged the pair to the water near the foot of the James River Bridge and dumped them into the water.

"Now the family told me that David Knobling never had

a weapon. But I'm thinking that this guy, my suspect, had access to all kinds of weapons in the house. Even though he was a convicted felon he still had access to weapons that were in the house."

There are some flaws with the theory. The angle of David Knobling's shoulder wound showed the point of entry to be the rear, with an upward angle of the bullet trajectory. There was no way for Sheriff Phelps to know that if the state police didn't share that detail with him. Still, it did not exclude some other form of the confrontation between Sammy, David, and Robin. Also it was raining on and off. If Robin and David were engaged in intercourse, why would they do it in the swamplands or on the wet sands of the beach when they had a perfectly dry vehicle to perform the act in?

Regardless of the details of the confrontation itself, Sheriff Phelps had unearthed an interesting piece of confession on the part of his suspect—someone had robbed David's wallet and was there, in the Ragged Island parking lot at the victim's truck near or at the time of the murder.

"Our suspect admitted going into David's wallet, taking money, hearing a noise, then he left. That's as far as we could ever get him. If I remember correctly, it wasn't conclusive on the polygraph—it seems that's what they told me. Inconclusive was the results of the polygraph. I got to questioning him real hard—that's when he admitted he got into the truck and stole the money."

Sheriff Phelps' first instinct was to arrest Sammy Rieder for the robbery, but he was looking at a much broader charge.

"I should have put him in jail, but I was trying at the time to solve a murder. It was just his word that he had gone in there. Again, I didn't have access to the evidence—immediate access. So I backed off."

The Virginia State Police were involved with the original investigation into the missing firearm and contributed a polygrapher for Sammy's interrogation. Sheriff Phelps shared the findings of his investigation with the state police, but it was more of a one-way street. From the sheriff's perspective, he was more than willing to share what he had gleaned.

"They put a task force together, the whole nine yards. Some of it we were included in on. We didn't get into the task force side too much, 'cause most of that was concentrated on the Colonial Parkway Murders. Most everything there was to do with those.

"They [the Virginia State Police] would meet with me. They would come, sit down with me, and discuss whatever they had. But most everything they did was towards the Colonial Parkway Murders. I kept thinking, 'My suspect just might have been involved in the parkway murders.'"

If that was indeed the case, the Isle of Wight Sheriff may have resolved one or more of the pairs of killings.

Did the state police ignore Rieder's admission because of an inconclusive polygraph test? That is certainly feasible. Polygraph examinations are only as good as the operator and the individual asking the questions. An inconclusive result is not positive, not negative. It doesn't provide enough information to rule someone out.

Fate often intervenes and inflicts its own justice. Such was the case with the mysterious Sammy.

"I never did see any confirmation on this—I was *told* this ... that he died. He ended up killing himself by choking himself to death in the bathroom, while he masturbated. That is what I was told caused his death. So my suspect died with me knowing that he stole the money and was involved with the pickup truck but I never proved that he shot these two people."

If the sheriff is correct about the approximate date of his death, it was in 1989, which was after the last of the murders tied together as the Colonial Parkway Murders.

There are several published studies looking into the correlation of autoerotic asphyxiation and serial killers. If, indeed, Sammy did kill himself in this manner, it would be a red flag for any behavioral scientist working the Colonial

Parkway case. Unfortunately, at the time of the Knobling-Edwards murders the possible connections to Thomas-Dowski were not suspected. By the time such logic could be applied, Sammy would have been dead.

As such, the digging done by Charlie Phelps may very well have been glossed over. We will never know until the case files are opened by authorities.

Rieder's own last public comment offers more questions than answers: "Why would I want to go out there and kill somebody I didn't know that good? I hope they find [whoever] did it. The way I see it, he had no reason to do what he do, or whatever it was."

Assuming Samuel Rieder had nothing to do with the deaths of Knobling and Edwards, the question remains—where were they from the time the left Robin's house to when the truck was first noticed at Ragged Island? That location and their motive for being there is critical. People assume the worse, but we simply don't know why they were there … period. It is also entirely possible that they encountered their killer elsewhere and were only at Ragged Island for the disposal of their bodies. The mishandling of the truck when it was first recovered, turning it and the evidence inside over to Karl Knobling, combined with the rain, may have obscured blood evidence that could resolve these nagging questions.

With no tangible explanation of the deaths of Robin Edwards and David Knobling, Karl Knobling's belief may explain that rainy night at Ragged Island. "My gut feeling is that David and Robin were in the wrong place at the wrong time."

THE THIRD

Richard Keith Call and Cassandra Hailey
Last seen early morning April 10, 1988
Remains unrecovered

CHAPTER 9

Richard Keith Call was born on March 8, 1968, to Barbara and Richard Call. To his family and friends he was rarely called Richard—he was Keith to the world. He was destined to be the middle of five children. The family originally lived in Newport News, then moved to the York County/Seaford area. In 1980 the family relocated to rural Gloucester County area. Keith's brother Chris was into equestrian sports, and the new home allowed them to keep horses and indulge in their son's interest.

Joyce Call-Canada, Keith's sister, recalls their close upbringing: "The older we got the bigger the house got. When I moved out they got a bigger house. When I was growing up we always had a three-bedroom house. I was the only girl so the boys would bunk together with the bunk beds, and I had my own room."

Gloucester County was large with land and small in population, with just under 30,000 citizens. Gloucester County was formed in 1651 and was home to a thriving American Indian community at one point and sported several plantations along the York and Piankatank rivers which flanked the county. Watermen made Gloucester their home, and recreational fishing remains popular to this day.

While Gloucester is a peninsula it is connected to York County by the George P. Coleman Memorial Bridge at Gloucester Point. If you cross the bridge you are only a few dozen yards from the entrance to the Colonial Parkway. Gloucester calls itself the "Daffodil Capitol of the World," complete with a festival and parade to support its self-claimed status. Crepe myrtle's dot the median of Route 17, which cuts the entire length of the county plunging out across the York River and into the heart of York County. Gloucester was a small community that clung tightly to its small-town feeling.

Keith Call's father worked at the Anheuser-Busch brewery in Williamsburg, across the York River from Gloucester. The brewery was one of the largest employers in the area, and Richard Call was a highly regarded manager. He worked the swing shift, a rotating shift, mostly days. Keith's mother was a stay-at-home mom; Barbara's focus was raising her children and taking care of the homestead. In some respects the Call clan appeared like an Anheuser-Busch Christmas commercial, home-centric complete with a horse.

Keith was a bright and energetic young man. He played T-ball and eventually baseball for a boys' team, the Red Sox. He liked sports, and the Call brothers shared a love of motorcycles, Doug Call, Keith's brother, remembers.

"We had YZ 80's. We would spend a lot of time riding motorcycles. We shared a bike. My dad got us a SL 70, a used one, we would ride the heck out of that bike. We lived over in Seaford until 1980, and he rode all around Seaford. Then they bought the older house in Gloucester, which Dad bought for the land, the house was kind of beat up. We rode around there too," Doug said. "We would ride that bike all around the neighborhood, all around the fields. We had a pretty good time on the motorcycles. Then he bought us a YZ 80 which was a bigger faster bike. We had that for a while. Eddie Brown [a friend of Keith's] had a motorcycle, and they would go riding and have a good old time."

In the 1980s, safety was secondary to fun. It was a decade when fun meant being with friends rather than befriending them online.

As a child Keith was very family-centric, and he and his siblings played with each other as siblings did. Joyce Call-Canada fondly recalls the day-to-day interaction she shared with her brother.

"I remember something funny. When I was growing up

and getting into my teen years, we still had phones attached to the wall back then. After school I'd be talking to my friends and trying to get a plan, something to do that evening, and then I would hear this snickering from underneath my bed. There would be my three brothers, all laying up under my bed … trying to find out the scoop of what was going on. I won't say they all did it always, but they did that for a while with me," said Joyce.

Christmas for the Calls was almost out of a TV special of the era.

"When we were growing up, Christmas was always an exciting time. We weren't sleeping—we were up all night. Granddaddy and Grandma—we would always go over on Christmas Eve. That was when everybody got together again … the extended family. A whole bunch of people. We would come home at twelve or one in the morning, and Mom and Dad would try and get us to go to bed and nobody could sleep. At the very least we were up before the sun—probably the only time of the year. We tried to get up at three or four in the morning, but they would make us go back to bed," Joyce said.

Vacations were family affairs as well.

"Our big vacations involved extended family—uncles, family, cousins, things like that—especially when we went to South Carolina. They liked to have fun, there's no doubt about that. That would involve a lot of the extended family. A lot of times we'd have to get two cottages—thirty or forty folks," Joyce said.

According to his brother Chris, Keith enjoyed boogie-boarding on these family jaunts.

As a young boy, Keith's spare time was devoted to the same thing that all young boys focused on before the discovery of girls—creating their own fun.

Chris Call recalls the days of their youth.

"We would go out and make forts. We always lived in a real rural area so we were always outside. We played hide-

and-go-seek, knock-knock-zoom [ringing the doorbell of a neighbor and running away], and living in the country we did stuff that kids shouldn't be doing. Of course nowadays you can't do things like knock-knock-zoom or make prank phone calls—you can't do that anymore. They didn't have caller ID or any of the other stuff," said Chris.

"For Halloween, we always went trick-or-treating. We all went together. We would make a costume that day and get those orange jack-o-lantern things to carry candy and would fill those things up several times—making runs back to the house, empty them off, run off all over the place."

There was no concern over stalkers or predators. In the seventies and eighties your neighbors were not potential threats, they were an extension of your parents' authority.

Keith attended Gloucester High School, and he had an almost Kirk Cameron of *Growing Pains* look to him, with classically styled 1980s hair. His parents instilled in him a strong work ethic.

One of his hobbies was sailboating. His older brother Chris owned a Sunfish sailboat, and Keith was fond of borrowing it to sail on the York River. He enjoyed the hobby so much that his first job was for Glass Marina. His brother Doug remembers his job there.

"We did cleanup and things like that. They built boats—fiberglass boats and that kind of stuff. He came home from school and was all, 'Doug is just sitting here watching TV, and I've got to go to work. Make him go to work.' I did get money for it, but I didn't want to at the time … there was a lot of fiberglass around there. Very icky situation. We would clean up the shop and stuff like that," Doug said. "When I came there he could graduate a little bit, he got to do some shop work while I got to do the cleanup. I think that was his ultimate plan. He got a bit of advancement you know. Forced labor there."

As brothers, Chris and Keith bonded over their love of the water. Chris Call remembers going out on the water with his brother.

"It was Memorial Day or Fourth of July. I would always be getting a ticket. 'Let's go out on the sailboat. We definitely can't get in trouble on a sailboat on the water there.' Come to find out we didn't have enough life jackets and the marine patrol pulled us over and gave us a ticket for that," Chris said.

The rivers were a constant source of entertainment in the era before smart phones, Xbox, and the internet. Keith and his peers hung out at the beach along the York River. It was a place to unwind and relax and was only a few short minutes from home. Every community had that one place where the kids could go and have fun, and the beach was exactly that for the kids at Gloucester High.

Keith was a deep and soulful thinker, a person that understood the deep connections within his family. He was a person that spoke up when he saw something wrong. When his brother Chris thinks about Keith now, he remembers one incident that stood out with his brother.

"Keith was a very sweet person, a very compassionate person. This is probably a strange thing that I have never forgotten about Keith and how compassionate he was. You can take this for what it is. When I was a senior in high school, Keith was probably in ninth or tenth grade. This is kind of awkward but has always stuck out and been very poignant with me and I'll never forget it," said Chris.

"I'm gay and I came out with my parents when I was a senior in high school, and everyone accepted it except my mother. My mother and I, well, it was very nasty—not nice. And here's Keith, a tenth-grader, and we live in a very rural area, and I remember he pulled my mother aside and said, 'You can't talk to your son like that.' I remember he wrote a paper for his class about the same situation. I remember he got an A on it. It was so moving and touching that someone like my brother would stand up for me and to my mother and write about it in a paper—spoke to how kind, compassionate, and caring he was. That was a very awkward thing to share with you, but that's the reality—and I always share it with my friends."

Of course as Keith got older his attention shifted from forts in the woods and motorbikes to females. There was only one person for him—Selina Brown [now Lehman]. In many respects, their story played out like the series *The Wonder Years* … a story of first love and the triumphs and tribulations attached to that condition. Her memories of Keith are among the most precious because of their origins, something everyone can identify with, first love.

"The years—the days—you can probably ask my husband—I can't even remember our anniversary. Yet I can remember that I started dating Keith Call on April 21 however many years ago. It must have been 1988 was the year he was abducted and April 21 of that year would have been our four-year anniversary. So I guess we started dating in 1984," Selina said.

"He was my first love. I guess I was sixteen when we met. He was maybe fifteen? We were in high school together. He basically grew up as part of my family … and I grew up as part of his family. You know—every picture you would see we were always together at whatever holidays … we would be at our house with my parents and vice versa. We grew up together. He was like a son to my mom and dad. You know—we were always together."

They went to each other's proms. There were no grandiose themes and kids spending hundreds of dollars on limos and clothing for the events. Their proms were at the high school, with forgettable themes and hand-made cheesy decorations. It was not about the dance as much as it was spending the time with friends.

"The big deal for us was what restaurant you were going to with your friends … you wanted to go to the best restaurant. I know for one prom we went over to … it was over by Willoughby Spit over in Norfolk—we had driven over there. It was his prom because I remember another guy from high school, Howie Edwards, went with us," said Selina.

"Then for mine—I can't even remember. I must have blacked that one out. It was my senior year, and I had gone through mono. I had mono at one time, and I had a horrible, horrible rash from head to toe. They said that it was stress-induced or something. It was horrific. Then it went away. Then right before my prom it came back out. I ended up wearing a white dress with this rash all over my body."

Keith didn't care—all that mattered to him was to be with his girl.

"We went to a beach—a beach party—afterwards. I think we were allowed to stay out all night long. I think we came home. Our parents trusted us so much they gave us a lot of freedom that we didn't have to hide things."

Keith's love of music helped guide their time together. He was a fan of U2 and Pink Floyd. His sister Joyce recalls that when they were filming teenagers standing in line overnight for tickets to a U2 concert, it was Keith that was jumping up-and-down in the background to get some on-air exposure in the pre-YouTube or Facebook days. Selina was there with him for the concert.

"We spent the night outside, it must have been 1987, and it was cold. We spent the night out in Norfolk in a parking lot. We stayed outside for some twenty-seven hours to get tickets. We went to see that concert together. Whatever he liked—he was determined and passionate about it. The concert we went to ... that was the Joshua Tree Tour. The CD had just come out, and it was really big. I remember getting ready to walk out of the concert and we were almost out when they started to play this one song—'Forty.' I remember we rushed back into the theater to hear it. I remember him really being happy that they were playing it."

Dating meant going to the Hillside Cinema in Gloucester, complete with two screens.

"I can tell you where we *didn't* go. We didn't go to the parkway. That's for sure. That never happened. The one thing I remember in particular—the first couple murdered—the two girls. So, nobody went to the parkway, you know, because people were murdered there."

Even with the passing of a year and a half, the Thomas-Dowski murders still clung to the memories of the locals across the York River from where the car was found.

"It wasn't necessary for us to go parking. Our families, well, we would stay at home, hang out in the den. I remember my mom buying us a VCR because she preferred for us to be there. Rent movies—back when you rented a VHS. I remember us watching *The Way We Were*—you know, because he did that for me. We would go to movies or parties that were local ... football games and the dances that were after football games. We pretty much stayed in the county," Selina said.

Call was drawn into a new emerging technology of the eighties—personal computers. In 1988, an IBM with 512k of memory and a thirty-megabyte hard drive, with less computing power than an iPhone today, ran $1,249—the equivalent of $2,500 by today's standards.

While PCs were making inroads at home, it was not with the powerful desktops but the smaller home programming computers. Keith's family purchased for him a VIC 20 Commodore computer, one that used the TV as its monitor. Doug Call remembers his brother devouring the technology.

"He had a contraption where he stuck the phone onto something to connect. I remember loading programs on cassette tape. It came with a book on doing your own programming. You had a whole list of code and if you got one thing wrong it wouldn't work," Doug said.

Despite the limitations of the technology, Keith managed to make the old-tech purr.

"I remember him drawing," Selina said. "He drew me a picture of Pee Wee Herman. I remember we saw that movie or we liked that show. There was a character on *Pee Wee's Playhouse* that was Penny—I think. I remember him drawing a picture of her, on the computer. I think I framed it. He printed it out, and I think framed it as a cute little joke or whatever. I remember him drawing with the computer, and I thought was something."

For the time period, Keith was pushing the limits of the home computing technology.

The senior Calls accepted Selina into their family and seemed to embrace her relationship to their son.

"I do remember going to *Good Morning Vietnam* with Keith—going across the river there. I remember a funny story about his father. We all went over to the movie theater together, over to the Newport News one. I think they were going to see a different movie. Ours was going to end sooner—the one Keith and I were going to see. I remember his dad saying, 'I'm sure you two will find something to do.' He said it and gave me this look, and I was so humiliated. That was because earlier that day he had found my birth control pills in Keith's pants. So it was like the cat was out of the bag at that point. I can remember his dad saying that like it was yesterday—his dad sitting in front of me. So funny."

Where some parents might have exploded, the Calls seemed to understand the throes of young love.

Graduation tends to be a pivot point for change for people, and such was the case for Keith. His parents purchased him a red Toyota Celica, and he received a watch as well. The car was his pride and joy (other than Selina) and he even had vanity plates for it: KEIFS.

With graduation came change in his relationship with Selina. She enrolled in the nursing program at Old Dominion University in Norfolk. While only a short drive away, it meant she was physically separated from Keith, though he visited her almost every weekend.

"Everybody loved him. He was the level-headed one—rational. We were the crazy college. Old Dominion

University has a nickname of 'Overdose University,' a big party school. We all had our fake IDs to go to the different clubs and stuff. He was always level-headed. He didn't get drunk or anything—he was the one that always maintained. He was the one that took care of all of us really," Selina said.

"We did a lot of the parties around campus. Halloween was a really big thing. We loved Halloween. I remember one year he had a patient gown with a dressing around his head. If we were in Gloucester we pretty much stayed at my parents' house, not dressing up or anything. The one I remember particularly is he dressed as a patient. We all dressed like nurses and doctors ... a whole big group of us."

Keith enrolled at Christopher Newport University, a smaller school in Newport News. With a student body of 4,420 in 1988, it was, at that time, more of a community college.

"Keith was the first one from the family to go to college," Chris Call said. "Christopher Newport has changed a lot since then. Back then it was a commuter school. It's come a long ways. It was more like a four-year community college."

Keith chose the school because it had an excellent and emerging information technology program. Having a degree related to computers in the late 1980s was almost a guarantee of a thriving career, and Keith Call was well on his way.

And while Keith Call's life was like an opening act of a John Hughes' 1980s movie, that wasn't to say it was perfect. Keith went on a road trip to North Carolina to Elon College to visit an acquaintance. As with most college visits, drinking had been involved.

"He had been drinking with some friends, whatever, and was extremely impaired," Selina said. "He had gotten his car keys—they had taken the keys from him. Somehow he had gotten his keys. Not really knowing what he was doing, and he got behind the wheel. Fortunately—or unfortunately—he hit a parked car—you know, how cars park alongside the road. Fortunately that stopped him when he ran into that parked car.

"I remember he was devastated. He felt like he had disappointed his parents. That just wasn't Keith. That was not him. He didn't drink and drive. We did drink—we did. You didn't have to drink and drive. He was responsible—a responsible young man."

The 1980s was a different time when it came to drinking and driving. Tough laws advocated by Mother's Against Drunk Driving (MADD) were only starting to be enacted state-by-state across the country. In the 1980s if you were pulled over for drinking and driving, the officer was less concerned with an arrest and more concerned with making sure you got home safely.

The elder Calls didn't have to push harsh discipline on their son over the accident; he inflicted his own mental punishment. Joyce Call-Canada remembers the incident. "They were pretty upset about it. I guess he got fined. I don't remember any big consequences ... that was the first time he had ever been in trouble for anything."

One thing everyone that knew him agreed upon was that Keith was not the kind of person to duplicate a mistake. Having had an incident drinking and driving once, he would not risk it again.

In early April 1988, Keith and Selina had a minor separation. It was not their first time. The two would agree to split for two weeks or so, even date other people. They always came back together.

"We had our little spats. We were young. We always gave in," Selina said. "I was the one, I would always call him. He meant so much to me. I said I was trying to prove to him that I would give him the two weeks. I would do whatever it took for us. I was insecure. I wrote letters and cards to him, to tell him how much I loved him, how I couldn't imagine my life without him, that I'd be nothing without him. He would always tell me, 'You don't give yourself enough credit. You're so much stronger than that.' Just always so encouraging and supportive and we just decided to take a two-week break."

For young lovers, it was a remarkably mature act in the evolution of their relationship.

Selina decided to go to Elon College with some friends on the weekend of April 9. Keith told her, "I love you. I'll talk to you soon."

"I told him I was going to Elon College that following weekend with my friends and he said, 'Be careful. Bad things happen when people go to Elon,'" said Selina.

Clearly he was referencing his drinking and driving incident there a month or two earlier.

In keeping with their agreement, Keith asked out a young woman in one of his classes, Cassandra Hailey. The two had agreed to go to a movie together Saturday night. There was a campus party at CNU and both of them knew someone there—so they planned on dropping by for a short time. It would be their first—and last—date. And from that point forward their names would be conjoined together as the result of a ruthless predator in the Tidewater area.

CHAPTER 10

The phrase "the girl next door" can be defined as an all-American girl who is dependable, approachable, and admired. If you were casting someone to play that role in a 1980s sitcom, Cassandra Hailey would be at the top of your list. She was a cheerleader and gymnast, even coaching gymnastics in her teenage years. She loved football games, not just because she was a cheerleader, but because she truly loved football. Cassandra was beautiful, inside and out; even modeling in her early teen years. She was responsible and dependable, traits she always upheld even as a child. Cassandra was close with her family, who taught her how to be down-to-earth. She was happy-go-lucky and was never without a smile on her face.

Cassandra Lee Hailey was born to Joanne and Glen Hailey on May 16, 1969, in Walton Beach, Florida. The story of how her parents met is the kind of story told over cocktails—the kind of funny anecdote you might see on *Mad Men.*

Joanne met a man she thought was named Bill Hailey when he was a patient in the hospital where she worked. The other patient in the same room as Bill introduced him to Joanne as Bill Hailey. She went on to believe his name was Bill for some time and would even write to her mother about Bill. One night when they were out at a club, a guy came up to Joanne and asked about Glen. After some confusion, it was finally cleared up that Bill Hailey's name was in fact Glen Hailey. She wrote to her mother to tell her she had gotten engaged to Glen, to which her mother replied: "What happened to Bill?"

Glen Hailey, who grew up in North Carolina, had been called "Sunny" his whole life. When he applied to the air force, he learned that his real name was actually Carol Hailey. He had never known that his grandmother had filled out his birth certificate while his mother was recovering from her c-section. Regardless of the multiple name confusions, Sunny joined the air force. He was admitted to the hospital after a bad motorcycle accident where he met Joanne, originally from Pennsylvania and was also in the air force herself.

Fast forward several years and the Haileys were expecting their third child. Cassandra was not in a rush to make her appearance into the world; she was at least two weeks overdue. When the Haileys named their youngest daughter, they made a conscious effort to not call her "Cassie." Instead, Cassandra earned the nickname "Missy" from her two older sisters, Teri and Paula. No one can recall how the nickname Missy came about, but her older siblings joked that the name came from the youngest daughter being "a mistake." Cassandra followed in her father's footsteps of never being called by her legal first name, family and friends almost always called her Sandra, Sandy, or Missy.

Cassandra was six years younger than Paula and eight years younger than Teri. The age difference between Cassandra and her older sisters only created a better bond when she was little; the girls treated her like their own baby doll. Cassandra was born in the tail end of her father's career in the military, and the family was ready to settle down after his retirement. Living a military family lifestyle, the Haileys were used to moving frequently during the girls' childhood. The family finished out their air force career in Las Vegas before retiring to Newport News.

Teri recalls her favorite memory of Cassandra in Las Vegas. "I had turtles—those little green turtles in a little box. We were getting ready to go somewhere, and I always put them outside so they could get fresh air. Well, Missy decided that she wanted to put them in the sun … in the Las Vegas sun. We went somewhere, and when we came back, those turtles were cooked," said Teri.

The family settled in a cul de sac in a tight-knit neighborhood in Grafton, a bedroom community in burgeoning York County in the 1980s. Cassandra got to experience the typical childhood upbringing that her sisters did not. She made lifelong friends in Newport News and didn't have to move schools or states during grade school.

Since she was the youngest and home most of the time when her older sisters were in high school, she told her sisters that she always "got the crap chores."

"Mom would have her clean out the ashes out of the fireplace. She said it made her feel like Cinderella. So we bought her a broom for her birthday," said Teri.

The older sisters continue to laugh to this day about the joke birthday gift.

"One time in Vegas, I was playing hide and seek with Missy. It was her turn to hide. I didn't go looking for her so she was hiding somewhere waiting for me to find her. She was six years younger than me so that was the last thing I wanted to do was play hide and seek with her. My friend came over and we left to go play. It was a long while before she finally came out of hiding," Paula said.

When Cassandra made her first appearance in grade school it was with a cast on her arm after an accidental fall from the monkey bars. A cast never stopped Cassandra from making friends or a fashion statement. She was always a model, even if it was modeling a cast.

The Christmas holidays were special for the Hailey family, and they tended to spend their Christmases at home. Mrs. Hailey, who's Italian, always made a lasagna dinner on fine china for Christmas dinner. The three girls would always get dressed up and take pictures—always one serious and one goofy picture—to send to relatives.

As Cassandra grew up, her personality and character shined. She was outgoing and "a friend to everybody." When she wasn't at cheerleading practice she was babysitting three small children, coaching gymnastics, or working at Regis Hair Styling as a receptionist or a local shoe store. No one forced Cassandra to get a job; she liked to be busy and constantly on the move. She was always very well organized and committed to all of her obligations. Cassandra attended modeling school for a period of time. She was a model for one of the hairdressers at a convention and let the stylist bleach and cut off her long auburn hair.

For Cassandra, the value of friendship was not measured in dollars and cents, but in the relationships themselves.

"One time, one of her girlfriends didn't make the qualifications to go to a school dance. She didn't get high enough grades to get a ticket, but Missy did. She wanted to make a copy of her ticket so that the other girl could go to the dance, too," her mother said. "I told her if she made a copy she may get in trouble or even get kicked off the cheerleading team. I always let my girls make decisions, but I always talked to them about the potential consequences. She ended up deciding not to go to the dance since her friend couldn't go."

Missy wasn't the type to brag, she kept her good deeds to herself.

"She used to work at Perkin's Restaurant as a cashier. I found so many checks she had written to her coworkers at Perkin's. Thirty dollars here and there to help them out."

Susan Scott had become Cassandra's best friend after they met at a gymnastics meet.

"I did gymnastics for my high school and she did gymnastics for her high school, so we kind of ran in the same circle. We didn't become great friends until I was dating someone at her school and hanging out with that crowd," Susan said. "She was an awesome person. I mean always smiling; always happy. Even when she got mad it was comical; she couldn't stay mad—it wasn't in her personality. Very bubbly, always smiling, just the kind of person you gravitate to."

Paula remembers her little sister as being non-judgmental and very giving. "She was so laid back. At the time she disappeared she was going to school and working like three part-time jobs. But you have never known that. She never seemed frazzled at all. She was always well put-together. She even did some modeling when she was younger—she always cared about what she looked like," said Paula.

After Paula was in a car accident, she called her youngest sister while she was at work. "I had to get somewhere, so I called her. She left work, came and got me, and took me where I needed to go. She would do anything for anybody. I mean it was out of her way and she just did it."

Working was important to Cassandra; she enjoyed purchasing her own clothes and filling up the family's extra vehicle with gas. Employment was a measure of independence in the world. Cassandra wasn't interested in purchasing a car of her own; she was perfectly content with the family's clunker of a Cadillac.

"One time she went to a gymnastics meet at one of the schools in Hampton. She wasn't too familiar with the area … she took off and drove around until she almost ran out of gas and still couldn't find the school. She came home crying that night. 'Mom, I couldn't find the school, and I kept running out of gas. I just kept filling it up and kept looking for the school, but I just couldn't find it.' She never asked for help or for directions, she just kept pushing on to find that school. She was very committed," her mother said.

Academics didn't come easy to Cassandra. She didn't enjoy schoolwork, but she did the best she could. She struggled with math and would call her friend Terry Kirby for help. Although he was a year younger than her, Terry and Cassandra struck up a secret relationship in middle school that carried on throughout high school. The relationship was so under wraps between Terry and Cassandra that her parents didn't know she was dating him until after she disappeared.

It some respects it was a relationship that was hidden

in plain sight. The Haileys were familiar with the Kirby family. At Tabb High School, Terry Kirby was a football and basketball star. Cassandra's older sisters went to high school with Terry's older brother, Wayne, who also excelled in athletics. The Kirby boys were popular in school, but Cassandra had her reasons for keeping her relationship with Terry—who was black—quiet.

Joanne Hailey remembers the attitude of the community towards interracial dating at the time. "Although it was the 1980s, there were still some places in Norfolk that black people wouldn't go to. One time, Terry was at our home when we got there. We were friendly to him, talked to him. My biggest fear when she was hanging around Terry was the reaction of the communities. Both of their lives were in peril because of the attitude of the people of the era. I used to substitute teach, and I knew Terry. He didn't drink or get crazy like his friends. He concentrated on his grades. He wouldn't do anything to jeopardize her. I just told her to be careful when she went out with him.

"In fact, the only time she ever lied to me that I know of was because of Terry. One time, she came home with a Christmas present. She said a friend gave it to her when it was actually from Terry. She was just afraid to say it came from him, I guess. She told me later on the gift was from him … and that's when I told her to be careful because there may be people out there that may not like it. All through school, he was her only boyfriend. She went to dances with other guys but didn't date them," Mrs. Hailey said.

"There was a lot of people still against interracial couples. Some people treated her really poorly—so called friends. Her close friends didn't. The girls on the cheerleading squad were very mean to her then. That was until Terry began to become famous, then they all wanted to be his friend."

As her best friend Susan Scott put it, "Certain people knew and others thought they were just good friends. Because of the stigma back in the eighties she knew who she could trust with the information and who to keep at arm's length."

Her awareness of the culture at the time speaks highly for Cassandra's emotional maturity.

Terry Kirby was being scouted by college football teams during his high school career, and he had his eyes set on the NFL. Sandy didn't want their relationship to be a distraction from Terry being scouted. His older brother went onto Major League Baseball as a right fielder for seven seasons.

"Living across the street from us was a family that was like Terry's second mom and dad. He was a football coach, and she was a principal secretary at one of the high schools. He [Terry] spent a lot of time over there. We were close with them as well. It came without really being said to keep him out of the papers because there was so much going on with the next step in his life," Paula said.

Like Terry, Cassandra loved football. Between her multiple part-time jobs and jam-packed schedule, she hardly had time for other hobbies but she always watched football. She loved going to concerts; one of her favorite concerts was seeing Cyndi Lauper.

"We loved everything—except country. We didn't like country—back then anyway. Everything you could dance to—good beat kind of stuff. Almost like teenagers of today," Susan Scott said.

Cassandra also loved listening to Prince and Pink Floyd. Her favorite movie was *Purple Rain,* and the girls watched *WarGames* when they got the chance. She spent most of her limited free time hanging out with friends or at parties.

In York County, there weren't many places to go as a teenager. A popular hangout spot for Sandy's friends was Heritage Square, a shopping center with a grocery store and a McDonald's, right off of J. Clyde Morris Boulevard (US Route 17). Teenagers would hang out in the parking lot until the police would chase them away for loitering. Heritage Square was synonymous with hanging out in the area, regardless of which high school you attended.

"You would meet up there and see what was going on that night. Was anything happening? Was anyone having people over at the house … any of those kid-things," Susan said of hanging out at Heritage Square with Cassandra.

The groups of friends would often go to Yorktown Beach, Nags Head, or Virginia Beach when they felt like getting out of town.

As a cheerleader, Cassandra was part of the social events tied to local competition. Pep rallies at Tabb High were held behind the practice field. There were bonfires before the big games against rival Poquoson High School. The booster club painted tiger claws all along the street and then would sit in front of each of the player's houses. Grafton had a small town feel to it, and that was part of its appeal.

Cassandra enjoyed being at home with her family as much as being out with her friends. "Her family was big. We hung out with her parents as much as her friends. Her sisters were older and were out of the house but they were there a lot," said Susan.

Cassandra graduated in 1987 from Tabb High School. She had a small graduation party and headed out to other friends' graduation parties.

"That's how it was at Tabb. Everybody was having a party. We used to have parties at our house during the year. We'd end up at the Kirbys'. That's where the best parties were all of the time. Missy went down to the Outer Banks the day after she graduated. A lot of her friends had cars so she didn't always have to drive. One of them had a Volkswagen, and they had six or seven girls in there. Back in the day when you did that sort of thing," Paula said.

Cassandra decided to enroll at Christopher Newport College (now Christopher Newport University) after finishing high school. She wasn't sure exactly what she wanted to study, so she decided not to declare a major her freshman year.

"She seemed to really like it. She was very curious about

things so it was definitely up her alley to dig into and be interested in academics," Susan said of Cassandra's short time at Christopher Newport.

"Our first year in college, she came over and stayed with me over the weekends. We went and did college kid stuff around campus because I went to Old Dominion University. She was just so ... *happy* all of the time. I have this one picture of her in my dorm room and she just looked, like, gut-laughing. We just laughed all of the time. You never saw her when she wasn't smiling—ever. She was infectious in that way. She lightened the room wherever she was. She was very easy to be around.

"I had a great time all of the time with her. I can't remember fighting like girls do. You know, how girls get into their little petty fights? She and I never did that. We didn't have to do anything in particular. If I couldn't do something one night or if she was working, it wasn't a big deal. We always found time the next day or so to see each other. I was a staple at her house for a long time," said Susan.

"Cassandra was so caring. She was just a good hearted, fun-loving person. She was never mean to anybody that I can recall. She was always there to help and support. She was just a great person. I love her parents to death—I love them to this day. It's very hard for me to see them because I know they look at me ... I'm sure I'm not a bad reminder ... but I'm a reminder none the less." Susan still gets choked up almost thirty years later.

Cassandra was not dating anyone in early April 1988 ... it was likely she simply didn't have time in her hectic life for another person—or that the right person had not come along. When Keith Call in her business class asked her out on a date, it seemed innocent enough.

CHAPTER 11

It was supposed to be a first date in name only, little more than that. Keith Call was not looking for a long-term relationship, and by most accounts, Cassandra was not out looking for romance either. Keith and his longtime girlfriend Selina were merely taking a two-week break. If anything, he probably viewed it as a good way to spend a Saturday night. Keith had dinner at home with his parents and his brother Doug that night. Despite being spring in Virginia, a cold front had moved in two days earlier and temperatures barely reached fifty degrees during the days with the nights getting even cooler.

Doug Call was at home when his brother was preparing to leave for the evening.

"This is the last thing I remember about seeing my brother. … He was going out on that date, and he went up to ask my mom for some money. And my mom handed him twenty bucks. And I sat and thought to myself, 'Huh, I think I'm going to try that myself.' My mom handed him some money and he walked out the door, and that was the last time I saw him," Doug said. "And it did work—she gave me some money too."

Keith left the Call homestead for the last time in his red Celica. He didn't go over to Cassandra Hailey's initially but instead diverted to his brother Chris's place.

"I lived about fifteen minutes away. I do remember that I was the last member of our family to see Keith alive. He came over to borrow some clothes because he was going on a date with this girl, Cassandra. He also wanted me to buy some beer for him. They'd changed the drinking age in Virginia from eighteen to twenty-one. So I was the last one to see him alive. When they found his car it was only five minutes from where I lived. I lived right across the point on the Gloucester side of the bridge," Chris said.

"I bought him the beer. I told everybody about it. If I hadn't gotten it for him, he would have gotten it from someone else. We used to go to Newport News and hang out outside the liquor store; you could always get someone to go inside and get beer for you back then. It probably was Busch beer, a twelve-pack. I remember purchasing it at Farm Fresh for him."

Chris Call set out for Richmond for a prior commitment, and Keith headed out on his own. From there he went across the bridge into York County and presumably to Cassandra's house a short fifteen to twenty minutes away. In crossing the bridge he would have driven past the Colonial Parkway entrance off of Route 17 on his way to Grafton.

The six-foot tall, 150-pound Keith Call was wearing his brother's white polo shirt, a brown and gray cardigan sweater, two-tone brown slacks, and shoes. With his short, dark blond hair styled just-so, he had to appear as if he stepped out of the movie *The Breakfast Club*.

When Keith arrived at the Hailey household he learned that it was Mr. and Mrs. Hailey's anniversary. Teri was there with her husband at the time to take them out to dinner.

"He was a pretty straight forward college kid," Teri said. "They were going to go to the movies first and then to the party. She [Cassandra] and Susan had been to a party in that complex I think the night before. The night before with her and her girlfriend she had called Mom and said that she was going to be out all night."

Cassandra was five feet seven, weighing approximately 135 pounds. She had auburn, asymmetrically cut hair and deep brown eyes. For her date she was wearing two-tone acid-washed blue jeans, a white, front-button blouse with three-quarter sleeves, and brown, ankle-length lace-up boots. She was also wearing a brown wooden bead necklace and two rings. In many respects, Cassandra stood out as an attractive college girl, like thousands of others, going out for some fun on a Saturday night.

Cassandra agreed with her mother to be home by 2:00 a.m. Being the third daughter bought her some leeway on when she had to come home. The strictness with each of the Hailey daughters lapsed a little more. Paula Hailey Meehan remembers her parent's guidelines: "Our rule was if you were not coming home, all you had to do was call."

Older sister Teri Hailey recalls a stricter set of rules given she was the oldest.

"I did not have that rule. I had to be home at midnight—not past. If I was late—I didn't get to go out for a while. And I was eighteen, and still, 'If you live in my house, it's my rules.' Each one of us got a little more lenient. I never ever did not get to not come home."

Teri remembers that night in April 1988 vividly.

"It really wasn't a date-date. I think it was they were just going out. They weren't going out to start a relationship. It wasn't anything like that," Teri said.

Keith and Cassandra left to go the movie. No one bothered to find out what film they were going to see. The thinking was there would be plenty of time for asking questions when Cassandra came home.

The last thing that Keith said to Mrs. Hailey: "I'll have her home at a decent hour."

After the movie, the pair arrived at the University Square apartments, across from Christopher Newport's campus. A photocopied sign on the apartment door ushered attendees to the gathering with the words, "Party Till You Puke." It was a typical off-campus affair—loud music, beer, and a lot of college students mingling and drinking.

When they arrived, Keith and Cassandra separated. Keith saw Gertrude Carter,[7] who was a mutual friend of his and Selina's, while Cassandra saw her former boyfriend, Terry

---

7   Name changed by the authors.

Kirby, and her best friend, Susan Scott.

Gertrude's recollection of the party was fairly comprehensive.

"I spent the party with Keith talking. He told me that I looked good, and I joked with him that he must have been drinking. He told me not a drop as he was driving. His speech and his behavior also indicated that he had not been drinking. He did not have anything in his hand [i.e. a drink or cup]. He talked a lot about his break up with Selena and that they were spending time apart for a certain period without calling each other and they would get back together," Gertrude said.

Keith told Gertrude he was not having a good time and could not wait to go home.

"He indicated that the person he came with was not ready to leave but he was. He left to go to the convenience market. A girl sitting directly across from us was dressed wildly. She had wild hair, makeup, a white shirt, and blue jeans with holes. I believe she had a black jacket, but that was to the best of my recollection. She was sitting on the couch with two black males that seemed engaged in conversation. They went out the door the same time Keith did, but I never associated them as being together [as they never spoke to one another]. He asked me if I would be there upon his return and I said maybe.

"He [Keith] returned, and we talked in the same spot. I never remember seeing the girl after that. Keith and I briefly spoke, and I told him I needed to get home. He told me he was leaving and that he had enough for the evening as he was not having a good time. I hugged Keith when it was time to go and saw the clock outside the apartment said 2:15 a.m."

Gertrude stressed that Keith and Cassandra did not spend time together while at the party.

"He stayed with me, and the conversation was forced and dragged. Keith and I were only acquaintances from high school," Gertrude said.

Cassandra's closest friend, Susan Scott, was there, and she remembers the party as nothing out of the ordinary.

"It was a bunch of kids hanging out, doing things they probably shouldn't," Susan said. "We were under the twenty-one rule. If you were eighteen by a certain [date] you could still drink. It was your typical college party."

Lisa Burns, a friend of Keith's on-again, off-again girlfriend, told Selina of her recollection of the party.

"I don't know if what she told me … I don't know if she was trying to make me feel better or what," said Selina. "She [Lisa] said that she saw him at the party and that he seemed elated to see her, because he didn't know anybody there. If Lisa had not been there, Keith wouldn't have known no one because Cassandra was off on her own. Lisa told me that … and again, she may have just been trying to make me feel good. I don't know, she said that Keith told her that he couldn't believe that he hadn't heard from me.

"He said to her, 'We've done this before but we never—' He's right, I always caved in."

Selina concedes that was usually the case.

"We had our little spats. We were young. We always gave in. I was the one, I would always call him. He meant so much to me. I said I was trying to prove to him that I would give him the two weeks. I would do whatever it took for us," said Selina.

"She [Lisa] said that when she was leaving, I can't remember, I thought she said it was one-ish, she went to tell him goodbye. He was like, 'No, you can't leave. Who am I going to talk to?'"

While accounts vary as to who Keith talked to and when, the party-goers also could not agree as to when Keith and Cassandra left. Various individuals have them leaving anywhere from 11:30 p.m. to 2:15 a.m. It was a college party, and at the moment, no one was watching the clock. After all, what could go wrong?

Being conscientious and respectful, it is most likely that

Keith planned his departure in time to get Cassandra home by the time she had told her mother. The Hailey home was only a few short minutes away from CNU. Even leaving at 2:15 a.m., he would have had her home close to her curfew time.

Susan Scott recalls what she gleaned from Cassandra that evening.

"They had been out to a movie, and they were not at the party that long. It just turned out bad all the way around from something that seemed so simple. It was a simple date," Susan said. "She came by the party ... she was going home. No matter how much I said, 'No ... just stay here with me. I'll take you home.' Blah, blah, blah. She just was, 'No ... that would be rude.' That's because that was her personality. So she said, 'I'll call you in the morning.'"

* * * * *

At Elon College, Keith's girlfriend was having a premonition of something wrong.

"So it was Friday night; we're having a great time with my friends. It was a girl I went to high school with—Holly— that we had gone up to stay with. Saturday, [we were having a] great time just hanging out. Saturday night we're at a party, and I got a pit in my stomach.

"I said to Holly, 'I'm going to go back to your room.'

"She asked, 'What's wrong?'

"I said, 'I just miss Keith really bad.'

"I thought that, well, this is just a week's gone by, I'm having a pity party or whatever. I just missed him, like, with every bit of my being."

The time of that sinking feeling in her stomach? Somewhere between 1:30 and 2:00 a.m.

The moon was in the last quarter and the overcast sky was just beginning to clear when they left. From the party, the most direct route back to the Hailey home in Grafton was on US Route 17—J. Clyde Morris Boulevard—also known as the George Washington Highway. They would have driven by the local hangout at Heritage Square, and there were unconfirmed sightings of them at a convenience store there. After that, however, the only person that saw Keith and Cassandra was their murderer.

At around 2:00 a.m., Mrs. Hailey woke up and checked … her daughter had not come home yet. She was concerned, but Cassandra sometimes didn't come home. When she was going to miss curfew, she would call. Joanna Hailey waited for the phone to ring but still did not panic.

Chris Call was one of the first people to see Keith's car after the party.

"I was coming back from Richmond with a friend of mine. We were coming back around 2:30 a.m. [Sunday, April 10] in the morning. It was Russian Orthodox Easter, and it was very late. We were coming back on the parkway to get to Gloucester Point off of I-64 there. I took the parkway all of the time. A funny thing happened. A van came out of the woods at Ringfield Park, which was a picnic area. I remember this van coming up behind us really fast.

"The speed limit on the parkway is forty-five. … It's about the only place I got a speeding ticket when I was eighteen. I remember remarking to my friend Ethan, 'You know that van must be doing sixty-five to seventy-five miles per hour to catch up with us.' I remember we got to an area where a car was, and that car was exactly where they found my brother's car when they found it a few hours later. Once we passed the car, that van slowed down and did a U-turn and went back. The van didn't pass. … I don't remember if it pulled in where Keith's car was," said Chris.

"That really struck me at that time as something really weird—you don't do that on the parkway, especially at 3:00 a.m. in the morning. When we went by the car I remember seeing a dome light on or the trunk was open and there was that little light on for the trunk. I remember remarking to my friend Ethan, 'Oh, they're probably out parking.' I had no idea it was my brother's car. I thought they were out parking and kissing—it was a lovers' lane area—as it was famously known as. I'm 99.9 percent sure that the car I passed was my brother's. When my father found it, and the park rangers about an hour later, that's exactly where my brothers' car was."

Two other drivers eventually came forward claiming to have seen the red Celica with the vanity license plate "KEIFER" in the turnout as well. One driver passed the car at 5:00 a.m. but did not notice the interior light on. Another driver passed it at 6:10 a.m. and noticed the light on.

Keith's father, Richard, was driving on the parkway on his way to the brewery at around 7:00 a.m. He passed the car parked at the York River Overlook turnoff, then turned around to check it out. It was disturbing initially because the driver's side door was slightly ajar. Mr. Call got out and checked the interior. The driver's side seat was folded forward, as if someone was getting into or out of the back seat. He returned the seat to its driving positon and leaned in the vehicle. Mr. Call saw Cassandra's purse on the passenger seat, his son's gold watch, and some cassette tapes on the console between the two front seats. He checked for the keys to the vehicle, but they were not in the ignition, nor were the keys on the front seat or anywhere else in the car. In the back seat he saw three beer cans on the floor, on top of a dull—perhaps gray—coat or jacket.

Chris Call remembers his father's account well.

"When my father found the car nothing seemed out of the ordinary. The keys were not in the ignition. He was kind of late for work. He kind of thought, 'Maybe they're out on the beach or something—doing whatever seventeen- to eighteen-year-olds do.' Nothing seemed out of the ordinary."

According to Chris, Richard's account differed from the park ranger's.

"When the park rangers found the car, the keys were in the ignition. Almost all of their clothes were on the front seat and the back seat—almost all of Keith's clothes and some of Cassandra's. I remember her bra, one of her boots, her purse, their wallets, the glove compartment was open. None of that stuff was like that when my father was there," said Chris. "He didn't see anything like that. He was even hypnotized and couldn't remember that."

Park Ranger John Seager was the first ranger on the scene. According to him, he found the car with the keys in the ignition and a folded set of clothing in the back seat. The rest of the scene was similar to what Chris Call remembers of his father's account.

So why the discrepancy? How could Richard Call have gotten it wrong—so wrong that even under hypnosis he couldn't remember the keys?

According to Danny Plott, a Virginia State Police detective who worked the case as part of a task force years later, at some point the park rangers found the car, gathered up some of the belongings, presumably to find some identification, and left the vehicle.

"The park rangers were the first ones there, and especially with Call and Hailey, they admit that they thought it was an abandoned vehicle and they inventoried it. Then they realized, 'Oh gosh, this might not be an abandoned vehicle,' and by their own admission—*one of their own's admission*—tried to put the stuff back in where he had found it," said Plott. "They don't want anything to do with it. I always wonder why one of them didn't say, 'Hey, we're in over our head,' and tell everything but they won't. I'm sure they're embarrassed."

At some point, the park rangers "tried to stage it. Or, they tried to put it back."

Danny further remembers, "Their interview sheets and what they [the FBI] saw—they just buried the park rangers about them going in and out of the car. One of them even said that he felt one of the park rangers may have taken something. They were some kind of pissed. I think that even the FBI at first, they thought one or more of the park rangers were behind it.

"I'm sure the rangers and the park service don't want to be painted as the people who were the bad people in this. I can tell you right now, in both Call-Hailey and Dowski-Thomas, their ineptness and ineptitude—I'm not saying we would have caught them if they'd left things away, but it's almost like you had to start over each time. Especially so with Cassandra and Keith."

Chances are the rangers innocently found the car, took some of the contents (clothing, keys, etc.) in an effort to locate or identify the owners. When they realized that both Keith and Cassandra were unaccounted for, they went back and re-staged the crime scene ... never bothering to tell Mr. Call they had done that. In the process, however, they managed to contaminate the crime scene twice and leave Mr. Call wondering for the rest of his life how he could have missed the clothing in the back seat of the car.

Keith's keys were allegedly located on the driver's seat, and a watch and eyeglasses case were on the dashboard. On the back seat there was a man's wallet with twelve dollars inside.

Then there was the clothing ... almost all of Keith's clothes, along with Cassandra's top, bra, and a lone brown boot. Her purse was on the passenger side floor. One thing was missing—Cassandra's wallet—though her checkbook was still in her purse. It was as if the wallet had been taken out of her purse. Call's shoes, wallet, and an alligator belt were also in the back seat. Some of Cassandra's jewelry, however, was never accounted for. The glove box was open—unlike when Mr. Call had come upon the vehicle—and the passenger side door was locked.

Ranger Seager had discovered Cassandra's checkbook in her purse and called the Hailey household in Grafton to see if she was there and perhaps could explain the apparently abandoned car. The Hailey family was stunned. No, Cassandra wasn't at home. The Call family was contacted as well—no one knew where Keith was either.

Other rangers gathered at the scene as members of the family trickled in, as did the media. Teri Hailey showed up, and her reaction to the park rangers was less than enthusiastic.

"I think they got their textbooks out of the Cracker Jack box. They let anybody walk all over the crime scene. Common sense would tell you—where the car's parked—how it was parked—there's clothes in the car—"

Being a law enforcement officer herself, Teri could not comprehend how the park rangers were managing the crime scene.

"So I'm a police officer so I'm going to think, or a rent-a-cop, if you want to call them that—the park rangers, I'm going to put two-and-two together. There's been a murder up here already. This doesn't make sense. Maybe this doesn't look like what it's supposed to be made to look like. I'm going to let every Tom, Dick, and Harry, walk up to this car—pick up stuff in this car, and walk all over what might be a crime scene," Teri said.

The park rangers immediately came up with their own theory, one that conveniently fit the evidence they saw. Keith and Cassandra had come to the parkway to make out, and in their zeal, they had gone skinny dipping. Almost immediately they fed that thinking to a dismayed press, who had already drawn conclusions similar to the family members—this had to be connected to the Thomas-Dowski murders.

Teri Hailey recalls the ludicrous idea.

"I'm going to assume they 'went skinny dipping'? Let's

see where the river is. I don't think they walked down that [embankment]. It was cold the night before.

"'Okay, maybe they walked this way.'

"Naked. Really? I don't think they would have done that either," Teri said.

Paula Hailey Meehan is quick to weigh in on the skinny dipping theory as well.

"I'm not trained in law enforcement, and *I* can figure that out."

The embankment at the York River Overlook was well over twenty feet down at a steep angle. Even in the daylight, navigating that almost straight-down drop would have been tricky—let alone naked in the cold and the dark. Still, the rangers held firm with their belief in the press who ran with the story.

* * * * *

Back at Elon College, Selina Lehman awoke after an uneasy night of sleep thinking about Keith.

"I woke up Sunday morning, still had that pit. We went to a soccer game that afternoon. Still, I was just teary-eyed. I cried the entire way back from when we left Elon. The girls in the car were all, 'What's wrong?' I just missed Keith so bad that I was sick. So we got back to ODU [Old Dominion University], we went up to our apartment, I grabbed the telephone. I wasn't supposed to talk to him for two weeks, but I grabbed the phone and went to the bathroom and called the house. I believe Doug answered the telephone. I said, 'Is Keith there?' And he said, 'No, he's not.' I said 'Okay will you tell him that I called?' I hung up the phone.

"It didn't sit well with me. I called him right back and Doug answered.

"I asked, 'Doug, where is he?'

"And he responded, 'Selina is he not with you?'

"I said, 'No, he's not with me—I just got home from Elon. What are you talking about?'

"Doug said, 'He's missing.'

"'What do you mean he's missing? Have you talked to Todd?'

"I remember that Todd was a friend of his. I remember specifically saying 'Todd' and Doug replied 'No—he's missing.'

"I walked out of the bathroom and my roommates were sitting in the living room, and they turned around and looked at me. That's when I saw the television. They were like white. It was on the news all over the TV," Selina said.

"I don't even know what happened. I don't know how I got from our living room to Keith's house. My girls came with me, God love 'em. We got in the car, and I drove. I drove from Norfolk to Keith's house, and again, I don't know how I did it. I think my brother in-law was there waiting for me. He got me, and I insisted on going to the parkway. Then he took me to the parkway, and that's when my whole life changed.

"Seeing the helicopters and the crime scene tape and his car and the media. To this day I have such a distaste for the media; it's immeasurable how much I can't stand the media. Their sensationalism and all that we went through."

Susan Scott, Cassandra's best friend, recalls how she learned what was unfolding on the parkway a few miles away.

"I got the call in the morning; I thought it was her [Cassandra]. My mom woke me up and said that Sandy's parents were on the phone. I was like, 'Okay ... '

"The first thing they asked me if Sandy was with me. I said, 'No.'

"They said, 'Okay, can you come over?'

"I was like, 'Sure.' I got up and drove over, and that's when I found out they had found the car on the parkway,"

Susan said.

"They *never* would have gone down the embankment to skinny dip in April. It was too cold. She never would have gone up there to park because she hated the parkway. And when I talked to her, she was going home. He [Keith] never would have gotten her to park on the parkway. Even if he would have talked her into going somewhere to park, it would have not been there. I don't think that after the evening, that was their intention. The intention [after the party] was to get her home."

With the pressure of the media arriving, it was becoming quickly apparent that the press saw this as more than just two kids missing. Keith's Celica had been found just over a mile from where Cathy Thomas's Honda had been found, in an almost identical turnoff. In an effort to take some control of the unfolding investigation, the rangers impounded Keith's car and had it taken off-site for further analysis.

No one from the National Park Service bothered to contact the FBI.

The view north on the Colonial Parkway as it appears today, looking north from the pull-off where Cathy Thomas and Becky Thomas were discovered.

One of the many scenic overpasses on the Colonial Parkway as it appears now. There are few access points to the park, especially after hours. Its isolation and lack of patrols by the NPS made it a perfect place for murder or to dispose of a vehicle/bodies.

Cathy Thomas in civilian life

*Cathy in the US Navy – one
of the first females to serve as
Surface Warfare Officers.*

*One of the last photos of
Cathy Thomas with her
friend Deb Hill. As with
everything in her life, her
career as a stockbroker
was a stunning success.*

*Cathy in the US Navy – one
of the first females to serve as
Surface Warfare Officers.*

Becky Dowski near the time of her murder. A bright and driven young woman from upstate New York.

FBI aerial photograph of where Becky and Cathy were discovered on the Colonial Parkway at the turnout near the center of the photograph.

FBI photograph of Cathy's car, barely visible having been pushed off the embankment. It is easy to see how the vehicle was overlooked for so long.

FBI photograph of the smashed back window of Cathy Thomas's Honda Civic. The National Park Service Rangers thought the two women might be injured as a result of an accident.

Current day image of where Cathy Thomas's car was discovered. There's no hint of the horror that took place here...from the brutal murders to the attempts to burn then submerge her car.

*David Knobling during
his time at the Frederick
Military Academy.*

*Karl and Judy Knobling with
David (the taller youth) and
his brother Michael in 1977.*

*One of the last photos of David
Knobling. He had a young
pregnant girlfriend and was
just starting a new career.*

*David Knobling at Christmas
in 1986, a few months
prior to his death.*

*Robin Edwards, a
spitfire youngster who
was more mature than
her physical years.*

*FBI photograph of David Knobling's truck. David always backed
his vehicle in, never left it unlocked, and it didn't require the keys
turned to accessories to play the radio...all signs that his vehicle was
staged for theft – the calling card of the Colonial Parkway murderer.*

Crime scene photograph of David Knobling's coveted Ford pickup at Ragged Island. It was left with the door open, the keys turned to accessories, and the radio on. David never left his car unlocked...and with the rain that night, a rendezvous in the marshlands seems unlikely.

FBI photo of Ragged Island. This image shows the James River Bridge and the roadway leading from the parking area to the river. The wooded isolation here is not dissimilar to that of the Colonial Parkway.

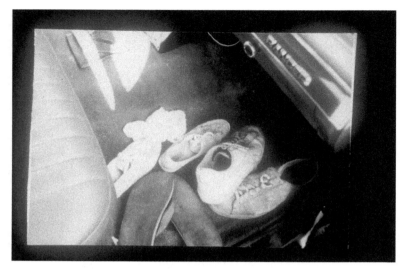

*On the floor of David's truck you can see the shoes
of the victim. Their removal was part of the control
that the murderer(s) exerted on the victims.*

*This crime scene photo shows Robin Edward's shoe that she
had doodled on, laying on the floor of David's truck.*

These crime scene photographs show the area where the remains of David Knobling and Robin Edwards were found three days after their disappearance.

This recent image shows the only marker at Ragged Island, a gunshot sign. The refuge still has a reputation for being a place for a romantic spot and drug deals.

At Ragged Island (as it appears today) this is the end of the roadway leading from the parking lot to the river's edge. Logically, this is the most easily accessible place at Ragged Island for the two young victims to have reached the water.

Richard Keith Call – Keith to his friends and family. A bright young man studying computer science at Christopher Newport.

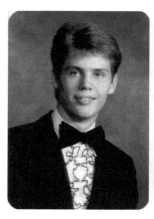

Keith Call in High School.

Keith was programming on leading edge home computing technology for the 1988.

Cassandra Hailey – every bit the girl next door – 1980's style.

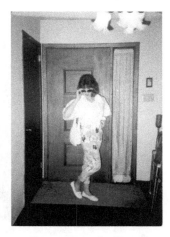

Cassandra Hailey, a hard-working student at Christopher Newport, Cassandra juggled multiple jobs, gymnastic classes, and many friends.

Cassandra, aka Sandy and Missy was fun loving, vibrant, and energetic. Her date with Keith Call was their first and only one.

These contemporary photographs show the parking area where Keith's car was discovered. His brother and several others saw it shortly after their disappearance and Keith's father found it the following morning as well. The real question that lingers...were Keith and Cassandra ever on the Colonial Parkway that night, or was Keith's car simply staged and abandoned there?

Keith's red Toyota. A number of people saw this on the parkway after the party, including his brother Chris.

FBI aerial photograph of the pull-over spot where Keith Call's car was found the day after their date. Its proximity to where Becky and Cathy were found a year earlier should have been a clue to the park rangers – but it was one they chose to ignore.

Annamaria Phelps came from a hard-working family in Amelia County, Virginia. She had moved to Virginia Beach with her boyfriend, Clinton Lauer and was struggling to get by but living the American dream.

Annamaria and her boyfriend's brother Daniel Lauer came back home for a short visit and so that Daniel could pack to move in with them.

Daniel's plan was to move in with his brother Clinton and Clinton's girlfriend, Annamaria Phelps. Their trip home on Labor Day weekend was only for a few hours. On their return trip to Virginia Beach they encountered their killer(s).

Daniel Lauer was from Amelia County, Virginia. He had some legal problems involving a marriage to an underage girl but was preparing to move on with his life.

A Virginia State Police photo of the rest area on I-64 where Daniel's car was found abandoned.

Daniel's Chevy Nova. The vehicle should have been in the east bound rest area, but was found in the west bound area where the killer(s) had left it.

The interior of Daniel's car. The killer taunted authorities by hanging his feathered roach clip on the half-opened driver's side window.

The back seat of Daniel's car, filled with his hastily packed personal belongings for his move to the beach.

A crime scene photograph showing the roadway leading back into the woods. The killer(s) drove Daniel and Annamaria back here in the darkness, killing them and covering their bodies in an electric blanket. Their bodies were found by hunters that came across the bodies weeks after they disappeared.

A Virginia State Police photograph showing the isolated logging trail from the air when the bodies were discovered.

As it appears today from the road, this is the lonely trail leading back into the woods where the victims had been taken and killed.

The bodies of Annamaria and Daniel were found six weeks after they disappeared, just over a mile from where his car had been located. This crime scene photo shows tent erected over their remains as investigators work in the rain to recover every clue.

A crime scene photograph of some of the investigators at the recovery site. In the center of the image is Danny Plott, standing next to Dr. Marcella Fierro of the Virginia State Medical Examiner's office.

Annamaria Phelp's locket as found on the logging trail. Was this a breadcrumb she had dropped, was it cut off during her struggle, or was it some sort of symbol that the killer left behind for investigators?

As it appears today, the location shown in the distance is where Annamaria and Daniel met their untimely fates.

Fred Atwell clearly rekindled the efforts of law enforcement on the Colonial Parkway murders with his release of the crime scene photographs to the media. He went from gadfly on the case to suspect, then, as seen in these images from his robbery trial – to convicted felon. What exactly does Fred Atwell know about the crimes…if anything?

CHAPTER 12

FBI Special Agent John Mabry was listening to the radio about 7:15 a.m. on Monday, April 11 when he heard the lead news story: "Rescuers are searching the Colonial Parkway for the bodies of a young couple whose car was found yesterday at the York River Overlook. Authorities fear the pair may have gone skinny dipping and drowned ... "

Mabry's mental response was to the point, "York River Overlook? I can't believe it. This is a nightmare." He, like the media, had drawn the connection to the case he had worked over a year earlier.

He raced to the federal building and inside found Joe "Wolfie" Wolfinger getting into his car. "Did you hear what happened?" Wolfinger shook his head. Mabry filled him in on the radio broadcast.

"You better get up there."

Since the Thomas-Dowski murders, the FBI leadership had changed in Norfolk, with Irvin Wells taking over that office. Irvin "IB" Wells is a man that has FBI ink for blood. He attended the Virginia Military Institute and went into the bureau working in Springfield then Champaign-Urbana in Illinois. He spent eleven years in Los Angeles and moved up in the flat organization structure of the FBI's management track—working in the Knoxville, Tennessee, division before moving onto headquarters in Washington, DC. Wells worked in the Intelligence Division, the FBI's counter-intelligence group. He was the assistant special agent in charge in Savannah, Georgia, then went back to FBI headquarters where he had been a special assistant to the assistant director, the bureau's number two man—and the person that ran the day-to-day work of the vast law enforcement agency. He was so good that he was retained by (and outlasted) three assistant directors before being moved to Norfolk as the special agent in charge at the time of the Call-Hailey case. In his career he arrested spies, ran crime squads and counterintelligence operations, and managed dozens of agents on countless cases.

Wells was no slouch. He had not been in Norfolk when the Thomas-Dowski murders had taken place but had been fully briefed on them. When word came of two young people missing on the Colonial Parkway, he saw the possible connection immediately. He ordered a command post established, and the FBI set up operations at the Duke of York Motel. Agents were dispatched to the crime scene to begin the arduous work. To the FBI, this was not a murder yet—this was a pair of missing young people.

The rangers' behavior was odd in Wells's opinion … from the way they handled the car to how they reacted to the FBI's presence.

"So we run into these guys, and they're defensive and they act like suspects! They were just such a strange ilk. They weren't like brothers in law enforcement. They were like, 'Who are you?'

"They were so odd that we were thinking, well … we believe there was an authority figure because, let's say Call-Hailey … somebody had to initially take control of these couples. Even in Dowski-Thomas, somebody had to take control because they fought back and awful things happened. I still think there were two. I don't think that one man could have taken control of those women," Wells said.

"Anyway, these park rangers, they were just odd and uncooperative. That's all I can say—uncooperative."

When pressed about what was out of place about their behavior, Wells cuts to the chase.

"One thing is we were law enforcement and they were uncooperative! I mean we are all working this together and we want to solve—and here they are being secretive, withdrawn."

Law enforcement was unsure about what had exactly happened to the missing pair but assumed they or their remains were nearby, so they brought in search hounds and John Branyon of Tidewater Trails Search and Rescue Group. Using the clothing garments found in the car, they did individual searches for each one of the missing students.

The team that scented one of Cassandra's garments then headed west alongside the parkway nearly a mile to Indian Field Creek, then they led the team to the landward side of the bridge. Ironically in going there they went past where Cathy Thomas and Rebecca Dowski had been found. The dogs tried to enter the water at Indian Field Creek, but shortly thereafter, they stopped.

Another team following the scent from Keith Call's clothing also went west but a much shorter distance. They turned right to the river and followed the shoreline back toward the overlook.

High tide at that time of the year was at 4:15 a.m., and the narrow beach where the trail for Cassandra led would have been covered with water between 2:00 and 7:30 a.m.

"The water would have moved the scent up into the rocks," Branyon theorized.

Branyon was fairly confident that his dogs had been on a solid trail. Ginger Branyon, John's partner, used three different dogs to follow the trial. The way that went after the scent indicated that it was strong, making it unlikely they were following a trail that had not been walked on by either of the missing persons.

The search dogs were trained not only for tracking but in cadaver search as well. The Branyons took three of the dogs out in a boat to see if they could follow the scent any further. All three definitely indicated they had picked up the scent of a dead body in the same two spots on the water. The York River had long shallow banks with a fairly steep drop off. Divers were immediately called in and waded into the cold, waist-deep water but found nothing. The dogs had detected a dead body in the water; that was all their handlers could confirm. Whether it was from either of the two victims would take several days to be potentially resolved.

Additional help came in the form of the York County Fire and Rescue team, which launched a two-day effort to search the York River. Dive teams from York and James City counties worked together in a tight search pattern covering a one-mile stretch of the waterfront. The local Nightingale emergency helicopter searched the shoreline, and groups of volunteers led by park rangers searched the woodlands from the pier at the weapons station at Cheatham Annex. The FBI brought in an airplane to augment the search. The fear was that if the bodies had been caught by the current, they could wash into the Chesapeake Bay and right out to sea. The coast guard put boats in the water as well, working a pattern up and down the river. By late Monday the water search of the York River was called off. Matters were left to aircraft after that.

The families were still chaffing at the theory that the couple had gone skinny dipping. Teri Hailey told the *Virginia Gazette* newspaper, "My sister was very modest. I've never known her to take her clothes off in front of anyone. To go swimming she would have at least left her underwear on."

In another interview with the *Daily Press*, she added to the narrative. "My sister and I are the same. If we can't see the bottom, we're not going in."

Teri was surprised that the two rings and the necklace Cassandra wore were not found. "I know she had the jewelry on because I asked to borrow the ring back that night. She wouldn't have gone in the water with it on. She wouldn't even take a shower with any of her jewelry on."

Joanna Hailey told the *Daily Press*, "They didn't go up there to go swimming, they didn't go up there to get in trouble. They're smarter than to go into the water on a night that cold."

By Monday evening the story was changing. The rangers'

skinny-dipping theory had been debunked by the media, the families, common sense, and finally by the FBI. Irvin Wells told the *Daily Press*, "We entered the investigation based on the mysterious disappearance and possible abduction of the two. There is no evidence or foul play or violence to suggest the two were killed."

Who had committed that abduction and why was still vague, even for those on the case.

Keith's car was processed—fingerprinted and checked for more evidence. It had already been touched by so many people because of the callous attitude of the rangers toward the crime scene, it would be tricky to perform useful analysis. Family members who might have touched the car, such as Richard Call, and the park rangers were fingerprinted to rule out some of the prints that had been found.

The clothing was inspected. There was no indication of blood. That offered a glimmer of hope that the clothing had been removed from Call and Hailey when they were still alive. There was no indication of blood in the car as well.

The command post at the Duke of York Motel was a model of FBI precision, Irvin Wells recalls. "We just set up a CP. The radio guy set up the radio. We have a supervisor there on the radio, and all of us are out in the field. We just try and coordinate what we are doing. There are some leads that have to be immediate. They try and ensure that our frequency is the sole frequency, not one that could be monitored by local people or other law enforcement agencies."

The FBI began to formulate its own theory. Joe Wolfinger, the assistant special agent in charge, reporting up to Irwin Wells, recalls from his memory what they believed had happened.

"I do remember that we pretty much thought they would have arrived, based on reports we had when they left the party, if they were accurate, they would have arrived at that point in Yorktown at the river, that little cul-de-sac or little cut off, around 2:00 a.m. or 2:15 or so. I'm sure if they left at 1:30 a.m. or 2:00, and I can't remember how long the trip was, I am sure they were drinking beer. They were young people.

"I don't think they went to the parkway to just look at the river. People do pull off. I remember the rangers sharing a lot of information about what they observed up there. I don't remember any dysfunction with them. But there may well have been.

"They [the rangers] helped us a lot. I mean you go to a place like that, it's a lovers' lane is what it is at night. There's all those cut offs, and you can sit and look at the river and do whatever you want to do. That's what it becomes at night. There's a whole cast of characters who descend on the place, and they're Peeping Toms. Most of them are pretty harmless people, and they're in their cars and they don't confront anybody. Some of them are obviously more dangerous.

"Who set upon them and where they were, we don't know. We used a ton of people—park rangers, FBI agents from the Norfolk office, Virginia State Police was heavily involved with us; we searched all around that car, searched the riverfront. …

"Call and Hailey could have been approached by someone with a gun, taken them somewhere else and dumped them. There's lots of places around there where they could have been taken.

"We probably had fifty people at one point walking through the woods looking for those kids; we had an airplane up. We covered a lot of ground, and we never found them. It's surprising with all of the hunters in the world that somebody didn't stumble over them at some point.

"I think they stopped where they stopped at two in the morning to make out and were taken from there. We didn't foreclose any avenue of investigation. Nobody ever bought into a theory that precluded looking for somebody else, something else, even the guy we talked about, even the Waterman Theory. You pursue something like that, that gets your attention, you give it a lot of focus, but you don't stop doing other things because that's there. I've been associated with many investigations, and I'm sure that Irv has too, where you're surprised to find out who did it. ... It wasn't one of the principle people that you thought—you know? So we never stopped keeping an open mind about who did it."

The beer cans on the floor of the back seat of Keith's car? Were they left there by the murderers? Irvin Wells offers a counterpoint.

"Or they were thrown back there, if you're being cavalier. I know that Call-Hailey was a first date. The fact that they disappeared ... I can't dismiss water all around. It had to be. I just know that water would be the way."

Under the FBI's theory, the pair went to the parkway to make out, were killed, and disposed of locally—there at the parkway. The presence of the beer cans on the back seat floor was simply explained as the two kids parking and having a few drinks. The missing clothing—well that was off due to the throes of young passion. The fact that Cassandra's door was locked, her wallet missing, and Keith's door left ajar allowed for a scenario where someone posing as an authority figure, approached the vehicle. Driver's licenses were asked for and possibly vehicle registration. The killer took control of his victims and marched them off somewhere along the parkway and murdered them. Their bodies were either disposed of in the York River or were still left to be found there in the brush.

This working theory, however, flies in the face of both of the victim's attitudes towards the parkway. Richard Call relayed to the press that "Keith was leery of the parkway. He had made statement before that he didn't like to go out there."

Cassandra had been more explicit with her best friend Susan Scott about the parkway. "She hated the parkway. Absolutely. Absolutely she hated it. She hated it at night. She just thought it was spooky."

When asked if Cassandra would have gone there to make out, Susan's response was adamant. "No! She *hated* the parkway. She thought it was spooky, and she hated it. We would take it between Yorktown and Williamsburg, sometimes at night, and she hated it. She never wanted us to stop the car … none of it. She wanted no part of it at night. I was never convinced they were there."

Other things about the theory disturbed the families. First was the clothing that was missing. Keith was shoeless; Cassandra would have been entirely naked, with one boot. In the chilling spring air, the thought that they had been possibly in the process of making love did not add up with the clothing that was recovered.

Richard Call and Joanne Hailey both agreed that the two must have been abducted between the party and the parkway.

"Keith would never leave his keys in the car," his mother, Barbara Call, told a gathering of the press that first week after the crime. "It was a high school graduation present, and he really loved it. His gold watch was a gift too."

Keith's father struggled with the fact that he had come across his son's car and had continued on to work. "I figured the kids had stayed all night at the party and had come to the parkway at dawn. It looked like they had left the car in a hurry. I thought maybe they had jumped out to go to the bathroom."

The rangers never told him that they had removed items from the car which was why he was not alerted immediately when he did his cursory inspection of the car.

Major Ron Montgomery of the York County Sheriff's Department sided with the families in his thinking. "They were never on the parkway. Cassandra was athletic. Her sister was a police officer. There was no sign of a struggle at the crime scene—no indication that they were there other than the car.

"I think they left the party and somewhere between Christopher Newport and Cassandra's home, whatever happened to them happened. Whoever killed them then drove the car to the parkway and abandoned it there.

"We put boats in the York River and searched there and the surrounding area. No signs of the bodies. No sign of anyone being there.

"It makes no sense to me that they would have driven there to park and make out. They were barely talking at the party. I think he was driving her home as planned—having left at 1:30 a.m. to get her home at 2:00 a.m.

"I don't think they were there [on the parkway] that night. Even if they were there, why park there? It's almost near the road, out in the open. If you were going to make out, you would be somewhere else, getting some privacy. Keith would have known that. Where they were parked was not where anyone would go to either try to get into the water or to make out."

Teri Hailey agrees with that line of logic. "It's in a pull-through. If you're going to stop and do *whatever*, you're going to go into one of these—you're not going to go to a pull-through one. We used to park up there. I know what we used to do. We would not park in one. We never ever, ever stopped in one of those."

The Monday after Keith and Cassandra's disappearance, the press was already making connections that law enforcement was not acknowledging. The *Times Herald* and the *Daily Press* both suggested in their evening editions that the missing youths could be connected not only to Thomas-Daily, but to the murders of Robin Edwards and David Knobling. It wasn't that law enforcement hadn't arrived at the same possible conclusion, but they refused to acknowledge any connections. It would be another week and half later before the FBI acknowledged to the *Daily Press* that there might be a connection to the Ragged Island killings. Even then, the phrase "serial killer" was conspicuously absent. No one at this stage, even the press, wanted to cause any more panic in the community than was necessary.

The FBI went to extraordinary lengths to attempt to gain new evidence. Camp Peary, the CIA's Farm for training, butted up to the parkway. The FBI broadened their thinking and began to wonder if the Russians might be able to help. Despite the fact that the US and the Soviet Union were still in the height of the Cold War, they did something remarkable according to Danny Plott of the Virginia State Police who had worked on the Colonial Parkway task force.

"The FBI, through the State Department, basically—to my knowledge—contacted Russian authorities and said, 'We know there is satellite photography of this training area. Just like there is satellite photography of other training areas. All we want, is on the days of these murders, even narrowing it down April something from such-and-such a time to such-and-such a time. Give us your photography—we'll never make it public—we're trying to solve murders—we'll sign any kind of things needed.'

"The Russians basically said 'Nyet!' So that was my understanding and what I was told … that the Russian authorities had been approached and they said no."

* * * * *

The links to other local crimes seemed to be further cemented only a few days into the investigation. On Tuesday, April 19, 1988, the news media lit up next with the announcement by Ron Little that he had been brought in by the FBI and was considered, in his own words, "a major, major suspect" in the disappearances of Cassandra and Keith. Moreover, he indicated that he was also being investigated for the deaths of Robin Edwards, David Knobling, and two other individuals—Laura Ann Powell and Brian Pettinger. His announcement to the press was shocking and seemed to only solidify the ties between Knobling-Edwards and Call-

Hailey in the public mind. At the same time it dragged in two additional murders into the mix—that of Pettinger and Powell.

Ron Little was a native of New Zealand who had migrated to the US a few years earlier. He was the president of Advanced Security and Investigation Services Inc., previously known as Liberty Security Services. Little had purchased the company in September along with an unnamed partner, who would later be revealed to be Steve Blackmon.

Little's company provided security for stores and businesses, though he was a self-styled private investigator— or so he liked to claim. When the FBI brought the thirty-three-year-old man in, he was working at the Ames Department Store as a security monitor. They seized his passport and his gun in the process of interviewing him.

Everything about Ron Little and the murders was suspicious, but nothing more than his going to the press with details about his connections to the crimes. In an interview with the *Daily Press* two weeks prior to the disappearances of Call and Hailey, Little claimed to have discovered a pattern in the murders that were taking place. He further claimed that the pattern identified both the killer and his next victim. With bravado, he said that he intended to confront the killer and warn the intended victim but refused to identify either.

Little lambasted both state and federal agents for their failure to connect the murders of Pettinger and Powell. Ironically, the only real connection that seemed to exist was their thin relationships to Ron Little.

Brian Craig Pettinger of Newport News was a twenty-six-year-old former security guard for Little's Liberty Security Services. Pettinger had left security work to become a dance instructor. On December 2, 1987, he left a party at a Hampton dance studio at 9:30 p.m. His truck was found two days later at a nearby mall parking lot. On February 1, 1988, his body was discovered in the James River off of Suffolk. His feet, hands, and neck were bound with rope, and the autopsy revealed that his cause of death was drowning. Pettinger was clothed only in his socks and shirt.

Pettinger had not left the party alone, he had gone with another instructor, Wayne Mack. Sergeant S. C. Hicks of the Suffolk Police Department stated, "We've always suspected that Mack was either there when it happened or knew how it happened." Mack immediately moved to West Virginia after the murder. When brought in for a polygraph, he failed it. He provided authorities multiple accounts of the evening, none of which jibed with the known facts and others' testimonies.

The case against Wayne Mack became terminally stalled when he committed suicide in June. In his note to his family he wrote, "I didn't leave any clues, so don't feel guilty." Hardly a plea of innocence. While Mack had been the favored suspect in the case, Brian Pettinger's death remained technically opened and unsolved.

Laura Ann Powell was an eighteen-year-old Gloucester woman who had also worked as a receptionist at Liberty Security Services two months earlier but was gainfully employed at her mother's video rental store at the time of her death. Laura and her boyfriend, Chris Cutler, got into a fight on their way to a friend's residence on March 9, 1988. On Route 614 she made Cutler stop the car and let her out. Cutler continued onto the party, then left to look for Laura. The next day his maroon Chevette was discovered at a convenience store with a flat tire and damage to the front end. A "large amount of broken glass and dirt" was found inside the car.

Chris Cutler admitted that he had been "in the vicinity" of the James River that morning after he dropped off Powell. A shirt was found in the back seat with blood on it that matched both Powell's and Cutler's blood types. When questioned with a polygraph, police indicated that his answers were considered "deceptive." While they felt they lacked enough to charge him with his girlfriend's murder at the time, they did arrest him for parole violations.

Cutler had been Powell's boyfriend for three years. He had a tattoo of a jaguar on his right bicep that matched one on Powell's left breast. His version of events was suspicious at best. He claimed that his car had been abandoned by friends who were using it to look for money to bail him out on a traffic charge and that the damaged front end of the vehicle was the result of an accident that he had suffered when he had fallen asleep behind the wheel months earlier. The bloody shirt? Cutler claimed the blood came from a blood test the police had administered when he had refused to take a breathalyzer.

Cutler told one interviewer: "Anything I've ever done, I got caught for. It surprises me that they would think I was smart enough to get away with this." He added, "Every place I've ever lived's got holes in the wall from me punching them instead of her. That's proof I never hit her." It was a thin defense at best.

Despite the fact that both of these murders could only be linked to Ron Little in the guise of a former employer, Little seemed content to flaunt it in the press. There was more that connected him to the Colonial Parkway Murders. Little claimed that Robin Edwards' mom, Bonnie, had worked for Liberty Security Services as a security guard. This was during a time prior to Little's ownership of the renamed company. Why he would reach out to the media to draw this thin connection is known only to him.

Ron Little had been married twice in New Zealand before immigrating to the United States in 1985. With only a twelfth-grade education, he and his partner, Steve Blackmon, styled themselves as the Tidewater-equivalent of *Starsky & Hutch*. Unlike the single television characters, Little managed to marry nineteen-year-old Wendy Nichole Nutter. Wendy was pregnant with their son at the time of the FBI inquiry. He hardly cast the appearance of a private investigator but was more of a self-glorified security guard.

Little was far from a perfect New Zealander before

coming to the US. In New Zealand and Australia he had been arrested for burglary, grand theft auto, and possession of Indian hemp. While he liked to promote in the press that he was a man with possible inside information, he did not bring up his drug or criminal background. In his discussions with the press regarding the Call-Hailey case, he seemed to be arrogant—telling the media that the FBI was "grasping at straws."

"I heard it was one of the greatest outfits in the world [the FBI]. They're in a bind … they have no clues. If the FBI wants to charge me, they should do it, or then should do it, or they should leave me the hell alone," Little said.

Joe Wolfinger of the FBI summed up the FBI's perspective of Ron Little. "Whatever stories I've seen about this have been generated by him."

Special Agent Steven Scheiner said, "I don't have any knowledge," in terms of Little being a suspect in the case. "If he were a suspect, I'd be aware of it."

Scheiner was quick to add, "Little must have his own reasons for stirring up such media attention. That whole situation doesn't even merit a response."

The FBI was not the only federal agency that wanted some of his time. On the same day that he met with the FBI, the Immigration and Naturalization Service also interviewed him. Little complained that he was "being railroaded" by the federal authorities. As it turned out, however, he had lied on his application to immigrate to the US regarding the fact that he was still married in New Zealand and had entered into marriage in the US. Moreover he was not allowed to purchase a firearm under the terms of his visa, so he was in violation of that as well. The immigration service said that his status as a legal resident of the country was no longer valid. Ron blamed his young wife, Wendy, claiming she had failed to file the right paperwork to establish his residency.

Ron then announced he was going to close Advanced Security and Investigation Services Inc. as a result of all of the publicity and the threat to his employees. "These are innocent people that are dying, and if this is what it's going to lead to, then I'd rather not get into it."

Realistically, the reason for closing the agency was most likely driven by the fact that he was subject to deportation.

Why would he go to the press, deliberately draw attention to himself, and be linked to a series of murders?

Larry McCann of the Virginia State Police offers one possible perspective. "Because he's taunting the police. He's saying, 'I'm smarter than you, you will never catch me.' That's a taunt. And for him to be interviewed, get through the interview, and then brag about that he's the chief suspect, well—that's a *huge* taunt. That's just throwing it back at the police saying 'Naa, naa, naa, naa—I'm smarter than you. You had me in your office, and I walked out.'"

For the public, it was easy to believe that Ron Little and his partner, Steve Blackmon, might have been directly involved with the Colonial Parkway case and the murders of Pettinger and Powell. Steve Blackmon's father was the chief of police in Newport News, and Steve got his job as a result. He won two medals for valor while there. He and Little were known for their crashing of local parties, and rumors of drugs and robbery dogged Blackmon when he accepted a job at the Gloucester County Sheriff's Department. While he was credited with saving a suicidal jumper off of the George P. Coleman Bridge, he was also twice charged with brutality—with both cases dismissed in court.

The senior Blackmon was fired from the Newport News Police Department after twenty-nine years of service. His son Steve secured a job as a deputy in South Carolina at the Florence County Sheriff's Department. In November of 1990 when two intruders broke into his house, Blackmon shot them. The subsequent investigation found that he was on cocaine at the time of the incident and that his story did not match the physical evidence. A jury agreed, and Blackmon was sentenced to fifteen months in prison for the deaths of the two would-be robbers.

The pair—Little and Blackmon—drew attention because of their fitting the profile at the time of who the FBI was looking for. Two men, one dominant—Blackmon—one more submissive—Little. Blackmon was a police officer, making it potentially easy for them to take on the roles and assume control of the couples. They had all of the regalia of police officers at their disposal, right down to the vehicles involved. For the public, it was easy to see why they were suspicious. Ron Little's running to the local press essentially bragging that he was involved with the cases, even going so far as to connect the dots for the investigators, made little sense unless he was, indeed, involved in the crimes.

Access to the gear and having somewhat seedy backgrounds alone was simply not enough to make the pair serious suspects. Danny Plott of the Virginia State Police offers another perspective, having reviewed Little's interview notes with the FBI. "People made a big deal of that, but I do not believe that, after reading it, it was almost like he was trying to become famous by interjecting himself in that investigation. And I don't know how you become famous being a suspect, but he was one of the first people that was supposedly a suspect. I mean, he worked at a gas station at one point providing security."

While the FBI disregarded him, the INS pursued charges against Little. From the perspective of the Call-Hailey investigation, he proved to be little more than a highly publicized dead-end and bore the responsibility for many in the public to draw untenable connections between the tragic deaths of Brian Pettinger and Laura Ann Powell to the Colonial Parkway Murders. In reality, their only connection was from the bizarre mind of Ron Little.

At best, the entire Ron Little affair was a minor distraction and divergence of resources during a pivotal time of the investigation. Another came in the form of a corpse in the York River. Joe Wolfinger of the FBI recalls a moment of excitement that occurred during the airborne search on April 14, 1988.

"We actually found a body. I can remember we had a plane or helicopter up, looking to see if they could see anything in the water or marsh or anything. They called us back in the command post there which was in a little hotel/motel. They said they saw what looked like a body, and as they got closer to it with the glasses on it, they said it looks like a black guy—an African-American. I remember thinking, 'Well, you know, if that's the body of one of the kids in the water and, well, they were white kids, well, it could turn colors—who knows?'

"Anyway they recovered the body and it was indeed an African-American guy. I thought he fell off a ship or committed suicide off a ship that was going up the river there to one of the navy points—the weapons facility.

"I thought it was a hell of a thing when you're out searching for a body and you find one and it's not the person that you are looking for. That's kind of a crazy thing."

It had been a Virginia State Police helicopter spotted the body floating about 300 yards off shore. A boater had spotted it at first, describing that there was a head floating in the York River. The coast guard sent a boat in, coordinated by the helicopter, and recovered the body. The incident was about two-and-a-half miles from where Keith's car had been discovered.

The body was that of a man and was badly decomposed to the point that it was conceivable that he could have been in the water for several weeks. He was wearing a short, waist-length leather jacket, brown-colored slacks, and tennis shoes.

On the Saturday after the disappearance, the *Virginia Gazette* newspaper printed a very plausible theory as to why the trained tracking dogs of the Tidewater Trails Search and Rescue Group had indicated a dead body in the water; it could very well have been the body that had been found, not

Keith or Cassandra.

The victim was a civilian mariner who had been missing for two to three weeks from a navy-operated ship that had been moored at the Cheatham Annex. His crewmen reported him missing, but no one was concerned enough to mount a search.

"One worker missed a movement out of Cheatham Annex a few weeks ago," Commander Richard Worthington of the Military Sealift Command out of Norfolk said. "No-shows are very common when we hire civilians to work on those ships. Civilians are under no legal obligation to finish an assigned cruise."

The body was recovered at the mouth of Felgate's Creek where it had come to rest on a sand spit. In two weeks it had drifted less than a half-mile from where he had been thought to have fallen or jumped in the water. The unfortunate victim proved to be just a bizarre dead-end for the FBI.

* * * * *

There had been no change in NPS policy in terms of patrolling the Colonial Parkway after the Thomas-Dowski murders. FOIA requests for any memorandum of policy changes yielded nothing. In a small park, it is entirely possible that the park service didn't write anything up. At the same time, in interviews in the period, despite the murders over a year earlier, the parkway was still not heavily patrolled at night. In total, at any time, there were seven patrol rangers and one investigator that worked the park. Chief Ranger Wally Neprash acknowledged that they patrolled on nights, mostly between Williamsburg and the Yorktown with two rangers, usually only until 2:00 to 3:00 a.m. There were times that the park was patrolled all night, but those instances were intermittent at best. If a ranger was sick, there was only one on duty. Putting this in the press basically broadcasted how vulnerable the Colonial Parkway was—though the killer was already well aware of its deadly exposure.

The families were reeling as to what to do. Each passing hour whittled away at hope. The Hailey family held a vigil at St. Joan of Arc Catholic Church to pray for the return of both children. The crowd filled the church and overflowed outside. Joanne Hailey told the gathered supporters, "If we don't keep these children in the limelight, people will forget. We're all here to help each other. I believe they're out there, and we need everyone's prayers to help ensure their safe return."

Members of the family went down to the apartment complex where they were last seen and hung flyers asking for information. The Calls offered a reward and pushed for the media to help in gathering tips. While tips did come in, none seemed to add to the narrative of what had happened to Keith and Cassandra. As Joanna Hailey told the *Daily Press*, "It is hard to just sit by the phone and wait, or wait for a knock at the door."

Barbara Call commented, "You feel very helpless. There's something you want to do, but you don't know what to do. If he [Keith] is dead, you would think that whoever did it would at least let us have him. If someone took his life, we need to have something. That's the hardest thing."

The Haileys were not just reeling from the disappearance of their beloved daughter but also from the surprise that Cassandra had kept her relationship with Terry Kirby from them.

"Mom and Dad found out when she disappeared. She kept that all pretty much under wraps that whole time," Teri Hailey said. "They wouldn't have cared. They really wouldn't have cared. I think she was going off of some other people's reactions. Daddy probably wouldn't have jumped up and down about it, but he wouldn't have cared. My dad is the least judgmental person. That's probably where she got it from."

Terry Kirby's connection to Cassandra was kept out of the local media. "It was something that they just wanted to keep out of the papers. It was never *ever* mentioned in the paper—their connection. He doesn't care now. We never mentioned it," Paula Hailey Meehan said.

Danny Plott of the Virginia State Police remembers speaking with Cassandra's boyfriend.

"I interviewed Terry Kirby. Terry was very forthcoming. He was BMOC [Big Man on Campus] there. He went to Tabb High School; he went to UVA. He had a professional career and was not a bad football player. We felt like he was very forthcoming. He basically said he had a relationship with Cassandra but knew nothing. I don't think he was bragging, but he said, 'I had a relationship—I was *really* popular.' I'll bet he was because he was the best thing to come out of Tabb High School ever."

Plott's comments are substantiated by Terry's career. Terry led Tabb High School to the State Championship in 1987. He was selected for *Parade's* All America Team and *USA Today's* All-USA Team after his senior year in 1988. He was a running back at University of Virginia from 1989 to 1992. In 1993, he was drafted for the Miami Dolphins. He went on to play a total of ten seasons for the NFL for various teams before retiring in 2002.

Unfortunately there was nothing at the party that he noticed that helped authorities narrow their investigation into Keith and Cassandra's disappearance.

The FBI was far from idle. They dusted off the profile from the Behavioral Science Unit from the Dowski-Thomas case—operating in the presumption that the same person may have committed both crimes. As Joe Wolfinger put it: "We pursued a million theories. And we got a million leads about weird people that hung out on the parkway. We identified a lot of people. We did a very vigorous investigation."

Irvin Wells recalls a substantial break that the investigators received related to the waterman profile. "Going home one day ... not an agent, but a radio technician who knew what was going on, sees this pickup truck, with oversized tires, rifle rack in the back, and the plate said EAT THEM.[8] So you think oysters, or women, whatever. So, interesting. We had hundreds of leads. So somebody checked that out."

Wolfinger recalls the instance as well.

"One night as our team was finishing up at the command post the electronics technician was next to a truck on I-64 heading I guess towards Norfolk. The driver in the truck was 100 percent the description we had had of this Peeping Tom [on the parkway]. He was a little more aggressive than the rest of them. He had approached people while they were making out on the parkway there. There was a couple, a boy and a girl, but the boy had long hair ... he could've looked like a girl. Well, they were actually kissing or something, and he came up to the window and said, 'Are you girls having fun?' or something like that. When he saw that it was a boy he backed off. So that prompted our interest."

Wells remembers the surveillance of the suspect.

"The truck was registered, I'll never remember the name, to this guy, who lived in a trailer with his brother, and one of them was a suspect in a murder in another county. And so we started doing what we call drive-bys with undercover agents. Just looking. That was pretty new after the Keith Call thing. And one of these guys was out spray painting the bed of his truck," Wells said.

"I am confident that we found the guy because our technician got the license number, we found him. We did a pretty good check on who he was and the agents were riding by his house to see what it looked like and he was actually out working on his truck. He was vacuuming the inside and had painted something. They stopped. It was a little bit of a crisis there because you don't want him—if there's evidence,

---

8   The vanity license plate has been changed deliberately.

you want to get it."

Time was clearly of the essence if the suspect was possibly destroying or obscuring evidence. Irvin Wells remembers the rush to get a warrant.

"So we got a search warrant to search their trailer because we thought evidence might be lost. The search warrant goes to a federal judge. You have to get probable cause, it's a big deal. It's not like we just got a search warrant. So we get a search warrant and search the truck which we couldn't find anything in, and the trailer. In the trailer was weapons, handcuffs, pornography, not that that means anything. Not all people involved in pornography are serial killers but many serial killers are involved in pornography.

"They got everything. We got his vacuum cleaner, and they did a search of his truck, and they found a gun, handcuffs, and I can't remember what else. He even admitted being at the next cut off around the right time. So he was seen by somebody else that night," Wolfinger said.

To the FBI, they had someone that had been a Peeping Tom on the parkway the night of the murders, who fit their profile of a waterman, who possessed some questionable material (i.e. handcuffs) that might point to their killer. The next step was to check his version of events and try to determine if he, and possibly his brother, were involved in the murders.

Joe Wolfinger remembers it vividly.

"The very best polygraph guy polygraphed him, after we did everything we could do with evidence. I mean everything you could do at the time with evidence. We didn't have anything else. It was obvious … and we did have in his interview he obviously lied [about being on the parkway that night]. He made up a story as to why he was there, and he was by himself that night. And he passed with flying colors … the polygraph. And while I'm not 100 percent on polygraphs, the guy that did the interview was the best polygrapher I know. He did all of the big espionage cases in

Washington. He did Aldrich Aimes, Bob Hansen, I think he did Hansen, he did every major espionage subject that we had. He might have done John Walker ... I think he did. So we had a first rate polygraph guy and a first rate FBI agent. So, what do you do? I still think that was a viable lead. But you don't live in a country where you can throw somebody in jail without any evidence," Wolfinger said.

Irvin Wells felt the same frustration.

"So these guys really did look hot. We brought in a polygrapher, one of the best the bureau had. Anyway, Barry-something was his name. He was sort of known as the bureau's 'polygrapher extraordinaire.' And he was responsible for polygraphing the John Walker case. And he said, 'These guys didn't do it.'

"We said, 'You better fucking be right.' And we walked away from him. I have always wondered ... to defeat a polygraph you have to be more sophisticated than—oh, and they were watermen! That was a big thing—they were watermen!

"He said, 'They didn't do it and didn't know about it.'

"I respected him—it's just the way things go. You get frustrated. That's the way investigations go. You get some people that look great and something happens," Wells said.

The hopes of closing both Call-Hailey and possibly Thomas-Dowski at that time ended with the polygrapher clearing the suspect.

The bureau began to turn their attention to the park rangers. After all, they had full access to the park and could operate without drawing suspicion. With uniforms and badges they could easily gain control of their victims. And there were complaints reported in the newspapers against one of the rangers in particular, Clyde Yee.

"For a long time, and I don't think he had anything to do with it, one of them, Clyde Yee, there was one ranger that was looked at very closely to start out with," said Danny Plott, who was part of the Colonial Parkway Murders task force.

The bureau was determined to not leave any stone unturned in their investigation. Yee was interrogated and polygraphed and passed with no issues, effectively removing him as a suspect.

What had been such a promising lead had suddenly evaporated. The FBI pressed on for weeks, but each possible tip turned into a rabbit hole with no reward. The bureau had to shut down the command post at the Duke of York Motel and slowly shift resources to other cases.

"My heart went out the Calls and to both of them, both families. Mr. and Mrs. Call just looked like they were just injured and hurt of course. Bless their hearts, I don't know how you deal with the loss of a child. That's the worst thing. My children are in their forties. I just don't know; it's just the hardest thing in the world to deal with. So I have sympathy," Wells said.

The remorse is deep and a matter of pride for the men of the bureau.

Joe Wolfinger said of the Call-Hailey case, "I always thought while we were investigating this, we were going to solve this case."

Irvin Wells responded, "I think we got spoiled because we solved so many."

"Yeah," Wolfinger replied. "The truth is Irv and I have a lot of cases where we solved them, and it's easier to talk about them than about this one, to say the least. If you're a homicide detective in a place where they have a lot of homicides, you can't expect to solve all of your cases. It's just not going to happen. So you've got to live with it. When you have a case like this … happily we don't have to live with a lot like these."

The case slowly chilled to a cold status.

The National Park Service seemed more focused on restoring confidence that the Colonial Parkway was safe, while still emphasizing some caution. Park Superintendent

David Moffitt warned that motorists should validate that anyone pulling them over would be dressed in a ranger's uniform. The implication was clear, there could be a false law enforcement officer working the parkway. If visitors were stopped they should "let the police vehicle pull alongside of them and identify themselves before opening doors or windows. We don't want a bunch of hysteria going around, but I think it's good that people know there is a potential for problems."

Chief Ranger Wally Neprash told the *Daily Press* that there were two unconfirmed stories involving people posing as police that had been circulating in the community. One involved a woman who claimed she was stopped by a ranger in an unmarked white car with a blue flashing light on the dashboard. This pseudo-ranger asked for her driver's license, looked at it, and told her to drive more slowly.

"It sounds like a routine traffic stop to me except that rangers at the park do not use white, unmarked cars," Neprash said.

Another story was about a woman pulled over by someone in an unmarked car in civilian clothes. The woman got a bad feeling about the man and sped off.

David Moffitt's response at the time: "You get the young kids who go out there and park and I think that's totally irresponsible. There are very weird people out there—not just on the parkway."[9]

In the community at-large there was an assumption that a person was impersonating someone in authority or law enforcement to lure in victims. Also the connections between the murders in the peninsula region seemed clear, even if authorities were not commenting on them as such. At the time, rolling in the Pettinger and Powell cases, they were referred to as, "The Peninsula Murders," in the *Daily Press*. The name was not destined to stick.

9   Evans, Bob. "Parkway officials downplay rumors but urge caution," *The Daily Press/Times-Herald*, May 7, 1988, A3

* * * * *

With a sensational as a crime as the disappearance of Keith and Cassandra, with possible links to other murders in the area, it was inevitable that individuals would emerge with tips from "beyond." Psychics and clairvoyants often are drawn to such cases offering their assistance free of charge— no doubt with the hopes of helping and possibly generating publicity for themselves. Over a half-dozen psychics reached out to the Calls and Haileys.

Barbara Call was doubtful of their insights, "We listen to what they have to say, but I can't say one way or the other whether I believe in them."

It was understandable that the families might have listened to what these total strangers had to say. The FBI leads were dwindling every day. As the media attention to the missing pair waned, the family members would have embraced any chance at finding them or their remains. What parents wouldn't do the same?

One psychic did not believe that the couple was in the car when it was taken to the parkway.

Another, concentrating on Cassandra, said the vision "brings a picture of the man who seems to be the murderer. A very twisted young man. I am able to see a shallow grave. Cassandra's hands and feet are tied. I see a wooded park and a large clearing. A bridge crosses a narrow expanse of water. The grave is near a barbed wire fence ... near a small waterfall."

Irvin Wells remembers the inevitable arrival of the psychics to the case.

"I think there's a dimension we don't understand in life. Those folks—the Haileys—they brought those psychics. I'm sorry it didn't work out; it would have been good if it could have. I would stick pins in a voodoo doll if it would help," Wells said.

FBI agent Joe Wolfinger, who was liaising with the Hailey family, remembers the intervention of the psychics more vividly.

"My problem was, after we finished the last few weeks of this case, was to deal with the family. They were very hard to deal with. I can remember driving over to see the mother of the girl, Mrs. Hailey, and I would answer her questions as much as I could. She wanted, I think, and even paid a psychic to help her find her daughter. I don't happen to believe that psychics can solve those cases. In fact if a psychic knew where the kids were I would be suspicious that the psychic had something to do with it. You know—kidnapping," Wolfinger said.

"I remember she said the psychic said they were on an island in the river and they were handcuffed or tied to a tree. I think she probably expected that we would dismantle the search teams we had and start searching islands. But that's a pretty hard thing to deal with … a grieving mother. So they were my problems. I would go see her, and she'd usually call the local congressman and say what an asshole the FBI guy was. It was pretty tough actually."

Ultimately, even the ethereal plane could not offer any tangible leads as to where Keith and Cassandra were or what had happened to them on that early bitter April morning.

* * * * *

One of the final footnotes of the immediate investigation played out in August of 1989. Ron Little's attempt at publicity for himself by tying himself to unsolved murders in the region had fully backfired. He was being deported. Little sent a six-page typed letter to senators, newspapers, and television stations saying that he was being unfairly targeted because he was considered a suspect in the murders of Pettinger, Powell, Edwards, and Knobling. He omitted mentioning Call and Hailey in his manifesto. The letter was a last-ditch effort to prevent him from being deported.

The Immigration and Naturalization Service filed twenty felony charges against Little, including false statements to buy firearms and falsely registering with the INS when filing for visas and citizenship, according to Willian Bittner of the INS. With so many charges, even Little's marriage to an American citizen was not going to be enough to keep him in the country.

FBI Special Agent Jim Watters responded to Little's diatribe of being persecuted: "I don't even want to justify that man's accusations with a statement. ... The FBI has interrogated hundreds of people in connection with these cases. The only one pointing a finger at Little is Little himself—and he seems to be doing it in a big way."

"If the guy was a suspect in any federal investigation, I don't care if it was drug smuggling or murder or what, someone would have filed an order to detain him in this country, not deport him," William Bittner said. "We never received such a request from any agency to detain him." Bittner was quick to add that several other law enforcement agencies were investigating Little for unrelated charges.

Ron Little was deported back to New Zealand just prior to the next pair of murders.

* * * * *

The agony of the families was a horrid mix of frustration, anger, and perpetual angst. For people less strong, the mix would have been toxic. Somehow the Calls and Haileys prevailed. Barbara Call summed up her thoughts as the momentum of the investigation waned, "If he is dead, you would think that whoever did it would at least let us have him. If someone took his life, we need to have something. That's the hardest thing."

Teri Hailey offered her thoughts to the media as well. "I think the hardest part is not knowing where she is. If someone is dead, at least you know where they are. You can visit them."

In January of 1989, visitors parking at the York River Overlook found several reminders as to what might have taken place there. Tacked to a tree was a faded handwritten note wishing a Merry Christmas to "Keifer." Over the past eight months, other nails in the tree posted roses and other remembrances. They were sad reminders of the two missing people—the only memorial that the families had.

THE FOURTH

Annamaria Phelps and Daniel Lauer
Last seen September 4, 1989
Remains recovered October 19, 1989

CHAPTER 13

Annamaria Phelps was born on the twenty-fourth of March in 1971—an Aries under the signs of the zodiac. The sign of the ram is known for rushing forward in life, without fear of consequences. No challenge is too daunting for an Aries. Filled to the brim with positive energy and exuberance, the Aries is an individual that is generous with a solid streak of optimism, mixed with a dollop of stern independence. If an Aries were to have any faults, it is stubbornness. An Aries does not go down without a fight, and even after they are down they are born scrappers who will continue to battle on. They build deep relationships with those around them, relationships built on respect and understanding. Strong-willed and stubborn—those are the hallmarks of this zodiac sign.

If anyone ever was true to their sign, it was Annamaria Phelps.

She was the youngest daughter of the Phelps family's four children. Her sisters, Cynthia Maria and Rosanna, were older, with her brother William being the youngest child in the family. While she had been born in Richmond, her home was in Amelia County, Virginia, just south and west of the state capitol—but a whole world away in terms of culture.

The population in Amelia County during the time she was being raised there was less than 9,000. Amelia was formed between 1734 and 1735, carved out of tracts of land from Prince George and Brunswick counties. It was rural farming land, where the cows outnumbered the residents. The county is best known as the nation's largest supplier of amazonite, a green quartz crystal hauled out of the Morefield Mine. In 1986 the county drew some short-lived regional fame when the Amelia County Fair boasted the largest potato pancake to be baked—a fundraiser for the German American National Scholarship Fund. While the pancake weighed in at over two tons, the fame it brought was little more than a footnote in the history of the county.

Robert E. Lee fought one of the last battles of the Civil War at Sayler's Creek on April 6, 1865, just before his surrender at nearby Appomattox, Virginia. While the nation and world referred to it as the Civil War, Amelia residents nursed the description, "The War of Northern Aggression."

The people living there were farmers, small businessmen, or individuals attempting to get away from the hustle and bustle of Richmond. That was the case of Annamaria's parents. Her father, William Phelps Sr., worked at American Filtrona outside of Richmond while her mother, Jewel, stayed home. Filtrona originally made filters for cigarettes but branched out in the 1980s, making everything from filters for cars, pregnancy tests, markers, and other consumer products. With Philip Morris a major Richmond employer and tobacco being a burgeoning cash-crop in the seventies and eighties, it was a good solid job, despite the long commute.

Annamaria's brother, Will, remembers his father's long hours away.

"My dad worked at night, and he did a lot of overtime. I'm sure it was difficult for Mom to get the four of us together and drag us anywhere," said Will. "He worked seven days a week. It was an hour drive to work and an hour drive back. That's two hours a day just in the commute. Then he might work a sixteen-hour day. He would do that sometimes three months straight—seven days a week."

Jewel was the foundation—the glue—that kept things together during her husband's long hours at work and on the road.

"Back before cell phones, my momma and daddy would communicate via CB radios. She wanted to make sure my dad made it safely," said Will. "My dad's handle was 'Flying Saucer'—because he had a very heavy foot. He had plenty of tickets, and he would drive around the curves fast with no brakes because he didn't want to wear out his brakes. He'd just coax it around—errr! Never mind the tires."

CB radios were the closest thing to smart phones and social media of that decade.

The family lived on six-and-a-quarter acres. Will remembers their upbringing and conservative roots fondly.

"My dad made good money. When he was growing up, he went from foster home to foster home—he told us many stories of when he would beg his neighbors for food. I think growing up in that kind of environment he kind of hoarded his money, I guess, in essence," said Will. "Looking back we were always embarrassed about the way we grew up but looking back at it, knowing how he was, he kinda—you know—going back to those days."

Their father turned the farm into a hobby and a playground for his children.

"When we moved to Amelia County, my dad had a fascination for digging. When I was a kid he loved to dig. He dug a pond out, by shovel and wheelbarrow. No heavy equipment. He did it all by hand. And he did that when he was working overtime. He would work sixteen hours, come home, and start digging in the pond [complete with an island], sleep for a few hours, and go back to work," said Will.

"He dug paths through the woods, and we had this big hill. And he hung a swing between the branches, and we would swing out over the hill, and it would look like—it felt like you was a hundred feet off the ground. He made a tire cable—people call it zip-lining now. Our daddy invented that. He hung a piece of cable and put pillows and cushions on the tree. We would hold onto the tire and slide on down to the end. He had a contraption on it so you could either sit in the tire or hold onto it."

Rosanna remembers her father's efforts to entertain his children as well.

"He dug numerous paths through the woods to make

bike paths for us and places to put different play areas for us to enjoy. I think he may have enjoyed them as much as we did," said Rosanna.

Will still marvels at all his father accomplished.

"My dad gardened too. He could grow anything. We always had animals. We had dogs, cats. We had ponies—a bull, and Dad would get in there and wrestle with it like it was a dog. We had goats and ducks. Annamaria had a pet—a dog Scruffy. Lab was the family dog. Scruffy was her dog. Momma would make homemade pies and homemade pudding. She used to can her tomato juice. She liked making her barbeque—it's just the simple things you miss," said Will.

"We admired Mom and Daddy both. They came from families that weren't that loved, and they found each other and had us and moved us to the country. Dad always worked a lot, but we had a camper. He always made sure we had vacations together in the mountains and at the beach. We just spent a lot of family time together."

Many people attribute rural living in the South with deep devotion to religion. That wasn't the case with the Phelps family.

"We went to church on and off. We stopped going as you got older. When we were younger, Dad used to drive the church bus. We moved to Amelia County. We didn't go a lot. Anna was really young when we moved. [I] remember Dad used to tell us, 'If you want to go to church I'm leaving in a few minutes. If you're not ready, I'll leave without you,'" said Will Phelps. "I don't remember the church in Chesterfield we went to. I want to say we went to the Baptist church. We really didn't have a home church after we moved to Amelia County."

Annamaria was as fireball of energy and vitality. Will recalls her personality.

"She was very spunky. Very, very full of herself. She always had a smart comeback but was comical. She always knew what to say back to someone, she didn't have to think about it."

Her sister Rosanna Phelps Martin Sedivy recollects with tear-wetted eyes.

"Mom would discipline her and I both at the same time, and I would cry because my feelings were hurt. Anna was on her lap and they would be laughing, and I would say 'What?' She didn't want anyone to stay mad. Her thing was getting them to laugh. She brought peace," said Rosanna.

Will remembers the exception to that: "Except in the mornings when you woke her up, if you wanted to wake her up."

Rosanna adds with a shaking head: "Or if you wanted her to go to bed either, she wanted to write or do anything to stay up all night. Boy she was ornery in the morning. But later on she would love you to death. She took a lot. But if you made her mad ..."

Independence was a hallmark of Annamaria's personality, as her sister Rosanna recollects.

"I'll never forget the time—Dad would work overnight so he'd come home in the morning. I guess Mom would go back to sleep after the older kids were off to school, and somehow William got hungry, and Anna would [try to] wake Momma up. Momma didn't hear them, and Anna set out to make him breakfast. Now she was four years old and he was two, and they had every ingredient in the kitchen in the living room, in a big bowl, all over the kitchen, everywhere," Rosanna said. "When Daddy came home it was too late to save anything he had to pull the carpet up. Back then you had to punish them for making this mess so he put them in the bathtub and that was their punishment."

Rosanna evokes memories of her youngest sister.

"I think she was a family person—somebody that loved her family unconditionally. She would have fought for her family tooth and nail—and that is what I intend to do for her. She could hold her own. Anna could take care of herself.

If you knew her you thought she was so easy going and got along with everybody. She was a truly happy-go-lucky person that loved her family and friends unconditionally."

Annamaria was not a person that acquiesced to being picked on as a child her brother recalls.

"I remember a time we were going to school—somebody got slapped on the bus. Somebody told me, 'Hey Anna's fighting,' and I turn around and it was a brother and sister. And she got all mad at me because I didn't help, but I didn't know that—she had taken care of it. She was mad at me for a long time because of that. I was sitting in the front, and she was sitting in the back.

"Mom had an incident where a bus driver told there was this kid on the bus that kept picking at her [Annamaria] and picking at her, and picking at her, and Anna would never say anything. Finally one day she heard this loud pop and she turned back and that child that had been picking at Anna had a smack across her face. And she [the bus driver] said she didn't say anything to the school, she deserved it," said Will.

When asked if her feisty attitude got her in trouble, her brother and sister both concurred.

"Yes! That spunky personality got her in trouble," Will said.

Rosanna adds: "I would have cried if I had to go to ISS [In School Suspension]. It was the worst horrible place ever. But she had good terms with the ISS teacher. She called that her 'homeroom class.' And not major, major things. You know, skipping class, things that are just mischievous things that—you know—nothing horrible."

As a child growing up, Annamaria did things that every kid did. She and Will commandeered their parents' video camera and would film themselves doing mock news and weather forecasts. She loved the popular movies of the era—*Superman, Star Wars, ET*—heavily leaning on science fiction, her father's favorite genre. It was not uncommon for the family to pile into the car and drive to the local drive-in theater. If anything racy came on the screen, William Sr. and Jewel would tell their kids to close their eyes until it passed. It was a simpler time when connecting with your family had nothing to do with social media or technology.

Around the time she turned fourteen the family moved into a new home, a double-wide. When the holidays came, her father, despite his long hours of work, went all-out. He strung Christmas lights through the kitchen, the dining room, the porch, all along the ceiling in the living area.

"Dad had to light up everything in the house. We had a big Christmas tree that barely fit in the house. The star was the ugliest star, but it would make the shape of a star on the ceiling. Our trailer was so small that the light from the star would overlap and hit the walls. It was beautiful to see, but the star itself was ugly," Will said. "Dad liked to put up lights all over the place. You couldn't see the green of the Christmas tree because it had so many lights on it. He had lights strung down the hallway. Anywhere where you could put lights, he put lights."

Jewel didn't have her driver's license until after Will was born—so William Sr. did most of the holiday shopping.

"Mom didn't know what we were getting until the night before Christmas. We could hear Mom and Dad in the wee hours of the morning playing with our toys—like the bowling games and stuff. When you made a strike and it made this noise ... and we thought, 'What is that noise?' They were in there playing with our games. We pretty much got everything we asked for and then some. At Christmas time we were very spoiled," Annamaria's brother said.

She had a humorous side to her as well. One time when her mother was taking a nap, Annamaria shut off the dryer, removed the contents, and instead put her younger brother in it. Will was angrier that she refused to turn it on rather than the pain it might have caused. Life in the Phelps homestead was like that of any other family in the seventies and eighties—where children created their own forms of entertainment.

Family vacations were special times. William took his kids often to the Smithsonian's National Air and Space Museum in Washington, DC. "For a long time I didn't realize there were other museums other than the Air and Space Museum," Will said.

Rosanna remembers the family trips fondly.

"We went up on in the Blue Ridge Mountains, Skyline Drive. Dad had a pop-up camper, and we would go camping. We went to Twin Lakes—it used to be Goodwin Lake back then—we used to go there a lot to camp. We used to go to Virginia Beach," Rosanna said.

Many hours were spent on the road.

"That was the pre-seat belt and all that time. I remember Daddy got a brand new car. Well, it didn't have air conditioning because back then—not everybody had air conditioning. We couldn't roll the windows down because Momma … curled her hair all night long—slept in curls, and had her hair fixed. And she would smoke her cigarettes and he would smoke his pipe, and [we] were riding down the road on a hot summer day, windows up, with us three girls in the back—'She's touching me, she's on my side, she's looking out my window … ' Poor Anna, she was in the middle because she was the baby girl. I can't imagine how pleasant a trip that was.

"We would have welcomed the windows down, but you don't mess up Momma's hair. Momma was a spitfire. I remember we were getting ready to go somewhere Daddy acted like he was going to squirt her or someone did squirt her and she refused to go anywhere—after we were all planning on going—because somebody wet her hair."

Annamaria was the same way about her hair as her brother remembers.

"She used to drive me nuts with this. We'd go to the lake, mostly Plymouth State Park, and she would spend *hours* fixing her hair. We would get to the lake and she wouldn't even get in the water because her hair was made up."

For the youngest of the Phelps daughters, her hair styling

was one of her few hobbies.

Annamaria was clearly bonded with her mother, Jewel.

"Anna would get out of doing anything—oh my word! She would just have to ask Mom, 'Can we do this?'"

"Mom would say, 'You do the dishes.'"

"She would spend four hours washing dishes. One night she finished doing them at 10:00 p.m. and momma said it's too late to go. I never saw anyone take so long to wash dishes in my life. And eating. It would take her forever to eat, too. We would get stuff you didn't want to eat, and Daddy was 'You have to clean your plate.' We would sneak our leftovers onto Anna's plate—that's why it took her so long to eat," her sister Rosanna said.

Family was everything to the Phelps clan—it was their heart and soul. As Jewel Phelps told the *Richmond Times-Dispatch*, "She had a heart as big as the United States."

Annamaria was more than willing in her youth to just be a part of her brother and sisters' lives. Rosanna remembers how "she loved to dance. When Will would play ball, Anna and I would run the bases. Will played baseball, football, ran track, but the girls didn't play sports." She added, "Anna kept the whole family together. She was the little peacemaker."

Instilled with a strong worth ethic, Annamaria got a job at the local Pizza Hut as a cook. Like many young women, as she grew older, her attention turned to members of the opposite sex. Annamaria was stunning. At five feet four inches tall, she had deep inviting blue eyes, with frosted blonde hair and a skinny 125-pound body. For an attractive young beauty, finding a boyfriend was destined to be easy.

In her case, that first true love was Jacob Newton. Her brother remembers his older sister's relationship.

"She liked—got attached—to boyfriends. Once she started dating somebody she got serious about them. She had one particular guy she got very serious about. She got pregnant when she was sixteen, and they lost her. The baby was a girl. And that broke Anna's heart. She really, really wanted that baby. She was really excited. I think she was due in February. Maybe she had her in February and she was due in July. She had her at almost five months—so it was very premature," said Will.

Anna had been involved in an auto accident just prior to her losing the child, which she believed contributed to her loss. It was her second accident; the first totaled her first car when she had just learned to drive. This time she had wrecked her father's car and in the process, had lost her unborn child … a devastating loss to such a young woman. Jacob Newton's parents, Buddy and Betty Newton, owned a roadside diner on Route 360. The loss of their would-be grandchild inspired the Newtons to donate a burial plot for the child, named Toby Ann Newton.

Annamaria filled the void of her lost child with the love of her nephews. Annamaria reveled in her sister's children, Robert, nicknamed Earl, and Ray, and insisted on taking them with her every chance she could. Rosanna remembers her sister's devotion to the children.

"We had a local place, the Tastee Freeze. She liked to go up there with them. She would take them *anywhere* with her. Anywhere she could take them: the mall, the local drug store," Rosanna said. Annamaria fondly wore a locket around her neck with a photograph of the two boys.

In the country, the drug of choice was marijuana, but according to her sister Rosanna, Annamaria was not into drugs.

"Anna had a personality a lot like me. We were two years apart, and we always shared a room. We laughed, giggled, and talked all night long. We hardly ever had an argument. Maybe once or twice, I can never remember arguing with her. We got high on life," said Rosanna. "We didn't use marijuana—we didn't have that kind of life. Our family moved us to the country so that we could be away from that stuff. My mom smokes cigarettes, and dad smoked his pipe. But as far as them having alcohol—they might have gone to a friend's house sometimes, once in a blue moon, and maybe had a beer or so. But there wasn't any liquor party—no drugs. None of that."

High school did not entirely agree with Annamaria. Some of that was attributed to her rebellious nature. While she attended Amelia County High School, Annamaria dropped out in the ninth or tenth grade. Her gaze was far beyond her hometown. Annamaria wanted to experience more of the world than her rural county could afford her. The way out of Amelia County was through her new love interest: Clinton Lauer.

Annamaria met seventeen-year-old Clinton in high school and began dating him after her romance with David Newton. Clinton offered her a new lifestyle altogether—a chance for Annamaria to spread her wings of independence. His sister's husband was in the navy and on deployment, and Clinton decided to move to Virginia Beach to help with her kids. Annamaria didn't need prompting—she moved out of her family's home in June 1989 to join him in his apartment.

She was a person that was all-in when it came to life, fearless about the future. Virginia Beach was—as it is today—the largest city in the state of Virginia and home to many navy personnel as well as a popular tourist attraction.

Clinton and Annamaria's life together sounded like a song by Rod Stewart or Bruce Springsteen. They were young, without a care in the world, living near the beach. Both of them got jobs at a local Wendy's. Even with the work, the minimum wage of $3.35 per hour was not enough for the young couple to make ends meet. It was a case of feast and famine—living meager paycheck to paycheck. They couldn't afford to have a telephone—they used a nearby payphone for their calls. There were times they missed payment on their electric bill and had the power cut off.

Matters got worse when their income was cut in half.

"They ended up firing her," Will said. "The way I understood it was because somebody had made a burger and it was not made correctly. And she took it home to Clint instead of throwing it in the trash. Apparently that's a big no-no. It's just really sad because of the people you can feed. They were having really rough times. Anna was talking seriously about coming back home. It was just getting rough. And we really wish she had."

It is hard for many of us to contemplate barely making a living in a new city, with the new love of your life—scraping for food just to get by. For Annamaria and Clinton it had to be both a time of stress and a time of excitement. They were not living large, but instead were living life together. In many respects they were living out John Cougar Mellencamp's song "Jack and Diane." They were two kids that were carving out a place for themselves in a harsh world.

Annamaria was trusting of the outside world. As it turns out, far too trusting. The outside world was changing and was already far more dangerous than she could have anticipated. While she and Clinton were not getting rich, they were working and struggling and prevailing. They had life by the horns and were riding it for all it was worth—living life to the fullest.

Besides, on Labor Day weekend of 1989, a potential solution to their financial problems seemed to have emerged. It came in the form of Daniel Lauer, Clinton's older brother.

CHAPTER 14

Out of all of the victims linked to the Colonial Parkway Murders, the one that is least known is Daniel Lauer. What can be told about him has to be reconstructed from snippets in interviews given over the years or research that often yielded only small nuggets of his life. Not every person was destined to stomp the earth and leave their deep footprints for future generations; some were meant to be silent sentinels to the passage of time.

Daniel was one of four children of Margie and Henry Lauer. In his early life he lived in Port Jefferson, New York. Eventually the family relocated to Truxillo in Amelia County, only ten miles from where the Phelps family lived. Truxillo, Virginia, was little more than a flat wide spot alongside the road—with a small general store and a baseball field. There was no downtown—only a crossroads among the flat farmland. For Daniel, a night on the town would have meant driving to Amelia Courthouse.

As his mother put it, "His life was wrapped around my kitchen table. He worked with his father, Henry, seven days a week and rode horses."

People that bond with horses are special. They are creatures that can sense the emotions of their riders. The bond between a horse and a rider is something unique among pets. To be a good rider, you must be one with your mount. As the poet Pam Brown wrote, "A horse is the projection of peoples' dreams about themselves—strong, powerful, beautiful—and it has the capability of giving us escape from our mundane existence."[10] Perhaps this is the best way for any of us to wrap our heads around Daniel Lauer's persona.

10   "Partnerships in Black and White," *Horse Connection Magazine*, April 23, 2013, pg 43.

Henry Lauer owned a painting business, and work became the center of young Daniel's life. He had hobbies. In his youth he liked to build models kits—mostly WWII vehicles, tanks, halftracks, etc. He was a solitary person. Like many young men in the country, he did a little rat-racing with cars—quasi-illegal but entertainment. He occasionally went roller-skating. Academics did not keep his attention, and Daniel dropped out of high school. As with many young men, his attention turned to young women. In this case his attention went to a local girl, Christina Sotos.

At the time, Daniel was nineteen years old and Christina was fifteen. They fell in love, and Daniel was devoted to her, despite their age difference.

As Margie Lauer said, "He wanted to marry the girl but her father said absolutely not."

Undeterred, Daniel and Christina got married the day before his birthday, August 22, 1988, at the Amelia County Courthouse—no doubt without the knowledge or consent of either set of parents. Christina falsified her age on the marriage certificate, claiming to have been born in 1970—making her eighteen rather than fifteen, and claiming that she too was from Port Jefferson, New York.

Daniel tried to start a new life with his young wife in the US Navy. He enlisted in Memphis, Tennessee, on September 6, 1988, and was sent for his recruit training in San Diego, California. His navy career was cut short, however, and he was discharged three weeks later—no doubt to face the legal ramifications of his marriage.

Like many first loves, it was a romance that was not meant to be. Daniel had taken his young bride across the state line into Tennessee and eventually the two were caught. The details of how and when the pair returned to Virginia were sealed given Christina's age at the time.

In the autumn of 1988, Daniel was convicted of contributing to the delinquency of a minor, a misdemeanor, for taking Christina to Tennessee. That charge was followed with the more serious felony conviction for knowingly signing a marriage license on which the young woman's age was incorrectly stated. Justice was swift in Amelia County, and Daniel spent the last three months of 1988 in jail and was told by the judge to not contact the girl until she was eighteen. There was a stubbornness about him though, one driven by his devotion to his now annulled ex-wife.

Daniel's parents took a more pragmatic view of his situation. "I told him to take off his wedding ring," Mrs. Lauer told the *Richmond Times-Dispatch*. "He said that while he was in jail he read the Bible and God said that when you get married, you get married for life. He halfheartedly went out with someone else, but there was no one else."

It was now 1989, and his younger brother, Clinton, had moved to Virginia Beach with Annamaria Phelps. They were struggling financially, while Daniel was doing well working for his father's painting business. When Clinton suggested that Daniel join them for Labor Day weekend, it was an offer he could not refuse. It was not just Labor Day weekend, it was also Greekfest, a time when all of the local colleges were out, and students flooded the Virginia Beach area for a week of drinking, partying, and basking in the last warmth of the summer before being shuffled into air-conditioned classrooms.

Lauer was making the trip in his new-to-him used car. He got it as a present from his parents on his twentieth birthday on August 23.

"He was just tickled to death [to get the car]," his mother said. It was his first car that was his and his alone. "All he talked about was this car."

The car was a six-cylinder, and "It didn't go fast enough," Daniel told his mother. "I'm going to put in a V-8."

Daniel didn't make the trip alone. His friends Joe and Jeanette Godsey agreed to accompany him. According to Joe Godsey's account in the *Richmond Times-Dispatch*, "Danny was scared to death to make the trip by himself. It was a long drive and he didn't' want to go it alone. Since me and Jeanette were his only friends in the county, he wanted us to go."

The Godseys had only known Daniel for a year, by Joe's own account. They left their three-year-old child with a neighbor but took along their eighteen-month-old daughter, Ashley.

At the Godseys' trailer, they climbed into Daniel's $600 gold Chevy Nova, splotched with black primer, a hint at a future paint job that would never come. The Godseys' daughter was strapped into the back seat. It would be years before Virginia mandated the use of child safety seats.

They stopped only once on the trip to Virginia Beach, pulling off of I-64 at the Fort Eustis exit to purchase some french fries and to use a restroom. It took another forty-five minutes to reach Virginia Beach because of the holiday traffic.

"Danny really seemed to know his way around the area," Jeanette Godsey said. "He was whipping around like he'd been there before, so I said to him, 'You seem pretty familiar to these parts,' and he told me that it was the only place he ever stopped when he was riding to the beach."

It was supposed to be a fun weekend of partying and a chance for Daniel to connect with his brother and Clinton's love interest—Annamaria.

Annamaria spoke fondly to her family of Clint's brother, Daniel Lauer. She bragged about his good-natured, helping attitude to her sister Rosanna, and Rosanna experienced it herself once when he helped her out.

"I remember Anna telling me that he would stop to help some random stranger change tires or help somebody do this or that," Rosanna said. "I remember fussing at her, 'You just can't stop and help anybody. You've got to be careful.'"

Very careful indeed. Little did Daniel or any of their small party realize that they had chosen the worst possible week, short of a hurricane hitting, to visit Virginia Beach.

CHAPTER 15

Labor Day weekend's Greekfest in Virginia Beach had traditionally been a time for the local college students to flock for one last burst of fun in the sun before classwork became a grinding chore. Prior to 1989 that had been the case. The local college student population swarmed to the beach area, and the resorts, while coping with out-of-control college parties, made a tidy profit from the throngs of visitors.

Greekfest had begun in the early 1980s as a large picnic party at Croatan Beach predominantly attended by black sorority and fraternity members from the local colleges. It had grown, as such things often do, by word of mouth— college-to-college. By 1986 a local promoter exploited it as a way to get one last boost to the tourism in the beach area before the drought that inevitably followed summer. City officials were worried given the size of the crowd for Greekfest 1989. While police had done little to beef up security prior to the weekend, rumors had been leaking out that the city had requested the Virginia National Guard to be on standby to help handle the crowds. Leaking that word out only seemed to be a self-fulfilling prophesy of trouble that was destined to arrive.

Riding on the summer of Spike Lee's racially charged film *Do the Right Thing* and with boisterous hip-hop music as a backdrop, it seemed there was an invisible undercurrent of racial tension in the air. The college-aged kids seemed drawn to the area like moths to a flame, as if they half-expected something to go wrong. By Saturday night tens of thousands jammed Atlantic Avenue in the heat, loud rap music blaring, drinks flowing. It was a powder keg destined to blow at some point. All it needed was a spark.

Against this backdrop, Daniel Lauer and Joe and Jeanette

Godsey arrived at the two-bedroom apartment where Clinton Lauer and Annamaria Phelps lived. They found it dark and the phone disconnected. They went down to the beach area to find it packed.

Joe Godsey recalls the trip, "Anna was flirtatious—she was a little flirt. We went to the beach because it was Greek Week, a big college thing there. When we drove around town, Anna had her legs hanging out the window. I didn't want anything to do with that."

By 1:28 a.m. matters had reached a critical mass in Virginia Beach. The crowd began chanting "Black power!" and someone hit a police officer with a bottle. A decision was made to outfit officers in riot gear. As the officers left Atlantic Avenue to put on their armor, their departure left the area virtually unprotected, and the crowd sensed that control of the area had shifted. An hour later the police returned, colliding with the students in an effort to regain control. It was a riot for no cause, no reason, but violent just the same.

Rocks and bottles flew. The windows of local businesses were shattered, and the urge to loot overcame the participants. Tear gas flew as more businesses fell to the surge of the rioters. It took several hours to restore any semblance of order. In the process only nine people ended up arrested for looting. By the time the National Guard arrived, seventy-two shops, thirty-one restaurants, and twenty-one hotels were damaged to the tune of $1.4 million dollars.

It was in this carnage that the small party gathered at Clinton and Annamaria's apartment. By all accounts they had been spared the chaos of the rioting, and since they didn't have power, may not have even known about the riot until later.

Sometime over the holiday weekend, the suggestion was made that Daniel should come and live with his brother Clinton and Annamaria.

As Daniel's mother would later remember, the lure of going to live near the beach was hard to resist. "You could live with us [in Virginia Beach] and escape your dreary workaday world in Amelia."

By Labor Day, September 4, Daniel made up his mind about moving in with his brother and Annamaria. He quickly made plans to travel back to Amelia County, taking the Godseys home. Annamaria chose to go along simply for a chance to see her family, if only for a short time while Daniel packed and loaded up his Nova for their return to Virginia Beach.

Anna was wearing gray stone-washed jeans, a short black T-shirt, and the locket with her nephews' pictures tucked inside around her neck. Daniel wore a white long-sleeve dress shirt, blue jeans, and tennis shoes.

Joe Godsey didn't offer much in the way of details about their journey home. According to him they took I-64 west for the trip, singing and making obscene gestures at anyone that annoyed them. Daniel was speeding, cruising along the highway at 85 mph. There was beer in the car, but none of the occupants were drinking. The Godseys' child Ashley was secured in the back seat for the journey to Amelia.

According to Joe Godsey, "No one wanted to sit in the back." Somewhere along the way Ashley's diapers had been changed, and diapers fell onto the floor of the back seat.

Daniel was excited. He was due to be paid by his father, which meant getting $800 in cash. This influx of funds into Clinton's and Annamaria's struggling household would restore electricity and provide some stability until he could find a job locally.

The Godseys were dropped off at their trailer first.

Daniel dropped off Annamaria with her family and went home to pack. He spent around ten minutes with his parents, gathering up his worldly possessions for the trip and his new life.

Mrs. Lauer asked him, "Danny, won't you need a blanket?" Daniel was going to take a blue one, but she insisted that he take a brown electric blanket instead. Henry

Lauer paid his son the money that he owed him … enough to get both of the Lauer boys and Annamaria back on their feet.

Margie Lauer recalled for the *Richmond Times-Dispatch*: "The last thing he said before he left was, 'Mom, I'll be back on the weekends to work with dad until I get a job that keeps me from coming.'"

In his car, next to the driver's seat was a crowbar, just in case there were any problems during the trip.

Daniel set off for the Phelps homestead.

Jewel Phelps helped pack up linens and canned food for Annamaria to take back to her apartment. Annamaria spent her time dancing with her three-year-old nephew. Her father voiced his displeasure at having to carry insurance on her wrecked car which she had abandoned in the front yard.

Jewel told one newspaper, "Anna was looking forward to meeting Clinton when he got off work. She said, 'Mama, I got a can of tuna fish so when I get home I can fix Clinton a sandwich because he doesn't have anything to eat.'"

Will Phelps remembers his sister's last visit at home.

"Danny dropped her off at Mom and Dad's. He went to his house and packed his clothes. He was coming to get his clothes anyway, and he brought her so she could spend time with us. She was off of work anyway. That was when she talked to me saying that her and Clint were thinking of getting married and she invited me back to the beach with them. I was so excited about going back with her; I really don't remember a whole lot. I was angry because I really wanted to go; I got my hopes up but couldn't. I wasn't mad at her or anything," Will said.

"Dad told them, 'Why don't you take 416? People were on I-64. They said, 'Aww, Dad, this is the only way we know.'"

Jewel Phelps's last words to Annamaria were to roll up her window and keep the door locked. No doubt the news coming out of Virginia Beach of the riots had her concerned about her daughter's safety.

Daniel and Annamaria left the Phelps home at 11:15 p.m. on Labor Day for the trip back to join Clinton in Virginia Beach. It was a slightly overcast night, with the moon in a waxing crescent. That made it a very dark night with a slow 12 mph breeze and the temperatures hovering in the sixties. The two proceeded as planned heading eastbound on I-64.

As you drive along I-64 through New Kent County, it is eerily similar to the Colonial Parkway in appearance. Trees fill the median and line the highway, and at night the headlights of the cars heading either direction form an almost creepy corridor through the pines. There are only two rest areas on I-64, one for either direction, across the highway from each other.

Now, the eastbound one is a wonderful building, a welcome center to Virginia, offering the first place to pull off and go to the bathroom for miles. Anyone pulling off on an exit would have found no businesses, only darkness and winding country roads. The rest area in 1989 was a split configuration, one roadway for cars, the other for semi-tractor-trailers. There were a handful of battered picnic tables and a public restroom that often left a great deal to be desired. Overflowing garbage cans from the holiday weekend's sheer number of visitors, would have added to the dreary ambiance. These are not the kind of places people hung out at for any period of time except for nefarious purposes or if they were unable to continue their trips.

It is not inconceivable that Daniel and Annamaria might stop at the I-64 rest area, if only to go to the bathroom. They had no reason to linger though. Daniel's Nova was in good running condition and had three-quarters of a tank of gas in it.

The next exit was less than a mile eastbound from the rest area—Route 155 that led north into New Kent, a sleepy little town a few miles away.

A truck driver said he saw them in the eastbound rest area in the early hours of September 5. A passing tourist reported seeing them at a picnic table in the westbound area about noon or one in the afternoon on the fifth of September but that account could never be fully verified. With the rioting in Virginia Beach, the westbound rest area would have been busy with people heading back to work or school after the holiday.

Daniel and Annamaria never arrived at their destination.

One state police investigator that worked the case years later, James "Doc" Lyon, recalls how Clinton had responded to his brother and girlfriend not returning home.

"Clinton got a girl that worked with him at Wendy's, and the two of them set out to find Annamaria and Daniel—thinking they had broken down on the highway. They stopped just short of the rest area heading west—they were low on gas and didn't have any money. They didn't even have a phone—I remember, I think, they used a payphone."

If they had traveled just a little farther, they would have spotted Daniel's car in a strange spot, in the *westbound* rest area, the opposite direction they should have been heading if they were on their way to Virginia Beach.

Clinton called his mother, Margie, at 9:00 a.m. on the fifth of September to say they hadn't arrived and again at 2:00 p.m. to let her know that Daniel and Annamaria still had not materialized. Mrs. Lauer contacted the Virginia State Police.

What no one knew was that Daniel's car had already been located. The Nova was spotted at 9:00 a.m. by a state transportation official and at 1:30 p.m. by a custodian. It stood out because of the way it was parked—left on the truck-side of the rest area, next to the exit ramp, parked at a strange angle near a "No Parking" sign, as if it had some sort of problem and had been abandoned. The road where it was parked was an acceleration ramp where trucks would lumber back onto the highway. The driver's side window was part of the way down and hanging from it was a marijuana roach clip adorned with feathers. The clip had always hung inside of Daniel's Nova, always from the rearview mirror. Now it was hung on the opened window.

After her second phone call with her son Clinton, Mrs. Lauer was beside herself. She filed a missing persons report at 3:00 p.m. on September 5. When the report came through it reached a Virginia State Trooper who was at the car and was about to have it towed away. He wisely cancelled the tow truck and checked the vehicle. The keys were in the ignition. The passenger side door was locked.

There was no sign of a struggle—no sign of Daniel or Annamaria—only the car left alone at an awkward angle on the exit ramp from the rest area. The crowbar remained next to Daniel's seat.

CHAPTER 16

A search for Annamaria Phelps and Daniel Lauer was coordinated by the Virginia State Police under a theory that the two youths had wandered off together and had somehow become lost. Tracking dogs were brought in to check the vehicle but could not detect any trace of either of the victims leading away from the Nova. The interior was a mess, but that was not the apparent work of a culprit rather than the rushed packing that Daniel had done.

Searching was difficult given the heavy forested growth surrounding the rest areas. Teams of officers fanned out from the westbound rest area, and checks were also made surrounding the eastbound area. No one found any sign or trace of the two missing people. For the remaining area, given the dense woods, the state police utilized a helicopter. It would have been like looking for a needle in a haystack with little hope of spotting someone from the air, but the effort was made. The search went on for three days but yielded no other clues.

Several items were identified as missing by the families. The brown electric blanket Daniel had taken from home and the money he had been paid by his father were missing. Annamaria had two matching wallets—one that contained her cosmetics and the other with her ID and money. The latter was among the missing items.

The car itself was in good running condition. The state police took ample photographs of it and checked the tires for soil samples that might tell them where the vehicle had been.

Larry McCann of the Virginia State Police Behavior Science Unit was one of the officers brought in on the scene. He didn't just take photos of the car. Having already started to draw connections between Thomas-Dowski, Knobling-

Edwards, and the Call-Hailey cases, he looked at the crime scene from what the evidence could tell him.

"I processed their car. We have nothing that ties them to the eastbound rest area. Their car is in the westbound area, parked at the far west," said McCann.

"On the driver's window, this window, the driver's, there's a roach clip there with a bunch of feathers that's hanging there. The feathers are hanging on the outside. That's a taunt. That's a taunt to the police. It says, 'Here's the car, I took those two kids, I killed them, here's the car, you'll never catch me.' It's a taunt. This is the mark of people that think they're so smart that they will never get caught. Cocky, brazen, and very thoughtful."

The disappearance in New Kent had overtones of the disappearance of Keith Call and Cassandra Hailey. The public and the press clearly started to see that and so had the authorities. Instead of announcing it, they instead cast doubt on the theory until they had something of substance. A Virginia State Police spokesperson told the *Richmond Times-Dispatch* there was no reason to believe the disappearance of Daniel and Annamaria "was connected with a string of unsolved and apparently unrelated disappearances and murders in eastern Virginia." Saying anything else might have caused panic, and some officials still had their doubts. New Kent was a long distance from the Colonial Parkway and Ragged Island—just under an hour drive depending on traffic.

There were challenges from the outset of the Phelps-Lauer investigation. The previous cases were all handled by different jurisdictions. The Richmond division of the Virginia State Police ran point on the Phelps-Lauer disappearance, while the Knobling-Edwards investigation was coordinated out of the Chesapeake division. They shared information—there was no real rivalry—but the efforts were not jointly coordinated from the start. With the FBI coordinating the other two crimes on the parkway, if it was the same killer or killers, they were certainly muddying the waters by having multiple jurisdictions involved.

Danny Plott remembers the early searches for the two missing youth.

"In '88 I became a special agent which is like the state police equivalent of detective. One of the first cases I was involved with was Annamaria Phelps and Daniel Lauer, the last ones killed. In fact, because of the other three, there was a whole lot more attention paid to it. Here we have a couple missing—we found their car in the westbound rest area, they'd been traveling eastbound," Plott said.

It was natural that some attention be paid by law enforcement to Clint Lauer, the one person that connected Annamaria and Daniel. Police would have been foolhardy to not look into him, but Clinton did not have any apparent motive for the crime.

Danny Plot was sent to Virginia Beach to interview Clint Lauer. "He was visibly upset. He was just as worried about his brother as he was about her. They were supposed to have been there—I'm not sure how much time had passed [at the time of interview]. They were both adults so it wasn't like we were looking for children. When they asked me when I wrote the report up, I said, 'I don't think he has any idea what happened to them.'"

There were many alleged sightings of the two missing people, which only seemed to fuel thinking that they had somehow run off together rather than had been the victims of foul play. They were spotted at a convenience store in Newport News around September 19, but police determined the person had been in error. The problem was that the Tidewater region was home to several colleges, and the victims looked like most people their age.

"I was sent out a couple of times in Williamsburg. ... They had thought they had found them. There seemed to be this young couple that was coming into an apartment complex every night sleeping. Of course all I did was scare the living bejesus out of a couple teenagers," Plott said.

Days dragged on with both families paralyzed as to what they could do other than wait. Daniel's car was turned over to his parents, who drove it just to make sure that it was, indeed, fully operational. It was—and still had three-quarters of a tank of gas—more than enough to make it to Virginia Beach. The question lingered for them all, "Why had they stopped at the rest area and what happened to them after that?"

The stress on the families was palpable. Annamaria's sister Rosanna remembers the period when her sister and Clint were still unaccounted for.

"They [the parents] did everything they could as quick as they could. Of course Mom was distraught and heartbroken because she knew that Anna would not just disappear and not tell her where she was going. She knew something was wrong," Rosanna said. "Mom was trying to work at the time, but she ended up getting so … she just stayed at home a lot waiting for her phone call—thinking that she [Annamaria] was going to call her. Where Dad was out riding around, looking around, taking William and my other brother in-law and any family member we could take to look. We actually looked around the rest stop area. We actually went past the road where they were found—drove past it several times. It's good we didn't find her like that."

Jewel Phelps spoke to the *Richmond Times-Dispatch* about the terrible days of waiting. "We're going minute to minute, second to second, just hoping and praying. We can't give up hope. If she could get to a phone she'd call. If she's being tortured, I'd rather they go on and kill her. We're hanging onto that thread of hope. Waiting is worse than death."

Four days after the pair went missing, Mrs. Lauer was wavering in her hopes that they would be found alive. "I guess I just feel that way because my Danny would have called. My husband went to work this morning saying, 'I better go to work because I might need this money for a funeral.'"

Then came the rain. As fall set in so did the first heavy rains of the season. Almost half of that September and October of 1989 it rained, some days dropping more than an inch. It was abnormal for that much rain in the period. Rosanna Phelps Martin Sedivy remembers those depressing rains.

"During that period of six weeks when they were missing it rained a lot. I was so upset. I kept thinking that she was out there in that rain. Even today when it really rains I get depressed," Rosanna said.

As the days turned to weeks with no sign of the missing pair there was a gloomy feeling that they might be like Keith and Cassandra—gone but never found.

A month after Daniel and Annamaria went missing, the Phelps family offered a $7,000 reward for information that might bring the pair home safely.

Jewel Phelps told the press, "I'm tired of waiting. It's been over a month and it's time to bring them home. She's worth more than $7,000 to me, and if I had more, I'd give it."

Word of the reward spread, but even the enticement of money did not bring out the critical information as to where they were.

October brought one change that had a dramatic impact on the case ... hunting season.

"It was early on in that hunting season. I think that hunting season, the hunters were turning up bodies all over the place. I can remember we were running a lot to body disposal sites. That was because killers had been prolific and now the hunters are the ones out finding them," said Larry McCann of the Virginia State Police.

Hunters didn't just walk trails, they went all over in the woods looking for the right spot to stalk their prey. They were an unacknowledged set of arms and legs probing all over Virginia.

Danny Plott sums it up: "If it wasn't for the hunters going back there, and people using that logging road, it might have been years before we found them."

On October 21, 1989, just after 8:00 a.m., two turkey hunters, members of a local hunt club in New Kent County went onto their club's private hunting reserve looking for wild turkeys. The access to the area was a logging trail or skidder road. It was the kind of road that you could take a four-wheel-drive truck up into. In some areas the wheel ruts were deep mud puddles from the recent rains.

The wooded area was just over a mile from the rest area on the north side of I-64 and was dense brush and growth. The trail ran up over a hill then back several hundred feet before splitting off into two directions. The woods were thick with trees and briars, cleared in several areas so that the hunt club would have good fields of fire.

To this day, sounds in those woods disappear instantly, absorbed by the brush. No noise from there can reach the ears of anyone living in the area nor are outside sounds, even those of the nearby interstate, able to reach the ears of those in that forest.

The bow hunters were back past the split in the trail when, some fifty feet or so off of the trail, they came across a ghastly scene. There, under the umbrella of the trees that were already shedding their leaves, was a brown blanket and two human skulls.

The hunters backed out and called the New Kent County Sheriff's Department, but in the age before cell phones and the remoteness of the location, it took nearly an hour to summon police to the scene at 9:20 a.m. Sheriff F. W. Howard and several of his deputies arrived and immediately recognized the possible connection to Annamaria and Daniel. The state police were contacted. As law enforcement began to arrive the cloudy day began to look more ominous. The rain began, a thick pelting that penetrated the fading leaf-cover of the forest soaking everything.

Danny Plott was one of the first state police officers to reach the site.

"They were laid side-by-side almost like they had laid down and gone to sleep. Now understand they had disappeared six weeks earlier so they were basically skeletal remains. Small animals had been there. Most of the big bones had been recovered but I think some of the finger bones were missing," Plott said.

The blanket covered most of the remains of Annamaria—but only partially covered Daniel. It was doubtful that was the original placement of the blanket. After six weeks, animals had clearly been at the site, doing what animals do with remains. The long days of dreary rains had not helped. When Virginia State Medical Examiner Dr. Marcella Fierro trudged up the hill and through the muddy trail to the where the bodies were found, a tent was erected over the remains to try and preserve the crime scene as much as possible.

Metal detectors were brought in looking for a bullet near where the bodies were found, one that might have dropped as a result of their decay … but to no avail. Sifting screens—identical to those used by archeologists—were brought in, and the soil around the bodies and on the trail were checked for even the most miniscule piece of evidence. The gathering of the scattered bones had to be done in a careful and meticulous manner—all the time with the cool autumn rain making the work muddy and adding to the grim atmosphere.

As investigators fanned out, a single discovery stood out—the small locket worn by Annamaria with her nephew's pictures was found on the logging trail some fifty to one hundred feet from the bodies. What was striking was that the locket was not attached to the necklace that held it—it was alone, almost if it had been placed there. While some bones were located nearby, it was the only piece of physical evidence that was separate from the bodies, causing investigators to wonder—how and why was it there?

Both of the victims' remains were clothed, and a lone

earring was found.

"Both bodies were clothed in light-colored blue jean pants and T-shirts," Tom Stanley, the special agent in charge of the Bureau of Criminal Investigations for the state police's First Division told the media in a press conference that evening. "The bodies were found at 9:20 a.m. No hair remained on either victim."

The mud-splattered brown blanket offered little evidence, other than it was electric; just like the one that Mrs. Lauer reported missing from Daniel's possessions in the car.

The state police withheld the positions of the two bodies from the families. Given the proximity to the rest area, the police were fairly certain that they had found Phelps and Lauer but did not want any missteps.

Tom Stanley told the press: "Visual identification is totally out of the question and fingerprinting is totally out of the question, so we have to go with dental and other methods of identification, so it's going to take some time. If we draw conclusions that it may be [Phelps and Lauer], we're asking for trouble."

Annamaria's sister Rosanna was on her way to the family home when the Virginia State Police arrived.

"The authorities came to the house to tell us. I thought they were after me because I didn't stop at the stop sign. I would have much rather gotten the ticket," said Rosanna. "I come up the hill then the state police came, pulled in the driveway, pulled in behind me. They went in all around me. They said they had found a couple and they weren't sure it was them because they had to do DNA testing, whatever testing, to make sure it was them. They were notifying us that they thought it might be them, and letting us know."

It took two days to get Annamaria's dental records and compare them.

Jewel Phelps told the media, "She's okay now. Nobody will ever hurt her again."

William Phelps Sr. was relieved.

"You can understand that at least we know what's happened and we can get on with things. We can get on with the hurt stage. But there are two things to be done. One is find the guilty party or parties, and the second is to see if there's any way we can reach these young people around here, tell them to be careful on the highways. You cannot stop to help people."

He firmly believed the two stopped to assist another motorist and were taken advantage of.

Daniel Lauer's body was identified several days later. Officers had to contact a doctor in New York for x-rays from when he had a sinus issue as a youth.

His mother, Margie, remembers when they received the word. "I guess we kind of knew it was Danny, but we kind of had our hopes up that it wasn't him."

Sadly and ironically, on the same day that Daniel and Annamaria were discovered, some of the family members of the other victims were pushing for more coverage of the other unsolved cases.

In February of 1989, Friends and Families Against Crime Today (FFACT) was formed. The families had gathered 12,000 signatures to get law enforcement to renew investigations into the pair of murders on the Colonial Parkway and other murders in the Tidewater area. Christi Muldowney, Kathy Knobling, and Lou Call were spokespeople for the group.

On October 21, while authorities were trudging through the wet forest off of Route 155, the *Virginia Gazette* ran an article that FFACT was pushing to get their cases covered on *A Current Affair* and other television programs.

Kathy Knobling told the *Gazette*, "It may be that we will never solve our cases, but now our main goal is to get these kids' pictures on TV in case anyone has seen something. We plan to go to New York and meet with representatives from CBS, *A Current Affair*, and *Good Morning America*. They've got to do something with our stories, if not, we'll go straight to *The New York Times*."

The families had no idea that two more clans were already being drawn into their ranks.

Even more bewildering was the fact that another party of hunters discovered yet another murder victim near the shoulder of I-64 three days later less than a mile further east. This body was badly decomposed but not nearly as much as Phelps and Lauer, still the state police could not identify the race or sex. The body was found in sweat pants, a light jacket, and tennis shoes. Given the difference between this and the Phelps-Lauer remains, police did not believe they were connected. Still, the discovery sent a chill through the community.

Commonwealth Attorney Thomas B. Hoover of New Kent County tried to offer some warning to those that lived in the area, deflecting the blame on the rest areas rather than a possible serial killer. "The rest area was known for crime—drug dealing, 'illegal encounters between promiscuous homosexuals.'"

Three years earlier two nurses, one male and one female, were on their way to a seminar in Northern Virginia and were robbed there. "The bottom line is it not a good place to stop, especially at night," Hoover said.

The state police also tried to throw statistics at the concerns for context. According to Tom Stanley in a press conference: "It's not unusual to find them [victims] lying along the interstate. The interstate is just a dumping ground. … I think the seclusion of the interstate in rural areas gives cover to those wanting to dispose of a body. Since 1984 five bodies have been found alongside or close to I-95 in Hannover and Caroline counties. I-64 also had that reputation. In New Kent in February of 1986 two men were killed in Chesapeake and dumped in the I-64 median about three miles east of Route 155. In James City County in May a New York City man was found shot to death off an I-64 exit ramp."

Blaming the rest areas or highlighting body dumping did

little to aid in the investigation. It was as if officials were going out of their way to downplay the horrific crimes.

The identification of the bodies was not the end of the investigation—but it turned the page on a new phase of it. First and foremost, someone had to determine, if at all possible, how Annamaria and Daniel met their fate.

* * * * *

Of all of the bones recovered, only one showed any sign of trauma. It was a finger bone, small, almost non-discrete in size—yet it told a story of what fate had befallen Annamaria Phelps. There was a cut made into it, a slice, one that had not healed at all, indicating that it was most likely inflicted at the time of the crime.

The neck bones of the two victims were also checked by the medical examiner's office to see if they showed signs of strangulation. The hyoid bone is in the neck and is the U-shaped structure that is fractured in one-third of all homicides by strangulation. In the case of Phelps and Lauer the hyoid was intact. That didn't mean they weren't strangled, only that it was less probable.

The medical examiner's office knew they needed some outside expertise given the six weeks of the bodies decaying. They turned to an unlikely source—the Smithsonian's National Museum of Natural History in Washington, DC. Dr. Doug Owlsey, the division head of physical anthropology at the museum, was recognized world-wide as one of the most prominent and influential archaeologists and forensic anthropologists. The remains were turned over to the Smithsonian for Dr. Owlsey's expert analysis. His determination was that the cut finger belonged to Annamaria.

While those files remain sealed, Danny Plott still recalls the results.

"I'm not sure if it's the right or left hand. By a finger bone, either the right or left hand, there was a knife cut. The knife cut into her hand, like a slice. His expertise [Dr. Owlsey's] said that he believes that was a defensive wound from her holding her hand up as the knife came. That's all we really have to say that probably a knife was used."

Plott goes on to postulate some of what happened that night. "Finding her necklace led us to believe that was a real good chance that was where they were killed. We think they were killed on the logging road, and their bodies were taken into the brush."

The state police theorized that that killer had not placed the necklace on the road as some sort of marker, but that it had been cut from Annamaria's neck as she had raised her hands up to deflect an incoming knife attack. There was nothing on the remains of Daniel Lauer to indicate a knife or gun attack. A bullet could have passed through his tissue without hitting bone. A knife attack, if it didn't hit bone, would not have left any indication after six weeks of the bodies resting in the woods.

Some time was given as to the theory that they may have been the victims of a robbery gone horribly wrong. Danny had over $800 in cash on him at the time of the robbery.[11] Was it possible that this was a drug deal gone horribly awry? The Lauers never ruled out that Daniel may have smoked marijuana—but he certainly was not a drug dealer, nor was Annamaria. At first glance, this was little more than a theory in search of the facts.

The Godseys were tracked down and interviewed, though Joe's interview came several days later—his time was unaccounted for immediately after the pair disappeared.

---

11   In differing accounts this dollar amount varies. Margie Lauer told the *Richmond Times-Dispatch* that Daniel only had $160 on him at the time of his disappearance. In other published accounts over the years, from the same source, the dollar amount wavers between $600 and $900 that he had been paid by his father for painting.

"It brings me to tears. I thought the world of Daniel. The state police, they jumped me at the county fair in front of everybody, telling me I had killed those two kids. I told them he was my best friend. ... You don't do that kind of shit with someone like that," Joe said.

Whatever the results of that interrogation, the state police let Godsey go.

The Virginia State Police arrived at a working theory, based on the little evidence they had, according to Danny Plott.

"If you look at those rest areas now, they are completely different. They used to be the old kind of rest areas; cars went around to the left, trucks went around to the right. ... Not only was the car found there, it wasn't found coming out of where cars parked. It was found coming out of where most of the time trucks or whatever parked," said Plott. "If I remember right—and God my memory's bad—it was maybe a gold Chevrolet Nova or something like that. It was parked, pulled off, like two tires on the pavement, two tires off—like someone broken down. They found it, they processed it. I don't think the car led much."

It wasn't the discovery of the car, but where it was located that was critical to the police.

"But they were coming *eastbound*. They had stopped—I believe they made a phone call from the eastbound rest area. Daniel made a call to someone. ... It may have been Godsey.[12] ... I'm not sure it was a friend or another brother, and that led us to speculate that there was a little something between him and Annamaria. Because he said he was going back to Virginia Beach with her, and basically the gist of the conversation, if I remember right, was 'Well, I think she likes me. If she offers it to me again, I'm going to take it.' Something like that."

From Plott's recollection, it seemed that Annamaria, who

12   The reference to Joe Godsey came up in a subsequent conversation with Danny Plott, but it is inserted here for clarity of the narrative.

was in a committed relationship with Clinton, was flirting with Godsey—casting doubts on Joe Godsey's version of events.

"Even if they were looking for a place to do that, you're not going to do that at westbound [rest area]. We wondered if that went on, did they pull down in that logging road, but neither one would have known where it was, you know, to enjoy each other, and were grabbed there. It just doesn't make any sense because this is just a dirt road and you had to go quite a ways back," Plott said.

"We think they were probably grabbed at the eastbound and then taken there. I think we tested the dirt on the tires, if I remember right, that logging road was like clay. I'm almost sure that there was no indication that that car had been down that logging road. I could be wrong."

The location of the bodies seemed to point investigators to more than one killer being involved.

"Here's another thing that makes me think that Phelps-Lauer had to be two fucking people or someone that was very strong because from that logging road, the edge of the logging road, to where we found their bodies, is about from where we were sitting to where my car is—it was a real hike [about fifty to one hundred feet]. They were carried by one or more persons. Neither one of them was real small; Annamaria wasn't real big and Daniel was six foot. Daniel was a pretty good-sized boy. I'm not saying that there's not plenty of men in the world that couldn't pick 'em up and take 'em. When I first walked up and saw them, I'm thinking, it's almost like they laid down side-by-side to go to sleep. Literally they were laid side-by-side, head-to-head, feet-to-feet. I don't think there was that much room [about a foot] between them," Plott said.

"So we think they were grabbed in the rest area and taken down to that logging road which; again, did they luck up or did they scout it? You can see it—but you don't know where you're going."

Daniel's window being part of the way down supports that he may have rolled it down to talk to someone that he assumed was an authority figure but really was his killer. Annamaria's wallet that was missing could have been an indication that she was taking out her identification, thinking that someone at Daniel's car window was, perhaps, someone in law enforcement.

As for the blanket, the murderer would have had to return to Daniel's car in the eastbound rest area and take the blanket back. It was possible that he would have brought it with him after he assumed control of Annamaria and Daniel but not likely. Whoever it was most likely returned to where he laid the victim's bodies out and covered them. Then he went back, drove Lauer's Nova to the westbound rest area and left it with the keys in the ignition, putting the roach clip on the window.

The killer then crossed the median to get back to his vehicle then left the area.

The assumption that Danny Plott lays out is that they were some distance from where the bodies were discovered by the hunters. The evidence for this is Annamaria's locket that was found there. The state police, at the time, assumed it had been cut from her throat at the same time she was protecting her neck from attack—leaving the defensive wound cut on her finger. If that had been the scenario, where was the locket's chain? No trace of it was found on the logging road.

Annamaria's brother, William, seems to substantiate Plott's theory. "She would put up a fight. That's not good in this situation."

There are competing theories to those that Plott offers. Larry McCann of the state police recently reviewed the photo of the locket. He offers the following:

"That is my ruler next to the locket so I took that photo and recovered that item, number 100 in the case—which tells me it is probably the first item collected that day. I tried to keep sequential numbering in related crime scenes and would usually start at the next 100. Now that I see it I 'sorta' remember it, but not where it was found," McCann said.

"Here are my thoughts:

"Since the victims were walked in at least some of the way, she [Annamaria] could have dropped it on the way in, or the offender on the way out.

"If she dropped it, was it because she was being manhandled or was it a breadcrumb to find her?

"If the offender dropped it, I would think it accidental. Why would he/they carry it out? Remembrance of some nature? Serial offenders are known to keep 'trophies' of their conquests, and I believe this to be part of a series. Disorganized offenders keep 'souvenirs' of their crimes and get rid of them quickly."

The blanket offers some insight into the killer's mind as well.

"I was there at the body recovery site. It was pouring down rain when I got there. Luckily the ME [Medical Examiner] brought a tent. It was just pouring down rain. Maybe he [the killer] put them on the blanket and drug them a couple of feet—but I doubt it, it was pretty secluded. I think it could be something else. It's called 'undoing,' another thing you will probably never read about. Undoing is when you feel a tinge of remorse for what you've done and you try and undo it. That might be it. If they were both on the ground and he pulled it up to here over their heads, that might be undoing. If he pulled it all the way over their heads, then that is concealment."

One thing does stand out from the state police's analysis of the evidence, whoever the killer was, he had prior knowledge of the terrain and the logging road. If he had taken control of the victims and had randomly pulled off on the dirt road, he had no idea if he would be able to get his vehicle out. The testing of the tires shows that Annamaria and Daniel were taken in another vehicle, presumably the murderer's.

Someone that did not stake out the logging trail in advance or have experience on that roadway would not have known if there was a house back in the woods or if it was possible to get the vehicle out. The murderer had planned for that logging trail as the place where the killing would take place prior to the murders. This was a killer that was staging his crime carefully, setting the proper stage and time.

All that was required was the selection of the right victims. This had all of the hallmarks of a predator, a stalker, someone who was a hunter—a hunter of human beings. This looked like the work of a serial killer, and there was only one local string of related cases—stretching from Ragged Island now up I-64 to New Kent County.

* * * * *

Authorities waffled on whether the murders of Annamaria and Daniel were connected to the other paired-homicides in the region. This was despite the analysis of Larry McCann who carefully stitched together a convincing profile of the killers—and drew the connections between the three pairs of murders and disappearances at the time.

In an interview with the *Times-Dispatch* in February of 1989, J. Robert Jasinowski of the Virginia State Police said, "Right now, I don't think there's a serial killer running around over there. That's just my opinion."

At the same time, Joe Wolfinger of the FBI responded, "We are concerned about the possibility that there could be a relationship between all those cases. To that end, we are working with other law enforcement agencies and sharing information and coordinating what we do."

Clearly the state police and the FBI were not on the same page.

While one team of the state police denied connections,

other parts of the organization saw them clearly. The state police had already begun to connect the dots and had included the FBI in their analysis. (See the Prologue chapter for more information.) For law enforcement it was a cumbersome relationship between the families of the victims and their own differing and often conflicting theories.

For the families it was a time of great frustration. Since June of 1989, the families were pushing for a regional task force to investigate the murders and lobbying the State Crime Commission. They saw the connections clearly, even if the police did not. To them, it only made sense to have a task force, even if the law enforcement agencies were resisting.

In that interim period between the disappearance of Phelps and Lauer and the recovery of their remains, law enforcement became more aligned. The state police and the FBI got together and reviewed some of their material. Larry McCann was present and came away from the two-day meeting saying, "There's a very good chance they are related."

Wolfinger of the FBI added: "The possibility any two cases are related is something we'll always keep an open mind about. The crimes occurred within sixty miles of each other."

In speaking about the meeting of law enforcement, Audrey Savage, mother of Knobling's stepmother, said, "I don't think Robin and David were meant to be found either. If it hadn't been for those tree roots at Ragged Island, them getting caught in them, they would have washed out to the sea and we never would have found them."

Even so, Larry McCann at the time was unwilling to include the Phelps-Lauer case with the other pairs of murders, "This is not related to that—it's just not."

Roger Rector, special assistant agent in charge of the Virginia State Police Bureau of Criminal Investigation, agreed. "I don't see the leads—neither do they [the FBI]—going in that direction at this time. They're similar, and then they're not at the same time."

On September 8, the Virginia State Police told the *Richmond Times-Dispatch* that "there was no reason at this point to believe the couple's disappearance is connected with a string of unsolved and apparently unrelated disappearances and murders in eastern Virginia."

Once more they had flip-flopped on the linkage between the murders.

By the end of October, Irvin Wells of the FBI was offering a slightly different stance.

"There is a lack of a 'signature' because different weapons are used. While we cannot say they are, we cannot dismiss the possibility that the four cases are connected," Wells told the *Richmond Times-Dispatch*.

New Kent officials were cold and only added confusion to the mix—worrying about their local tourist trade to the media rather than consoling the families.

"We're trying to do everything possible we can to make New Kent look positive and get positive press. That's why any negative press concerns us," said County Administrator H. Garrett Hart III.

With three bodies turning up in the county in a short period of time, the concerns were about the future of potential racetracks to be built in New Kent. They were worried investors would be scared off. "It won't be because of this unless we get some rash of bodies, where one turns up every week. I don't think there's a killer stalking people in New Kent County."

Behind the scenes, as details about the knife were shared between the state police and the FBI, a different picture was emerging than was presented to the public.

Robert W. Meadows of the FBI commented to fellow agent John Mabry: "Slashed like Dowski and Thomas with the bodies carried away from the car like Call-Hailey and Ragged Island. Damn, you could take the crime scene photos from this one and narrate Call-Hailey."

No apparent motive. "But there's a motive, you can bet your ass."

On the roach clip taunt, Mabry commented, "Really sticking it to us, huh? Don't think we can find you?"

The nature of the investigation was morphing into one where the deaths of Annamaria Phelps and Daniel Lauer were part of something bigger, more menacing—a serial killing spree.

Pressures from the public and the families of the victims could no longer be ignored. Danny Plott recalls the task force.

"Shortly thereafter [Phelps and Lauer] the FBI and the state police formed—not a *formal* task force—but a task force," Plott said.

Representatives included an FBI agent from Norfolk and a state police investigator from the Chesapeake office. The Lauer-Phelps killings took place in the jurisdiction of the First Division of the Virginia State Police out of Richmond—while the murders of Knobling-Edwards were covered by another division.

"So it was us three. Other FBI agents worked it, other state police special agents worked it, but that was the main—the three of us. To tell the truth, most of the time it was myself and the FBI agent, Bob Meadows," said Plott.

The task force essentially shared information opening between the two state police divisions that covered their two crimes and the FBI, which handled the two cases tied to the Colonial Parkway. They did not jointly investigate but merely shared information. Nor did they bring in other agencies that had some experience in the region.

As Ron Montgomery of the York County Sheriff's Department put it, "I was never part of the task force. The task force was set up by the Virginia State Police and the FBI. I simply had to turn over my files to them. Local law enforcement offices were not included. I've met with them a few times over the years, but they were running the show.

We have joint jurisdiction to investigate in the park now, but we didn't back in the 1980s."

Danny Plott tends to agree that York County and other jurisdictions were not invited to the proverbial party between the state police and the FBI.

"All I'm saying is he [Ron Montgomery] was never part of any of the actual investigation through the state police and the FBI. … This does not mean anything about the York County's Sheriff's Office or their agency, to me they're all very professional," Plott said.

The initial task was daunting. Both law enforcement agencies had to read through the voluminous files each had gathered on the possibly related crimes. They were not just familiarizing themselves with their investigations that had gone on, they were looking for possible links and connections, perhaps persons of interest that crossed from one case to another. It was a mind-numbing task of reading reports. The FBI alone by 1990 had put in over 10,000 hours investigating the homicides, and that material had all been meticulously documented. The state police had to scan several filing cabinets worth of reports that had to be digitally stored for the FBI's access.

Patterns were looked at—everything from the phases of the moon to weather. If it was the same murderer in all four cases, was there anything that this killer did that might point to when he might strike again? Everything from satanic worship to witchcraft was at least considered. No patterns could be found.

Some law enforcement officials were quick to accept Larry McCann's analysis and the presumption that this was indeed a serial killer.

Mark Johnson, one of the detectives working for the campus police at the College of William and Mary told the press, "We're just waiting for September or October because we all agree that's when it will happen again."

Others, like Ron Montgomery of the York County

Sheriff's Department, disagreed: "I haven't seen a bit of evidence that ties these cases together other than they were couples that were killed. The fact that they were couples was the only commonality I ever saw."

The fact that law enforcement couldn't agree on the most basic premise did not instill confidence with the public or soothe family angst.

The concern for the public was tangible. This killer was still on the loose and apt to strike again. With even the low-key formation of a task force there was an expectation to produce some sort of results. The problem? There was not a lot of new information. When the *Virginian Pilot* and the *Ledger-Star* released their speculation as to who the murderer was, they introduced a prevailing thought: the killer could be disguised as a police officer.

Danny Plott remembers, "I think that was one where we made a mistake. We were trying to do the right thing ... where we said it might be an 'authority figure.' Immediately the media took that and ran that it was a renegade police officer. What we simply meant was: Cathleen Thomas, Naval Academy grad, not a shrinking violet. Rebecca Dowski, scholarship softball player at William and Mary. These were not little nerd girls that were shrinking violets. The only ones that were going along close to being scared were Cassandra and Keith. If you put in Knobling and Edwards they were not living-on-the-street kids but they were kids where Robin was twelve ... twelve going on twenty.[13] God bless her. And Phelps-Lauer, again, country kids not going to go along with what you say. Now what we meant was, if I walk to two people in a car and I have a gun, I'm an authority figure. I have authority because of that gun."

People began to call in to local authorities with reports of possibly bogus police officers pulling over people. Plott offers his context for such incidents: "That's actually a

13   Author's Note: Robin was twelve at the time of her murder. Danny Plot was speaking figuratively.

common thing. Not so much now, with all that is going on. We constantly arrested people for impersonating a police officer. When I talk to them I tell them, 'It's not near what you think it is brother.'

"Unfortunately that leads to today. I have women friends that if they are not sure it's a police officer, they ask, 'What do I do?'

"I say, 'Don't go above the speed limit and find yourself a well-lit place.'

"The good thing about today is the availability of cell phones cut that down. When I was a young trooper in Emporia, we had a guy grab a couple of young women when impersonating being a police officer. Grabbed 'em and raped 'em."

None of the tips or apprehensions of false officers resulted in any tangible leads for the task force.

As the year 1989 came to an end, the police forces were still not entirely aligned on whether the murders and disappearances were connected or not. The families were more organized; thanks to the formation of FFACT, they were keeping the press focused on the murders. Lost in all of this was the formation of tangible leads and tips that would close any of the cases.

It took over a month for the Virginia State Medical Examiner's office to release the remains of the last two victims, under the condition they would not be cremated. The Lauers launched a protest; they wanted Daniel cremated. The final resolution was never made public. The Phelps family was donated a burial plot by the Newtons, the family of her first boyfriend. Annamaria's remains were laid to rest next to her prematurely born daughter.

Jewell Phelps only commented to the Daily Press, "It'll be over for her. They've done enough with her."

As to the murderer of Annamaria Phelps and Daniel Lauer, Jewel Phelps was blunt with the media, "I want to catch them. I don't want Anna to die for nothing."

GONE BUT NOT FORGOTTEN ...

CHAPTER 17

Serial murders are a fascination that have always caught the public's attention, especially in the 1990s. Ted Bundy had been put to death in 1989, and his wanton killing spree was still fresh in people's minds. The Green River Killer was still on the loose and made national news with each recovered victim. The fascination with serial killers was on the rise, so it was not shocking that the murders in eastern Virginia garnered news coverage nationally.

The media seemed to struggle with what to call the seemingly connected murders in the Tidewater region. Murder sprees and killers needed a name, like the Boston Strangler, the Hillside Stranger, the Night Stalker, or Zodiac Killer—something to sell newspapers and titillate readers.

In Baltimore's newspaper, the crimes were referred to as the "Lovers Lane Killer." The *Richmond Times-Dispatch* called them "The Peninsula Murders," but that did not stick either. It was either the *Virginia Pilot* or Andy Fox of WAVY Channel 10 that first started using the term "Colonial Parkway Murders." Both had been covering the crimes since the discovery of Cathy Thomas's car on the parkway. Out of all of the descriptions, this seemed to be the one that stuck in the public consciousness best.

With the start of 1990, law enforcement was still waffling on whether the crimes were really connected or not. In a January 21, 1990, interview with the *Richmond Times-Dispatch* Tom Stanley of the state police said, "We are concerned. Do we have (a serial killer) or do we not? Right now, we have no basis to connect any of them. There are similarities, but there are differences too."

In the same piece Joe Wolfinger added, "We don't have anything that would suggest that is what's going on here."

At the same time a task force between the FBI and the Virginia State Police was quite active. For the families and the public at large, it seemed confusing and disjointed.

The families, individually and through FFACT, did not relent. When the two-year anniversary of Keith and Cassandra's disappearance came up in early April 1990, the group organized a vigil in the parkway, gathering a large crowed at the Indian Creek Bridge and inviting the press. Most of the families had some sort of representation there. Joanne Hailey summed up the feelings: "It's never gone away. It's always there. People say it'll get better, but it won't get better. It's just an empty spot that never goes away."

The truth was that the task force was still working the cases. Working under the theory that Keith and Cassandra's remains were likely still on the parkway, a search was organized.

Danny Plott remembers the efforts that were made at the time.

"I took a company of marines. I was with them, I think fifty to sixty marines, and went to those areas adjacent to those areas where the car was. We walked and walked that, as far as we could. That has been done several times. These were all marines out of the naval weapons station there— their security detail there. We walked arms-length apart and walked down there and back and found nothing," Plott said.

"I'd probably feel the same way that the family does. I read some place that we made no effort to find the bodies. Whatever. It was searched shortly after the car was found. It wasn't searched as extensively as it was later on because there wasn't enough personnel. I was with the marines doing it, I think, in '89, probably '90, not long after Phelps-Lauer."

Law enforcement tended to work each pair of murders separately. There is some logic behind this approach. If you solve one pair of murders, you can then determine if the same perpetrator had the opportunity and means to have killed the other victims. If the cases are, indeed, the work of a serial killer, you solve one, you solve them all. If the cases are not related, at least you have solved one pair of murders.

The problem with this thinking is that it can become siloed. Investigators become fixated on their case and fail to see the bigger picture of how they might be connected. The mentality shifts to: "These cases can't be connected because we have a working theory on our particular pair of murders." No one wants to be wrong, so the tendency becomes to not draw probable connections between the cases.

With the Colonial Parkway Murders, this led to a disjointed set of messages from investigators. They began to hedge their comments about the links between the cases. At the same time, behavioral analysis from both the FBI and the Virginia State Police clearly pointed to probable connections. With no central authority to control what was said to the public, what emerged was individual officers interjecting their own thinking. The lack of a true centralized task force with central leadership and communications resulted in a confusing and bewildering string of communiques to the people of the Tidewater and the victims' families.

The task force began to gradually leak information regarding the killers in hopes of generating leads. There was an unspoken fear with the public. Serial killers took time off, and that was the case with the Colonial Parkway Murderer. There was a cooling off period between the murders. If it was indeed the same murderer, he would strike again in either the spring or—more likely—in the autumn.

In the July 24, 1990, *Richmond Times-Dispatch*, Larry McCann, the person whose profile best detailed the thinking of the killers, talked to reporter Mel Oberg about the suspected pair of murderers, hoping that the less-dominant one might come forward.

"There's a second person out there. That second person is looking for some way to get out of the bind that he is in. There's something going on between this second person and the perpetrator that needs to be resolved. He needs to come forward. What we're looking at here is a puzzle, and this guy has the big piece."

McCann was careful in his choice of wording. He was offering the supposed accomplice a way out of the situation he found himself trapped in, possibly a hint at a bargain that might be struck. If it was a pair of killers, trying to convince the more dominant person would have been a waste. Larry McCann aimed his guns at the weakest link in the chain hoping to compel that person to come forward.

When asked if he thought the killer had schizophrenia, "I would say that if he had multiple personalities, he would be so poorly integrated he couldn't pull off these crimes. I'm not a psychiatrist. I'm a cop, but this guy must have his mess together because he's doing a real good job."

After routine checks of VICAP—the Violent Criminal Apprehension Program—Tom Stanley added, "We have had no reports back that there are any crimes outside this immediate area [similar to this one]."

But the public was reminded to take care at all times, especially when in a remote area. "Control was taken of the victims early on," Irvin Wells of the FBI told the newspaper. "A weapon in the face could be control. The task force warns anyone being pulled over to make sure the officer is in uniform and a marked car. If not, ask for the officer to display badge and identification. We recommend everyone be alert and we urge people not to find themselves in remote areas."

Despite the pleas for one of the killers to come forward— no one did.

Autumn came and there was a nervous waiting on the part of the citizens of the area to see if the murderer would once again strike. Nothing happened. The pattern seemed shattered, but there was no sense of jubilation—only wonder about the murderer striking again.

McCann continued his press with the media a few days later with a small press conference that was covered by a number of sources.

"The passage of time doesn't mean any false alarm, and it doesn't slow us down any at all," he said.

When McCann spoke about serial killers he was most passionate, offering the behavioral model that was accepted in 1990.

"They never stop. They either die, go to jail, or move."

In regards to why the Colonial Parkway Murderer hadn't struck: "I don't know, but I'd like to think he's in jail somewhere."

As the year came to an end, the vacillating on the connectivity between the murders still was an issue that the task force allowed to be played out in public with the media. Most of this was driven by the fact that in the case of Robin Edwards and David Knobling, the state police believed they had a solid theory as to who did it: the mysterious Mr. Washington. In the case of Annamaria Phelps and Daniel Lauer, they didn't have a means of connecting that crime with the others. In fact, in terms of physical evidence, there was nothing at the time that connected the crimes. What connected them was a pattern—the murders of pairs of young people at isolated locations. From a behavioral sciences perspective, the cases were clearly part of a pattern. The lack of linkable physical evidence caused law enforcement to hedge.

Irvin Wells of the FBI told the media, "While we cannot say they are (connected), we cannot dismiss the possibility that four of these cases are connected."

The Virginia State Police wavered with their bets as well. J. Robert Jasinowski, special agent in charge of the Bureau of Criminal Investigation in Chesapeake, said of a connection, "You can't say there is; you can't say there's not."

Joe Wolfinger of the FBI was far more pragmatic. "One murder is a lot as far as I'm concerned. ... We've asked ourselves if there is a serial murder at large here and that's something we're very concerned about."

Tom Stanley was pressed whether the string of murders

were possibly linked to a cult. "We can't go with the cult theory because usually there's some sort of sacrifice or mutilation."

He added, "I think a lovers' lane connection is valid. They are out of the way. Ragged Island is accessible but secluded. The parkway has that characteristic again, although a lot of traffic is in and out of there.

"As time goes on these things work against you."

* * * * *

The task force scrambled to Hannover County, Virginia, just after the Fourth of July in 1990 when the bodies of two young people were discovered. Deborah Ferguson was a Virginia Commonwealth University art student, and James "Jim" Sherrin was a former student there. Their bodies were discovered behind the Park & Ride in Old Town Mechanicsville. Like the parkway victims, they were not killed there, their bodies were dumped there.

Lt. Howard L. Wray Jr. of Hanover told the *Daily Press* on July 7, "They (the task force) stick their noses in everything that happens within an hour and a half of the Peninsula."

Most versions of the last few minutes of their lives center on a drug deal that may have gone bad. It is that possible motive that seemed to exclude them from being included in the murders in the Tidewater.

The murders of Ferguson and Sherrin remain open to this day, but there was enough dissimilarity to rule out their murders with those of the Colonial Parkway Murders.

* * * * *

Behavioral profiling of criminals is often characterized as

an inexact science. That is incorrect ... it is an *evolving field* of study and is often the best tool investigators have to help them narrow their search of tips and theories. As the body of knowledge about serial killers grows, so does the impacts to the profile of who might be the killer. The original profile of the Colonial Parkway Murderer is coolly analytical.

Larry McCann, trained by the FBI's best, felt that the murderer was an organized killer. As he described it to the press, "If we look over the list of organized characteristics his [the killer's] smooth technique and the victim's lack of struggle indicated that he's an organized killer. The behavioral evidence suggests a second person is involved and may be participating against his will."

John Douglas, chief of the FBI's Behavioral Science Unit, wrote the proverbial textbook on serial killer profiles. He says this about an organized killer: "The offender may use impersonation to gain access to the victims. ... His demeanor is not usually suspicious. He may be average to above average in appearance, height, and weight he may be dressed in a business suit, uniform, or neat casual attire. He frequently uses his or the victim's car in the offense."

McCann's profile felt that the nature of the crimes pointed to two individuals working together; one dominant personality, the other more submissive. Much of this was driven by the fact that these crimes always involved pairs of victims. Pairs of victims drove the thinking that extra hands were going to be needed to maintain domination over the victims.

Jack Levin, professor of sociology and criminology at Northeastern University, was quick to point out that by 1990, nearly 30 percent of serial killers operated in teams. They were often brothers, cousins, and friends.

Douglas offers more details: "They generally are two extremes. You have a master/slave relationship, dominant/ passive personalities. They usually are two males, but there have been exceptions. They are almost always police buffs."

One of the very few things that the members of the task force agreed upon is that it was most likely that they were looking for a pair of murderers—not a single person.

James Fox, professor of criminal justice at Northeastern University and author of *Mass Murder: America's Growing Menace*, characterizes serial killers from a slightly different perspective.

"He is a sociopath. He lacks any degree of remorse, conscience or empathy. And, he is a sexual sadist acting out his fantasies. Nearly three percent of all men are sexual sadists, and most sociopaths don't kill. But, when you have both, then you have someone who has no inhibition against acting out these sadistic fantasies."[14]

This killer exerted extraordinary control in each situation. One thing that never changes in the discussion of the Colonial Parkway Murders profiling is the control aspect that was applied to each of the situations. In the case of Thomas-Dowski, control of the situation allowed the killer to tie up both victims to the point of strangulation. In the case of Knobling-Edwards, control most likely came at the end of a pistol barrel—leading the victims to the water's edge where they met their fate. Only when control was lost, i.e., David Knobling broke free, did the murderer face any real challenge. While we don't know the circumstances of Call-Hailey's disappearance, clearly some sort of control was implemented to force the victims to strip and eventually be killed. With Phelps-Lauer, control was needed to get the victims into the vehicle of the killer to take them into the woods. The Colonial Parkway Murderer was all about control.

In the case of Robin Edwards and David Knobling, their shoes were found in David's truck. The removal of the shoes could be interpreted as a method of control. While there was a sandy beach area at the end of the boardwalk at Ragged

14   Robertson, Bronwyn, *Denbigh Gazette*, October 4, 1990, pages 4 and 5.

Island, no one would have gone out on the long wooden boardwalk barefoot—and the other venue alongside the bridge was less sand and more gravel.

In Keith and Cassandra's case, most of their clothing and shoes were removed—again as a means of controlling the victims. In some respects, the forced control through these means may point to one killer rather than two. Two people would not necessarily have to take such measures to control their victims, where a lone killer might remove shoes and clothing to ensure a higher degree of control.

That control can be implemented in many forms. A gun would have been the most likely form. If the murders were all connected, we know that the killer had a knife, based on Thomas-Dowski and Phelps-Lauer, and a gun, per the deaths of Knobling-Edwards. The killer also had rope. When the original profile of the killer in the case of Thomas-Dowski was done by the FBI it seemed that the killer was disorganized—that the killer was grabbing things out of the back of his truck to conduct the murders … the rope, the knife, the diesel fuel, etc. As time passed it began to look more as if the murderer planned the killings, preparing a suite of implements that might be needed to complete the task.

Larry McCann offers a key insight into the killers' method of selecting victims: "They think things through, and that may be why it's only every year because it's so well thought out and everything has to be just right. So the two guys are out there, they're ready to do it, but it's not perfect so they wait and wait, and finally after a year, okay, it's perfect, bingo, we got a couple."

In other words, the killer was a stalker. It was possible that he interacted with many couples before he found the "right" victims. Most of the people that he interacted with probably had no idea how close to death they may have come. It also meant that the murderer was methodical and highly selective. This was a hunter, a stalker, picking his victims carefully against a set of mental criteria that only he fully understood or comprehended.

A key telling aspect of these crimes was that the murderer appeared to commit the crimes separate from where the bodies were recovered. In the murders of Cathy Thomas and Rebecca Dowski, they had been killed in one location and their bodies placed in the car for disposal. In the murders of Robin Edwards and David Knobling, their bodies were found some distance from Knobling's truck and there was no evidence they had been killed where they were found. We only know that there is a separation between the disposal of the remains of Keith Call and Cassandra Hailey and Keith's car as evidenced by their bodies not being found with the vehicle. If the state police theory is valid, even Daniel Lauer and Annamaria Phelps were killed in a different spot than where their bodies were found—separated by upwards of one hundred feet.

These were acts of concealment. In all of the cases, efforts were made to dispose of the bodies. The first attempt with Thomas-Dowski was a series of errors: the failure to ignite the diesel fuel and the botched attempt to push the car into the York River. With Knobling-Edwards the bodies were likely put in the James River and thanks to tidal forces, washed ashore. The murderer hid the remains for six weeks in Phelps-Lauer. The only time the killer succeeded in a concealment attempt was in the murders of Keith Call and Cassandra Hailey.

Larry McCann offers some insights into the movement of the bodies.

"While I don't know what the killers were thinking when the victims were moved about, I do know the mechanics of the actions reveal information about the killers. By herding the *living* victims, at least one of the killers show they were confident in their ability to control the victims. Control could have been gained and maintained in many ways: by having multiple killers; overwhelming size of the killers; the killers having weapons; faux police stop to gain control, then multiple killers and/or weapons to keep control," McCann said.

"Bottom line is that the killers showed confidence in their ability to stop, move, and kill strong and feisty victims, and to stay at the scenes to move the bodies then move at least one car quite a distance from the bodies. They had so much confidence that they committed the same crime again and again, and in the same area.

"The movement of these victims stretches beyond 'MO' and into 'signature,' which is something not necessary to commit the crime but something the killers feel driven to do. Some would delve into psychiatric exposition about signature; I prefer to view it more simplistically as evidence that links multiple cases to one offender."

Finally, in three of the murders, the cars were left with the keys either in the ignition or in plain view, with the vehicle not concealed. Was this an attempt to induce someone to steal the cars, to further cloud the investigation, or is it a deeper psychological perspective of the murderer? If the killer was hoping someone would stumble across the vehicle and steal it, it most certainly added a level of cunning and a desire to beat the investigators by muddying the crime scene with an auto theft.

McCann's perspective on this behavior points to the attitude of the murderer.

"It shows confidence blooming into arrogance—at least one of the killers is so confident he can move the car and not get caught, so arrogant that he is much smarter than the police, that he taunts us with the car movement, leaving it in an obvious place, and the feathers.

"By leaving the keys in the ignition he is not only inviting the vehicles to be stolen, but relishing the idea of the dead ends that would be thrown into the investigation by the car being even farther from the scene and the trouble one more of his victims will feel."

* * * * *

There was a tendency, mostly by the media, to link the Colonial Parkway Murders with other serial killing sprees. That's natural and in some ways logical, but often those links were nothing more than being sets of serial killings. True connections, even behavioral, require much more. One that gained some attention was the Gainesville Ripper killings at the University of Florida in 1990. In late August of 1990 five people, four of them students, were brutally murdered in Gainesville, Florida. The timing for the citizens of the Tidewater region was chilling—it was autumn, a year after the Phelps-Lauer murders. To some it seemed as if the killer had moved further south, perhaps to evade publicity.

The Gainesville Ripper only murdered one pair of victims, the others were killed separately. Also those murders were in a narrow span of time, not with the typical cooling off period that most serial killer's demonstrate. Breaking and entering was the trademark of these crimes, and it was that modus operandi that led to the relatively quick capture of the Gainesville Ripper, Daniel Rolling.

* * * * *

Joanne Hailey contacted the media on July 26 with a letter written to the killer. It was a direct appeal from one of the family members to the murderers.

To whom it may concern:

There are many things in our life that disappoint or hurt us. Some things we never forget; others hurt us so bad that we want to strike out and hurt someone just as much as we've been hurt.

To the person that chose to strike out and hurt the young people in our community—Cathleen and Rebecca, Robin and David, Sandra and Keith, Annamaria and Danny—I'd like to say:

I am sorry someone hurt you. Whatever happened should not have happened to you or anyone else. I'd like to help you get through that pain for I am feeling that same pain. You have chosen to strike out, not only to these young people, but to me and their families. The pain is the same. We cannot put our pain to rest until you do.

Someday I might find forgiveness for what you have done. As a mere mortal, I find that hard to do with so much pain in my heart, but you should know there is one greater than any of us who will forgive you for anything.

I pray to My Almighty God that He will reach down and touch your heart and heal it of its pain, that through that healing you will find the strength to atone for what you have done. I pray that atonement will begin with your letting me know the whereabouts of my daughter, Sandra Hailey, and her friend, Keith Call.

An anonymous phone call to me, the newspaper, a clergyman, or from anyone who you feel you can trust, can be the first step toward that healing. I am asking you to please let me know where our precious Sandra and Keith are. My number is in the telephone book. I wish I could convince you of the peace you will find when you have resolved this hurt. Please let us help you find that peace.

Sincerely, and with the Peace and Love of our Savior Jesus Christ,

Joanne Hailey [15]

Mrs. Hailey told the media that her telephone was unmonitored. The entire community took pause with the <u>letter, wondering</u> if this killer, like other serial killers, might

15   Crocker, Ronnie. Mother's Letter makes personal plea, *The Daily Press*, July 26, 1990, A12

respond in some way.

No response from the killer was forthcoming.

On Saturday, April 13, 1991, the families assembled to commemorate the disappearance of Keith and Cassandra at the York River Overlook where Keith's car was found. Nearly sixty well-wishers joined the family members with a short, cold prayer service. Bonnie Edwards spoke out the most vocally. "We're not going to let anybody forget about this until we found out who is doing these murders. We hope no one else has to die before they find out who is doing this. I think this group today shows there's an ultimate judgement he's got to face and there's no escaping that one."

The people of the peninsula did not forget. The murderer did not respond, nor did he strike again.

In the summer of 1991 there was a rash of reports to authorities regarding individuals posing as police officers pulling people over. One person pulled over a sixteen-year-old motorist on Oyster Point Road in Newport News and ordered a field sobriety test, examining her license and searching her car.

Someone in a fake unmarked police car with out-of-state plates operating on I-64 brought several complaints—including one involving a woman who was pulled over by someone posing as a Virginia State Trooper.

Another man reported a security guard stopping him on private property not protected by private security.

From Newport News to Hampton Roads, over twenty reports came in of false police officers operating in the area.

The reports all had a thread of commonality. The man was described as wearing a dark uniform, about six feet tall, clean-shaven, muscular, with short black hair. It was only because a member of her family was an officer and she was familiar with police procedures that she realized that the man was not a legitimate officer. His vehicle was equipped with red and blue flashing lights, adding to his credibility.

Immediately it was presumed that this might be the

Colonial Parkway Murderer, possibly out trolling for another potential victim. The information was shared with the task force, and while no arrests were made, the incidents dropped off after appearing in three local newspapers. If you were going to pose as a police officer in the Tidewater area, it meant you were going to fall under the scrutiny of the task force as a possible murder suspect.

At the start of 1992, the work of the task force dwindled as did the influx of incoming leads. That wasn't to say there weren't occasional bursts of activity. Some tips had trickled in over the life of the task force, mostly about where Keith and Cassandra might be buried.

For example, a woman walking along a beach of the James River next to the Colonial Parkway discovered several bones. "We had some cadaver dogs found no bones in that area of Williamsburg," Danny Plott said. "Quite possible they were shallow Civil War graves there at one time, and then the bones are gone. We didn't find anything." The woman finding bones on the beach, even one at the other end of the parkway, offered a momentary glimmer of hope for the families and investigators.

The two recovered bones were sent to the Virginia State Medical Examiner's office who determined they were not human but animal. Yet another dead end.

By this stage the families did not rely on the state police or the FBI as their main conduit for information. They stayed in contact with each other. Most kept detailed notes of their conversations. They shared their information with each other to ensure they were being told the same thing. It was frustrating to them that they had to take ownership of this responsibility, but information flowing out of the task force was so minimal, every little nugget of data, no matter how trivial, was seen as a piece of a larger puzzle.

Housewives and working fathers took on the roles of detectives because they felt not enough attention was being paid to their cases. They were drawn together in a strange way ... their only shared bond being that they had all suffered the same loss at the same time. It was, in many cases, all they had in common—the horrific crimes. Some, like the Hailey family, hired private investigators that tried, without police cooperation, to piece together what might have happened to their loved ones.

"The FBI seemed to be taking it personally that these families wanted to know. If I remember right anytime they asked us to meet with them, we tried. We didn't tell them that this was being worked day-to-day because it wasn't. Anytime we had any information ... and I'm sure the FBI did the same thing, these files were passed onto new agents. You never know what a new set of eyes will see," Danny Plott said.

"By 1992-1993 I had very little to do with the cases. We had leads—when a lead came up we would work on it. In 1997 I became a supervisor in the same office and even then ... I think we called them inactive. We only called them inactive to put them in a file until we had another lead. Often I would take new agents that came in and say, 'Read this. Tell me what you think.'

"Most of them would come back and they would say, 'Oh my God.'"

As the 1990s advanced, Brian Hamblin of the FBI told Bill Thomas, Cathy's brother, that that status of the investigation was more than stalled.

"This murder is at the bottom of a very dusty pile."

John Mabry of the FBI told the *Daily Press*, "There were times we would develop what we all would agree was a really strong suspect. There were some that just seemed so promising—the 'right person.' But none of those panned out. From a personal perspective, when you go through that it really is an emotional letdown. When it just doesn't pan out—and in all fairness to the suspect—you just move on to the next person."

The National Park Service was less concerned about

solving the murders as they were the public confidence in the Colonial Parkway. In a 1996 interview with A. J. Plunkett of the *Daily Press,* Chief Ranger Jim Burnett said, "We're doing everything we can to ensure that when people come to the parkway, they're safe."

Without external stimulus, the Colonial Parkway Murders might very well take on the status of local folklore or a Wikipedia entry on the internet. That incitement was to take on strange and interesting forms that no one could predict.

CHAPTER 18

The Colonial Parkway Murders took on a bizarre twist with the release of *All That Remains*, a fictional thriller/ mystery in 1992. Patricia Cornwell, a highly renowned author, was at the time living in Richmond and working as a computer analyst at the Office of the Chief Medical Examiner. Her novel, about her celebrated character medical examiner Kay Scarpetta, dealt with a serial killer in the Tidewater area who killed couples.

The opening of the novel takes place at a rest area on I-64 in New Kent County where a pair of young people has mysteriously disappeared on Labor Day weekend. Their bodies are found in the winter in a nearby dense woods, and the lead character performs an autopsy on the remains. It appears to be the work of a known serial killer, the "Couple Killer."

The details of the autopsy and the rest-area scenario were eerily similar to that of Annamaria Phelps and Daniel Lauer. In the book, Scarpetta, after many twists and turns, learns of a link to a suspect at the CIA's "Farm" at Camp Peary. Of course in the fictional version, the protagonist solves the murders and the book ends with the death of the killer, thus ending the spree.

The novel was a bestseller. Cornwell's character of Kay Scarpetta was already well established and adored by her fans. Little did she realize that the book would have two impacts related to the real case.

The first was outrage from some of the victims' families, especially Jewel Phelps. Having obtained a copy of Annamaria's autopsy report, she felt it was clear that Cornwell had used her position in the medical examiner's office to access that material and use it as a the basis of her character's autopsy in the book.

She told the *Daily Press's* Ronnie Crocker on September 27, 1992, "That is the hardest book I ever read in my life. I put it down, walked the floors, smoked cigarettes, drank coffee and cried and cried and looked at that book. I wanted to pick it up, but was afraid too.

"Why don't she leave us alone and let us grieve in peace? What right does she have to make fame and fortune because of my Anna's tragedy and heartache? Where are our rights?"

Margie Lauer felt differently about the novel.

"As far as I'm concerned, the book can't do any harm. I just hope somebody can read and remember some little thing. That's the best I can hope for," Margie said.

Kathy Knobling captured another tone.

"My first reaction when I heard about it was, 'I wonder how they end the book?' We haven't gotten an ending to our story," said Kathy.

In August 1997, William and Jewel Phelps sued Patricia Cornwell over the book. They claimed that Cornwell had illicitly used their daughter's autopsy report in her novelization. The Phelps' attorney stated: "It's a violation of the law and my clients' privacy. She must say how she obtained the information."

The lawsuit, however, fizzled over time and never produced the results that were intended. What it did do was keep the Colonial Parkway Murders in the minds of the public.

* * * * *

When a case goes cold, there are times when it momentarily flares up—where something external brings it back to the surface. For the families of the victims, it can be a momentary burst of hope and a resurfacing of the pains they have been through. For law enforcement it is a crunch of activity, hoping that an expansion leads to resolution.

Such a flare-up of activity took place in 1996. The murders of two women in a nearby national park made the public wonder if the killer might had resurfaced far from the Tidewater region.

Two female hikers, Julianne "Julie" Williams and Laura "Lollie" Winans, entered the Shenandoah National Park at Front Royal in the Piedmont region of Virginia, some three hours from where the Colonial Parkway Murders took place. They were young—Williams was twenty-four and Winans was twenty-six—and not from the area—Williams was from St. Cloud, Minnesota, and Winans was from Grosse Point, Michigan, attending college in Maine. The girls were not alone, they had Winans's golden retriever named Taj with them.

For them it was supposed to be a nice relaxing hike in one of the countries' premiere national parks. The girls were lovers but were not public with their lifestyle. Their families had no idea of the nature of their relationship at the time.

They entered the park just prior to Memorial Day weekend and were last seen by someone other than their murderer on May 24. They made camp one-tenth of a mile from the popular Skyline Drive and a half-mile from the Skyland Lodge. The location was close to people but at the edge of isolation.

Memorial Day, May 27, passed and nothing was heard from the women. Taj was found wandering near the lodge on June 1. Rangers went to their campsite and were stunned at what they found.

In a sleeping bag that appeared to have been tossed down near the bank of a creek was Julie Williams. Winans was in their tent, some seventy-five feet away, also dead. Their deaths did not come quick or without brutality. Their murderer had stripped both victims of their clothes then bound and gagged them. Their throats had been slit to a near point of decapitation. Winans had her wrists bound with duct tape and her ankles tied off with a pair of long underwear. Williams wrists were bound.

One of the rangers on the scene was none other than Clyde Yee, having transferred from the Colonial Parkway.

The National Park Service did not make any announcement to warn park visitors for thirty-six hours. With the park packed for Memorial Day, it is likely they didn't want to panic the visitors—but at the same time that left thousands of others at risk of being potential victims without any knowledge of the risk. It was a move that was going to haunt the National Park Service after the investigation.

The FBI stated publically they were looking at the "substantial similarities" between the murders in the Shenandoah and that of Cathy Thomas and Rebecca Dowski. At first glance, the case seemed to fit the pattern of the Colonial Parkway killer. The crime was committed on federal property—assumed by authorities to be the case with Thomas-Dowski and Call-Hailey. It also involved a couple, and like Thomas-Dowski, they were lesbians. There was a knife employed—which was known to be the case in Thomas-Dowski and Phelps-Lauer. But the similarities ended there.

This was labeled quickly as a hate crime—it seemed that the victims were chosen because they were gay. It was not a lovers' lane situation—this was a camp site. There was no staging of a vehicle either. In the murder of Williams and Winans, there was no deliberate attempt to conceal or hide the remains as happened with the Colonial Parkway cases.

The Shenandoah murders went cold until July 9, 1997. On that day, Yvonne Malbasha, a single mother from Canada was bicycling in the park when Darrell Rice, a resident of nearby Maryland, confronted her. He began stalking her from his blue Chevy S-10 pickup. At one point he forced her off of the road.

"The vehicle came so close I could actually feel the heat

of the engine," Yvonne said.

Rice then threw a soda can at her, grabbed at her chest, and screamed, "Show me your titties."

There was no doubt in Yvonne's mind that Rice intended to rape and kill her.

Rice tried to throw her into his truck, but she managed to squirm free and evade him. Malbasha contacted the rangers who took her description of the vehicle, the license plate number, and the clothing that Rice was wearing. The rangers acted quickly. A blue Chevy S-10 was spotted at the Swift Run Gap exit to the park, but the man behind the wheel was wearing a different shirt and the license plates didn't match. On the front seat was a shirt that did match her description of her assailant. When interrogated by authorities, Rice admitted that he had confronted Malbasha and had changed his license plates to evade authorities.

Darrell Rice was convicted of his assault on Malbasha and sentenced to 135 months—eleven years—in jail.

Checks of video tapes of vehicles coming into and exiting the Shenandoah Park showed that Rice's truck entered the park and was there at the time that Williams and Winans were murdered. Further investigation pointed to the fact that Rice was extremely prejudiced against gays and women in general.

Circumstantial evidence certainly pointed to Rice as the murderer of Williams and Winans, and despite what is shown on television programs such as *CSI*, murder convictions are often successful on circumstantial evidence alone. In 2002, Darrell Rice was indicted for capital murder for the slayings of Williams and Winans. According to prosecutors, he targeted the pair of women because they were gay.

The physical evidence did not link Rice to the crime. A hair sample found in duct tape from the crime scene did not connect to him. The lack of physical evidence caused the charges to be dropped. This did not exonerate Rice, it simply meant that at the time, the authorities lacked evidence.

In 2011 Darrell David Rice was released on parole. Investigators have not given up on the Williams and Winans case and consider Rice their prime suspect. His hatred of women in general and his family connections in the Culpeper, Virginia, area allowed other agencies to consider him a possible suspect in unsolved crimes in the region.

The Route 29 Stalker murders is another spree of unsolved serial killings in the Piedmont Region of Virginia. Route 29 is an old roadway, stretching from Washington, DC, through the Bull Run Battlefields, snaking west and south down through Culpeper and into Thomas Jefferson's hometown of Charlottesville. Starting in 1996, a number of women along the Route 29 corridor were pulled over and at least one of them was killed. The pattern for this murderer was to flash his headlights to get a victim to pull over, telling her there was a problem with her vehicle. He would then offer her a ride … and in at least two cases used the friendly lift as a prelude to assault and murder.

The evidence of this came in February of 1996 when Carmelita Shomo was driving on Dumfries Road in Manassas. A truck pulled up behind her and flashed its headlights. She pulled over, and a man approached her from the vehicle telling her there were sparks coming from under her car. This "Good Samaritan" offered her a ride to get help. He traveled a short distance and pulled off the road, attacking Shomo. Carmelita struggled to get free, but her ankle was caught in the seat belt. Her assailant pulled away, dragging her down the road some distance before she got free. At first it appeared to be an isolated incident, but then a string of young women disappeared.

Alicia Showalter Reynolds had been driving on Route 29 traveling from Charlottesville to Baltimore on March 2, 1996. She was last seen alive climbing into a dark Nissan pickup truck just a few miles south of Culpeper. Two months later her remains were found in a field in Lignum, Virginia, in a shallow grave, off of Route 3, which connects to Route

29.

Twenty-year-old Anne Carolyn McDaniel of Orange, Virginia, left a group home on September 18, 1996, and was never seen alive again. Four days later her burned remains were found near Mt. Pony, only ten miles from where Alicia Reynolds remains were found.

Samantha Ann Clarke, a nineteen-year-old from Orange, Virginia, left at 12:30 a.m. on September 13, 2010, to meet with an unknown party. She was never heard from or seen again, and her remains were never found.[16]

Police have suspects in mind for these murders, but again, lack the evidence to connect their suspects firmly to the deaths. There is a belief that Darrell David Rice was responsible for at least some of the so-called Route 29 Killings. Their reasoning was sound. Carmelita Shomo identified Darrell Rice as her assailant and in 2005 he pleaded no-contest to the charges, returning again to prison. Rice knew the area well and had a propensity for violence against women. Lacking any tangible physical evidence, there was a reluctance to push for charges against him. Since Rice has been in jail, the Route 29 Stalker crimes have stopped.[17]

Armchair detectives look at Darrell David Rice as a perfect person of interest in the Colonial Parkway Murders. While the pattern of murders is very different, the argument could be made that the killer changed his modus operandi.

16   Samantha Clarke was repeatedly in contact with Randy Taylor, including one call just prior to her disappearance. Taylor has been convicted of another murder and is a suspect in Clarke's demise.

17   It should be noted that there is no "official" list of crimes that compose the Route 29 Stalker murders which leads to some confusion. Alexis Tiara Murphy often is associated with these crimes though Randy Taylor has been convicted of her murder. Hannah Graham is also attributed to some lists, but Jesse L. Matthew plead guilty to her murder and that of Morgan Herrington whose name also is attributed to being part of the Route 29 Stalker cases. Adding even more confusion, Richard Marc Evonitz, a convicted serial killer in Spotsylvania County, Virginia, was convicted of rape and murder in three cases not far from Route 29.

From the timeline perspective, it fits. If Rice is indeed tied to the Route 29 killings, his murder spree started after the murder of Annamaria Phelps and Daniel Lauer.

The FBI and the state police were not ignorant; they tried to draw connections between Rice and the unsolved Tidewater murders. One key problem was age. Darrell Rice was born in 1968. At the time of the murders of Cathy Thomas and Rebecca Dowski, he would have been 18 years old.

Age alone does not rule out Rice. He was unfamiliar with the Virginia peninsula area. The reason he is considered a suspect in the Route 29 Stalker crimes is that he had intimate familiarity with the region. One thing that can be safely assumed about the Colonial Parkway Murderer is he knew the area where he operated and knew it very well.

Finally, Rice was a loner who seemed to be driven by hate and rage against women. The victims in the Colonial Parkway Murders were—75 percent of the time—male and female couples. Rice's pattern was to go after lone women, and in at least the case of Carmelita Shomo, he did not demonstrate the kind of control that a lone killer would have had developed if he had been the lone killer in the Colonial Parkways cases.

Rice alone is not the only suspect on the Route 29 Stalker cases. Randy Taylor is considered a suspect in Samantha Clarke's murder … it clouds the issues as to which crimes really are tied to a single serial killer along the Route 29 corridor. This string of murders may actually be the work of several independent killers—and may not be connected at all.

The vast differences in the pattern for a serial killer would have been far too significant to consider the Route 29 Stalker and the Colonial Parkway cases connected. Serial killers perfect their craft over time. Generally they don't change the things that work. They fix things that go wrong. In the Colonial Parkway Murders, the killer shifted to use a gun. He got better at concealment of the bodies—perfecting it in the case of Call-Hailey.

One of the major differences between the cases is how the killers gained control of their victims. For the Colonial Parkway Murderer, the control aspect was part of his success. The Route 29 Stalker, if it is indeed Rice, would have had to break with something that worked very well in the past if he had also been the Colonial Parkway killer. It seems highly unlikely that such a dramatic change would take place.

The other regional serial killing cases were carefully investigated by the FBI and state police, but no official has ever implied publicly a connection with other murders. At best, the review of those cases proved to be a distraction for law enforcement officials.

Little did they realize that the largest distraction was yet looming.

CHAPTER 19

With the families of the victims there was a shift over the years. The emotional toll that the unresolved justice took on them, especially the parents, was incredible and often came at a high price.

"I knew that this would kill my parents," Chris Call said. "It would shorten their lives. The way my mother worried and fretted about things, I knew she would die of cancer. My poor father, not only did he have to worry about his son being lost and murdered by a serial killer, but he had to deal with my mother who'd kind of gone off the deep end—trying to take care of her. His job at Anheuser-Busch got kind of stressful. I kind of knew that he would have a heart attack, and he did—that's what killed him. They both died at sixty. They didn't handle it well."

Bill Thomas's parents had planned on purchasing a home in Annapolis and retiring there, near his father and Cathy's alma mater.

"I knew they moved out of the house sooner than planned. Looking back at it now, I'm sure that was just a reminder for them … with Cathy's room there left just as she left it."

Bill adds, "Our mother Evelyn—after losing her youngest child, her only daughter, her best friend Cathy—died at age seventy-five never knowing who had killed her daughter. Mom was never the same after Cathy died."

Ginny Dowski Minarik remembers the impact on Rebecca's mother.

"Mom lived in Poughkeepsie. Sadly Becky's death just tore her up. She ended up selling the house in Poughkeepsie—obviously it was too big. For a short time she lived with Bob's younger sister, just under him, Karen, in the Carolinas," said Ginny. "Sadly she developed some dementia and heart issues and passed away about a year and a half ago … never knowing what happened to Beck."

Some parents found an inner strength to prevail despite the loss. Susan Scott recalls the impact on the Hailey family.

"It was hard on her parents. I'm really surprised that it hasn't taken more of a toll. They kept the house for so long, kept the candle lit … always holding out hope," said Susan. "Especially when you hear the stories of people found ten years later. Like the three girls that were found in the room in Cleveland. You think about that, you think about it."

The torch of remembrance for the families began to shift from the parents to the next generation. The siblings of the victims were now shouldering the burden. Some do it as a means of filtering who gets to the parents. Others have discovered themselves to be thrust into the role of the spokesperson for their family when it comes to the murders.

And each anniversary it resurfaces—especially those in five-year increments—the reporters and film crews arrive and ask for the memories of the murders, ask the families to lay bare their loss. It is a solemn responsibility. The brothers and sisters have walked a tightrope between ensuring that the story does not fall from the press entirely, while having to try and shield the pain of their loss.

For the families, they felt alone. As new officers took over the cold case files, they would reach out to them and try and forge relationships. "For a long time it was a revolving door in terms of agents handling the case for the FBI," Bill Thomas said. "We would get one for a while; they would move on, we'd get someone else."

For investigators it was almost as daunting to jump into the cases. Doc Lyons remembers when he took on the Phelps-Lauer case.

"The case file on just these murders was fifteen to twenty files full and is hard to read. It's *War and Peace* times four. I got involved in 2004," Lyons said. "I'd had some luck working murder/suicides. My success was on cold cases. I solved one that was seventeen years old and another that was twenty-two. It was the first no-body conviction in the state. The Dempsy case. I went out and we found the bridge of her [teeth]. That was all we found. One was a hit and run, over twenty years earlier." He pauses momentarily. "I told Rosanna I would solve this before I left. I let her down."

Help started coming in from unexpected sources. John Morse of John Morse Investigations, a private investigation firm in Virginia, reached out to Bill Thomas and offered his resources, free of charge, to the Colonial Parkway victims to explore their cases, "Because I thought we might be able to help," Morse said.

It was countless hours of work, but Morse proved to be an asset to the families—often unearthing new information that was passed onto the authorities.

Engaging with John Morse you get a perspective of a fresh set of eyes that looked at all of the murders, regardless of jurisdiction. He was not burdened with the theories that had been pursued by authorities in the past. Some of what he uncovered is remarkable. But like others, he struggles with seeing all eight murders/disappearances as being done by the same killer.

"I don't think these cases are connected. I'll stop short of saying it was bad police work—it certainly was shoddy work on their parts," Morse said.

"To me the one case that stood out as not being part of this was Phelps-Lauer. There was significant distinguishing behaviors that we saw in that case. This was the only case where robbery seemed to be tied to it. There was a sign of remorse with the covering of the bodies—that is usually an indication of someone that had guilt associated with what they did … not a total stranger. He [the killer] knew them."

Morse, working from memory, indicates that the person that the authorities should be considering is Joe Godsey.

"If my memory is right Daniel Lauer had between $600 and $800 on him from his mom and dad. Godsey knew he was coming into that money. Now, if you were broke in the 1980s and suddenly had cash like that, what would you do? I think they were either out buying some pot to smoke or flip to make more money," said Morse.

Joe Godsey was one of a very small circle of people that knew that Daniel Lauer was about to be paid by his father. That group was only the Godseys, Daniel, Annamaria, Clinton Lauer, and the Lauer parents. The missing money points more to a murder for a robbery motive rather than a serial killing.

Morse's investigators discovered another vital connection. Godsey and another member of his family were connected to a hunt club in the same location where the bodies were found. This might have provided him familiarity with the area. While Morse was working from his memory and not his notes at the time (and hence is not quoted on this part of the interview) this information has been independently confirmed by two other sources.

When asked about the other cases, another that stands out with Morse is Call-Hailey.

"This is one where I can't connect the dots. I think they went to the parkway to make out or they were doing that elsewhere. Someone, in my mind, went out of their way to make this *look* like it was connected to Thomas-Dowski," said Morse. "Out of all of the cases this is the weakest because we simply lack the bodies. I believe they were dumped in the river."

On the Edwards-Knobling case, Morse found himself drawn into the same theory that the state police was pursuing.

"They either pulled off to get drugs or to make out. There's a lot of hearsay that there was a drug deal in the works. That spot there is well known for drug deals and sex.

"They were placed down and shot. The assumption is that she was shot first and David took off running, was shot in the shoulder, then in the head. They had no shoes on, they were in the vehicle. The shoes being off seems to be a thing if these cases are connected—the lack of shoes. It's probably a control thing. One officer told me that maybe they went out on the beach area to play around in the sand."

Morse's investigation was intriguing in the new angles— i.e. Joe Godsey—that were brought to the forefront. He still had a bigger role to play in the case ... but it would be a few years before that occurred.

* * * * *

In December 2009, twenty-three years after the murders of Cathy Thomas and Rebecca Dowski, the first of two blunders by the FBI in the case played out in the media. In 1992, Major Ron Montgomery of the York-Poquoson County Sheriff's Department sent one of his officers to the state medical examiner's office to collect some skeletal remains that were in evidence ... remains that had nothing whatsoever to do with the Colonial Parkway Murders. When that investigator came back and checked the material, he discovered that two small boxes containing the rape kits from Rebecca Dowski and Cathy Thomas had been sent back.

Montgomery secured the rape kits per protocol in the evidence room and contacted the FBI, both by fax and by phone, over a two-year period to try and return them to the bureau. In March of 1996, the FBI's response to Montgomery was that the kits should be destroyed. Frustrated that they were unwilling to take the kits back, Montgomery followed the FBI's request and the kits were incinerated. Word of it finally leaked out in 2009.

Neither Cathy nor Rebecca had any indication that they had been raped, so the swab samples may or may not have contained any DNA evidence. The initial testing of the rape kits had been done by the Virginia State Medical Examiner's office and had never been turned over to the FBI.

For the families of the victims it was not an endorsement for how their cases were being handled. While the technology for detailed DNA analysis did not exist when the samples were gathered in 1986, every year the technology advances. There was no way to know if the kits were subjected to analysis in 2009 what they might have revealed.

"There's no way to demonstrate the depth of my family's frustration with the Federal Bureau of Investigation," Bill Thomas told Mike Mather of WTKR. Per Mike Mather's report, Thomas had asked the FBI to fully disclose what evidence they had from his sister's case, but the bureau, per their long-standing policy, refused to do so.

The destruction of the evidence, useful or not, was the tip of the iceberg. It was about to be eclipsed by one man—Fred Lee Atwell.

Atwell was from the Hampton area—a Tidewater good ol' boy through and through. The Williamsburg resident never graduated high school, dropping out of school in the tenth grade. His first arrest was in North Carolina for burglary and larceny. Atwell broke into his uncle's house under the auspices of stealing some food. He was paroled from that charge after serving six months of a two- to six-year sentence.

Freedom didn't settle well with the young Atwell. Upon his return to Hampton he was prodded by an accomplice into stealing a television set and some stereo tape players. It had been a sting operation. "The police had a bug in the TV and they followed me and popped me." For his blunder he received a four-year sentence, and he was released early for good behavior.

Fred worked as a paid informant for several years before he became a deputy in Gloucester. He claimed that he was tempted by some former compatriots to take part in a robbery, but he turned them in. It was his turning point, where Fred claimed he was making the shift from the dark side of crime to the light side of justice.

Atwell obtained a job at the Gloucester County Sheriff's Office on February 2, 1981, despite his pair of felonies—having obtained a pardon by the Virginia governor so that he could at least own and carry a handgun as part of his duties. According to a newspaper report, "The State Criminal Justice Service Commission, which monitors police standards, turned up no instance of a person with a felony record working as a sworn officer." [18]

The fact that a former felon had been hired as a deputy might have raised flags, but Fred had instilled himself in the community. The then-thirty-two-year-old Atwell claimed that he had also served as an informant for the FBI, which may have bolstered his credibility. He also helped the ATF on two cases that led to convictions, convincing them in his early career that Fred was reformed from his criminal ways. As an officer working for a $9,600 salary, Atwell liked to brag that he had been shot at, threatened, and had even had a bomb attached to his car.

The *Newport News Times-Herald* ran an article questioning the legitimacy of the Gloucester County Sheriff's Department in hiring him. Atwell even offered to resign when the article came out, but Sheriff Ruben Emerson refused it. "I wish I had five or six more like him."

Why would anyone hire a failed, if not bumbling felon as a law enforcement officer?

John Morse offers his insight on the matter: "You have to remember that in the 1980s, the Gloucester and York sheriff's departments were all crooked. They were not mature but kind of backwater communities. Cronyism was prevalent. Most were involved with running drugs. Many turned a blind eye to crimes where it was in their interest. Atwell should have never made deputy in a sheriff's department."

After several years of being a deputy, Atwell left the Gloucester Sheriff's Department. For a short time, he made

18   Paust, Mathew, "Ex-felon shifts career to police work," *The Free Lance-Star*, May 21, 1981, page 6.

his living as a bounty hunter, also known as "fugitive recovery"—something he was not licensed to do. His involvement with the Colonial Parkway Murders began much later. Atwell, for reasons only he fully knows and comprehends, began to incorporate himself into the murders. He reached out to the victim's families and seemingly was launching his own private investigation.

Joyce Call recalls Fred dipping his toe into the cases.

"Yeah, he kind of inserted himself into the case. I knew who he was; everyone in the county knew who he was. My dad knew him. Actually my dad was friends with an old deputy whose name was John, and Fred was actually friends with John which was how we met him. … He just inserted himself into the families at that time."

Paula Meehan, Cassandra's sister, was confused by his involvement.

"I kept saying, 'Why is this guy so involved with this. He's not related to anybody.'"

Bill Thomas told *The Huffington Post*, "He always tried to insert himself into the investigation and into the families."

Atwell's private "investigation" into the parkway murders was vague at best.

"Fred would call me all the time, almost weekly, and talk for hours at a time, but in the end, I really didn't end up anywhere. I always felt like he was holding back, that he knew something but would not come out and just say it," Cathy's brother Bill Thomas said.

Atwell figured out ways to string the families along, Joyce Cal remembers.

"I think after I got used to him I thought he was a really strange character. And then sometimes I didn't like him, you know. I don't really think I could trust him. But he was always coming up … 'Oh I found out this. I just heard from so-and-so.'

"So I was 'What did you find out?' I just had to find out. 'What do you know now?'

"I don't know if he was making it up or did he really know something," Joyce said.

In 2009 Fred found himself at the center of the Colonial Parkway investigation, though not in the way he may have originally intended. Mike Mather a reporter for WTKR broke the story.

"It was one of those weird reporting moments ... where you get a call from somebody who had something he thought was valuable and had not been successful getting reporters to pay attention," said Mather. "I took a chance and met him in a parking lot. He handed me a CD which had a small little contact sheet on it, and as soon as I saw even the contact sheet I knew everything was absolutely legitimate."

The handing over of that CD would launch one of the strangest series of twists and turns related to the Colonial Parkway Murders and would draw Mike Mather into a firestorm of controversy.

"He was a Gloucester deputy for quite some time. Even after that positon he hung around and was closely associated with law enforcement—and that is a pretty broad term. There was a private investigation or guard-like agency that asked Fred to come teach a class on the Colonial Parkway Murders. Fred was a deputy in and around that timeframe—I don't know exact specifics of when.

"He declined because he said he did not work directly on the parkway. And the security company owner said 'I have some materials you could present. Could you look at them and see if you want to change your mind?' Basically here's some stuff that you could talk about.

"He gave to Fred a series of slides, and Fred recognized them for what they were and made copies of them. From what he tells me, he spent a considerable amount of time from that point on trying to convince the FBI, trying to have them investigate this or take it seriously. Now I will tell you, initially it seemed a little dubious. How could somebody call the FBI and say, 'I have slides from probably the most notorious series of unsolved crimes in maybe state history; you should come get them and do an investigation on it'? That was my initial thought. But in my next several months of dealing with the FBI, I became 100 percent convinced that what he was telling me was true."

Mather was intrigued with the concept that the crime scene photos were out in the public. Rather than just rely on Atwell's account, he engaged the FBI himself.

"It was interesting. I contacted the FBI for a contact. I don't know what was in their mind at any point, but their forward-facing line to me was that this was no big deal … these pictures have been out, it's not a big deal at all.

"'We're not particularly interested in them, who really cares? Must be a slow news day.'

"All of those things. That persisted for a while, and I did some research to see if these had been out there or anything like that had happened and I came up with no stories, blogs, anything that reveal this.

"As I told the FBI, 'With or without you, I'm going forward with the story,' their candor changed tremendously. It was going to be … I could be prosecuted. 'It would be improper to publish evidence from a crime.'

"It was a one-eighty from 'No big deal' to 'You had better not.' I had a rather lengthy almost aggravated conversation with some FBI folks in Norfolk.

"I hung up the phone. About twenty minutes later I had a call from Fred Atwell that the FBI was in touch with him … racing over to his house to get all of the remaining copies. So they went from extremely dismissive posture to flipping it around to this is a big deal and you could be in big trouble for moving forward."

Atwell distributed the CD with the horrific images to a number of media sources but none seemed interested in the story with the exception of Mike Mather who recognized the egregious breach of evidence handling and trust.

Atwell told WTKR, "I took them to the FBI and the state

police and nobody's done nothing."

He had been trying for a year to get law enforcement to act, and only then did he go to the press. The story of their loss of control of the evidence was a dark-mirror of the level of control that the murderer had demonstrated over the victims.

The release of the photos shattered any trust that law enforcement had with the families.

As Joyce Call told WTKR, "I was floored. I was in disbelief for a while."

What had been an annoyance they had disregarded had suddenly become a very public embarrassment for the FBI. To the families it was gut-wrenching. The FBI—the stewards of their case, the nation's top law enforcement agency—had let evidence out of their control related to their loved ones. For an agency that prides itself on precision, they were suddenly facing a public relations nightmare of the worst kind, with aggrieved family members taking to the press and airwaves to complain not only about the photos but about the lack of attention that the cases had been getting.

To many of the families, at the time, Fred Atwell was seen as having done something good. The parkway murders were in the news again, albeit for the wrong reasons.

For Atwell, however, his relationship with the FBI soured immediately. Someone inserting himself into the investigation—a local with a criminal record—appeared more suspicious than heroic. Atwell went from gadfly to person of interest.

Fred told Mike Mather in an interview in April of 2010, "I did not do, I had nothing to do with the parkway murders." He did concede, "The profile fits me. I am on the list."

He was hauled into the Norfolk office of the FBI and questioned. His notebook on the murders was confiscated. Most people would have kept a low profile, but Atwell kept going to the media which only put him under more scrutiny. Atwell told the media he was being targeted while the FBI was relatively close-mouthed about the matter.

The FBI had to mend bridges with the families—the cases were too high profile and their mistake too public to simply sweep under the rug. They essentially moved the case to the top of the tall pile of cold cases overnight. A full review of the murders they were responsible for was promised as well—with fresh sets of eyes looking at the evidence.

The Virginia State Police were less supportive in regards to the cases they were responsible for: Phelps-Lauer and Knobling-Edwards. While the FBI promised a top to bottom review, it took getting the press involved to finally get the state police to offer to do the same with their victims' families.

A reluctant but renewed sense of vigor and energy to solve the Colonial Parkway Murders kicked in. For the first time ever, at government expense, all of the families were brought together in the Williamsburg area. It was a welcome but awkward gathering. Some of the families had gotten together before, one-on-one, and had maintained remote contact via the phone and email. Now, for the first time, they were face-to-face. Their only connection to each other was a terrible string of tragedies and painful loss. The bureau provided packets regarding how they would be communicated with and what DNA testing could be done, and a candid discussion was held on how cold cases were handled and a commitment to stay engaged with the families of the victims. It was an attempt to mend the fence after the release of the photos, but with most of the survivors, it did little to change their confidence.

The families, in some cases, found themselves supporting the man that had brought so much focus to their cause, despite the FBI's focus on Fred.

Joyce Call-Canada told WTKR, "That's crazy, outrageous. Never in a million years. I know in my heart that Fred Atwell had nothing to do with it. I don't know why they would be spending any time on Fred Atwell. Unless the FBI is able to provide some credible information to my family about why they think Fred Atwell, an old friend of the Call family, would be involved in the Colonial Parkway Murders, this seems like a complete waste of time."

Bill Thomas offered the most popular perspective at the time, "This smacks of retribution."

Fred's response to being considered a suspect was simple.

"I didn't do it. They can come get my DNA any time they want it. I will be glad to give it to them. I don't have a problem with that. I have nothing to hide about the parkway. They have 132 suspects, so why don't they look at them instead of me?"

The bureau confiscated Fred's notebooks on the murders for review as well. It took the intervention of WTKR's investigative reporter to get the FBI to turn the books back over to Atwell three months later. While the FBI stated publicly they did not foresee Fred's arrest, it was also very clear they were keeping him on their radar.

In a normal set of murders, that would have been the end of the matter—but the parkway crimes proved once more to be the exception to the rule. Fred became involved with a fundraiser for the families of the victims. The intent was to raise money for rewards and to keep the story of their lost ones at the forefront in the media—and hopefully generate new leads for investigators.

Joyce Call remembers the raffle in December of 2010 with a mix of sorrow.

"We had some kind of a fundraiser at Pop's Drive-in," Joyce said. "He [Fred Atwell] brought the Corsica—that was supposed to be the car donated [for a raffle]."

Most of the families of the victims took part in the events, selling raffle tickets.

Atwell showed up at the event with a small vending trailer where he cooked food for attendees. He kept a large jar out for the "Colonial Parkway Victims Fund." Fred asked the Call family for the $270 for "DMV fees" for the vehicle.

To all parties involved it seemed as if nothing was out of the ordinary.

The raffle was held, and Fred himself drew the winning ticket. He called the phone number of the winner but did not immediately connect with him. The family members all wanted to make the awarding of the car a publicity event for the press, but Atwell was elusive. He claimed to have difficulties in connecting with the winner, and as time passed, suspicions began to grow.

According to Joyce Call, "We started getting a really funny feeling about it. I called the dealership, and they said, 'Yeah, we know Fred. He took a car on a test drive.'

"That's when I started getting a funny feeling about the way that he was acting. My aunt and I called up there. They said that it was a test drive, that car was not a gift."

John Morse got involved on behalf of the families as well, looking into the winner of the raffle. As it turned out, it was a relative of Atwell's. The families confronted Atwell, more in hopes of how to manage the expectations and the public's perspective.

"We didn't want it out in the press. We were trying to spare him from all of that. But he, with his big ego and everything else, told on himself. We were going to try and make it nice and quiet—the authorities could go over there and question him and let him tell them what was going on, what happened," Joyce Call-Canada said. "Well, he found out what we had done. He called Mike Mather himself at Channel 3, going on and on about this raffle. We were hoping to keep it hush-hush, do what the authorities were going to do to you, and keep it out of the newspapers. That's what we were hoping anyways. I just didn't want his name all plastered out there."

Atwell's on-the-air confession with Mike Mather was capped off when he then turned himself into York County authorities.

"I should have stopped it, but I didn't," Atwell said.

Initially the families tried to rally behind Fred, but as more information became available via John Morse, it was clear that was not the best course of action.

The money he took for the DMV fees from the victim's fund—Atwell openly admitted to Mike Mather that he pocketed it to reimburse himself. No comment was ever made about Atwell's tip jar and its contents. That act of cashing the check under false pretenses alone is a felony in the state of Virginia. More importantly the families had to cope with the taint that Fred had brought down on their cause. Rosanna Phelps Martin Sedivy recalls the embarrassment.

"We were all completely naive. It made me feel horrible that I had to look at these people that we had gotten money from and I feel like I did so many people wrong," Rosanna said.

Her brother Will Phelps added, "I feel ashamed."

John Morse is more pragmatic in his memory of the events.

"Fred's involvement in the car raffle thing is a classic move of ego for ego's sake. He's the kind of murderer that returns to the crime scene or the fireman that starts fires then puts them out," Morse said.

While he decried that the FBI was out to get him, Fred Atwell was his own worst-enemy.

Even while the raffle fraud was unraveling around him, Fred was attempting a new angle to potentially profit from the parkway victims.

In early 2010, Atwell contacted Bill Thomas under the pretense of working on behalf of "a foreign interest." This alleged interest claimed to know where the bodies of Keith Call and Cassandra Hailey were buried. For $20,000, Fred agreed to broker an arrangement with the mysterious party to get the remains recovered. He even provided Thomas with a map of the general area where the bodies were allegedly buried.

According to Thomas, "The whole thing didn't feel right.

I mean, we had a reward out there already … so why did he need the money? If he knew who had buried them, he should have just turned that name over to the police. Why ask for money?"

At best, to Thomas, it felt as if the Atwell was extorting money and using Keith and Cassandra's mortal remains as a bargaining chip. At worst, it was extortion from the families of the victims.

The effort seemed to further erode Fred's credibility with the families, if there was any left after the raffle scheme.

"We're still trying to deal with it. It's unexpected. We really felt he was on our side and then found out he was not," Jennifer Phelps, sister-in-law of Annamaria Phelps, told *The Huffington Post*.

Fred Atwell's long dark spiral was far from over. The self-inflicted pressures had to have been tremendous, and it was inevitable that something had to give. Fred separated from his wife. Facing felony charges in York County and strapped for funds, Atwell went to Roanoke, Virginia, where his daughter owned a house. By his own admission, Fred was living in the woods and had gotten into his daughter's empty property for shelter. He was in need of medicine that he could no longer afford as well.

In desperation, he turned to a financial advisor who was helping his wife, Wanda Sears, with the intent of robbing her. Atwell showed up at her place of work on August 30, 2011, with a pistol in what appears to be one of the most feebly executed armed robberies ever. Depending on the account, Fred either pointed the gun at her or at the ceiling, then coerced her to provide him with cash. Ms. Sears said the amount was only $60, while Atwell insisted it was $161. He had asked her to draft him a check for $1,000 but then realized he would have to cash the check, so he refused to take it. Both claimed that he did not threaten her, and Fred even said that on his departure, she gave him a hug. Fred asked her to go into the bathroom, unlocked, while he made his getaway.

Despite Ms. Sears not wanting to press charges, the State's attorney had little choice in the matter—a felony armed robbery had taken place. A warrant was issued for Atwell's arrest.

Fred fled to Georgia. He dyed his Santa-like white hair and beard to a jet black. For a long time he was living in the wild as a homeless person. At emotional rock-bottom, Fred allegedly contacted a suicide hotline and claimed that he wanted to be suicided by the police—shot by them as the means to end his life.

The Gwinnett County Sheriff's Department in Lawrence Georgia apprehended Fred at a Bass Pro Shop on September 1, 2011, and extradited him back to Roanoke to stand charges for robbery and the use or display of a firearm in the commission of a felony.

There was no rigorous defense mounted by Atwell as he pled guilty to all charges. He admitted in court that he had no idea why he had even come to Roanoke in the first place. The only point of contention that was raised was the amount of money taken—Fred claimed it was $100 more than what the victim said.

The Commonwealth's attorney even tried to downplay the crimes.

"I admit that this is an odd case. If you were talking about somebody going into a Holiday Inn or holding up a convenience store and holding up a person at gunpoint and taking the cash, I'd be asking for a lot of time here. However this was a robbery. He placed the lady under threat. She said later she was not afraid, but she did call the police. As he admits, he took the money at gunpoint. Regardless of the amount—she says it was $60 or $161—or if he had taken the $1,000 he asked for. It's still robbery."

Atwell's attorney did what he could to mitigate the damages, but it was the legal equivalent of Sisyphus pushing the boulder up the hill. The Commonwealth's attorney's request to the judge was three months under the minimum recommendation, but it was still a hefty sentence thanks to Virginia's rigid guidelines.

Atwell was sentenced to ten years, suspended after he served five years for the robbery, plus three years for use of a firearm.

In one of his parting comments to the judge, a contrite Atwell said, "I was wrong for what I'd done, and I've got to be punished for it."

His legal woes were far from over. The fraud trial in York County took place weeks later, and Fred pleaded guilty to the charges there. This piled on additional years to his sentence.

Mike Mather, who has spent a considerable time with Fred Atwell, was perplexed by Fred's final descent into crime.

"Of all of the mysteries of the Colonial Parkway, this is the one that is the hardest for me to grasp. I just don't really know how or why it happened," said Mather. "Fred shared with me an awful lot, and I believe 100 percent that he was under tremendous, tremendous pressure. I mean there were times that agents called him into a meeting and accused him of being the Colonial Parkway killer. He wore that."

Mather sees Atwell as a mix of hero and victim for his involvement in the case.

"He was very concerned about being under the pressure of being named as somebody. He came right out and said, 'Here's the meeting I was just in. I offered to take a lie detector test, and I didn't do it.'

"I had FBI agents telling me things like serial killers insert themselves into investigations—which is absolutely true."

Mather tries to put Atwell's actions into context.

"I really think he was—my opinion is unchanged—he was trying to do the right thing, trying to help these families. I think he did a tremendous service to these families, to justice. If anything moves forward and there are any suspects developed in the case, and the case is actually closed, it will be entirely due to his insertion into this case.

"I was convinced that the FBI, despite their rhetoric and talking points, were doing *nothing*, not moving forward not one inch on this case. I believe, but do not know, that Fred was so interested in helping these families and doing more for them, that he let that part of it get ahead of him," said Mather. "I believe 100 percent that his intention to raffle a car was legitimate and was bonafide. I think when it became apparent that it was not going to happen, he couldn't get a car donated or he couldn't parlay his work with the families into a donation from a car company, he literally did not know what to do next, and proceeded. Obviously that was a major mistake."

John Morse saw the impact of Fred's actions on the families and has his own questions about the man's motives.

"Think about this—why would he take off to Roanoke to try and rob a woman for $100? Fred was in law enforcement. He knows the ramifications of escalating like that. It is an extreme reaction to being called out on the raffle. It doesn't make sense," Morse said.

As Bill Thomas reflects, "I've always felt that Fred knows something about the cases ... but he seems hesitant to come out and say it."

Bill adds, "As bizarre as Atwell's involvement in the Colonial Parkway Murders was, we still owe him a debt of thanks for blowing the whistle on the FBI losing control of the crime scene photos. Without that scandal, the Colonial Parkway Murders investigation would have never moved forward."

Mike Mather concurs with Thomas's consensus, seeing Fred's role as crucial to the ongoing investigation.

"I've spent an extensive period of time with him, and he is quite a character. I will say, quite unequivocally, that the case would not be opened in any real sense without Fred

Atwell."

Doug Call sums it up best. "He stirred the pot for sure. I don't know. The crime's not solved—so it didn't help so much."

Whatever secrets Fred Atwell has, he is keeping them to himself. An attempt was made to engage him in prison but no response was forthcoming. Atwell remains in prison until 2020.

So what real influence and impact did Atwell have on the case? Well, most certainly, his release of the crime scene photographs was the impetus for the FBI to reopen the cases and start reviewing the evidence anew. Surely that is a positive. The other side of the coin is that Atwell tried to profit from the Colonial Parkway Murders at the expense of the families' reputations and emotions. For that crime, there is no low but certainly a moral cost.

At worst, Fred is a gadfly who poked into these crimes, inserting himself in an unproductive and clumsy manner. At best, he was a distraction for authorities. The hours spent cleaning up his mess and looking into his own background most certainly could have been better spent looking into other suspects.

Joyce Call poses the most nagging question regarding Fred Atwell that remains unresolved: "I wonder why he's so interested in it?"

* * * * *

In June of 2010, a former homicide detective with the Milwaukee Police Department, Steven Spingola, offered to come out and investigate the Colonial Parkway Murders. Spingola was not offering his services free of charge but was minimally charging the families for his week of time.

As Bill Thomas put it, "They managed their costs for

us—ate at Burger King, stayed at Motel 8—that kind of thing."

Spingola brought a fresh set of trained eyes to the cases, spending a week interviewing officers, family members, and anyone relating to the cases.

There were several things that Spingola made public as a result of his investigation.[19] His meetings with Fred Atwell provided new insights into Fred's own "research." According to Spingola, Fred believed that an associate of Liberty Security, Ron Little's company, was in attendance at the party that Keith and Cassandra attended before their disappearance. This is a claim refuted by Ron Montgomery, according to Fred. If that is indeed Atwell's contention, it is clear that his perspective was that Little was somehow connected to at least that murder.

A confidential tipster reached out to Mr. Spingola and said that he had seen Keith and Cassandra at a 7-Eleven in Tabb, off of Route 17, only a few blocks from the Hailey residence. If accurate, this sighting narrows down where the couple may have been intercepted.

In the Phelps-Lauer case, Spingola made two points of note. One, he criticized the search done by the authorities after Daniel's car was found at the rest area. He contends, correctly, that the authorities should have done a grid search centered on the car, for at least a mile. If they had done that, the remains of the two victims could have been discovered sooner, along with vital evidence and information that could have helped investigators.

The second revelation was a note, allegedly in Annamaria's handwriting, pointing to a meeting with a named person at a rest stop in a blue van. The note had been found by Annamaria's sister in-law Jennifer as part of the

---

19   Spingola, Steven, *Predators on the Parkway*. This digital paper, available on Amazon.com, is a twenty-nine-page summary of Spingola's investigation. While it lacks depth, it does provide a good document summarizing his findings.

investigation. It included a phone number, and in Spingola's mind, this might be a vital clue to a possible drug deal. The note was turned over the Virginia State Police.

The state police spokesperson Corinne Gellar said, "The note and the nature of the note was reviewed by police at the time of the murders. It didn't lead to any significant finds, and so the note is nothing new to the investigation."

Finally, one observation that Spingola said was critical was that the windows were partially down on three of the four vehicles of the victims. In two cases, the glove box was open. To him, this pointed to someone posing as a police officer or other authority figure, approaching the victims and asking for identification such as driver's registration.

The person that got the last word in on the Spingola investigation was Jewel Phelps. In an interview with the *Virginia Gazette*, she expressed disdain over the publishing of Spingola's report in book form without the family's input.

"That slimy no-good snake had no right to write things about the victims and make accusations when they can't stand up for themselves. I would have never given him that note if I knew he'd be using it to make money."

* * * * *

After the FBI's mishandling of the crime scene photographs, the families were understandably skeptical about their commitment. Agent A. J. Turner committed to light the proverbial fires on the case. Their first step, doubling the reward to $20,000.00 for information leading to an arrest on the Colonial Parkway Murders.

New detailed analysis found fingerprints and trace evidence that the FBI believed could be useful in the case. All reports from both the FBI and the state police were digitized, and they were going to use intelligence analysts to review the files.

Agent Turner told the victims' families that despite the absence of concrete evidence linking the cases, agents still believed that all eight deaths were the work of a serial killer or killers.

In 2012 the Call family planned a public hunt of the parkway by volunteers and trained search dogs. The intent was to comb some of the areas not covered by prior searches as well as once more bring the murders into the minds of the local citizens. The National Park Service declined the formal request, saying that they would allow it but would limit the searching group to fifteen.

Joyce Call told WTKR television, "There's more than fifteen family members!"

The search was halted before it even began—the victim of insensitive bureaucracy.

"One thing we don't want to do in a national park is interfere with the visitor experience," James Perry of the National Park Services said.

CHAPTER 20

Theories abound when it comes to the Colonial Parkway Murders. Some are fueled by rumors and social media, while others are often fed by inconsistent statements from authorities. Others grow because of wild things posted on the internet, a questionable source at its best. Any book on the murders has to address the theories, no matter how ridiculous they may seem, if only to put them in the spotlight and acknowledge their existence.

The Ron Little and Steve Blackmon Connection

The threads that connect Ron Little and his two companies—Liberty Security Services and Advanced Security and Investigation Services Inc.—to at least one of the parkway murders *does* exist. Bonnie Edwards did work for Liberty Security Services at one time. Atwell's accusation that one of the pair might have been at the party where Keith and Cassandra attended has never been validated by any source. Certainly men in their thirties would have stood out with the college-aged attendees. Even if Mrs. Edwards had worked for Liberty Security, that alone is not enough of a connection that would have led to the murder of her daughter.

John Morse, who investigated Little's viability as a suspect, came up dry.

"Little is a fantasy. Little was not much more than a glorified security guard working at a gas station/convenience store called Little Suzy Gas Station. He had a funny accent, and that seemed to make him appealing to a lot of women. He wasn't afraid to use his 'powers'—his accent—to lure in women. He and Blackmon saw themselves as Crockett and Tubbs from *Miami Vice*. Blackmon was definitely a bad cop," said Morse.

Steve Blackmon was indeed a bad cop. He was capable of killing, as he demonstrated later in life. There are many rumors of him being involved with illegal drug sales while a deputy, but those were not substantiated by actual charges. The fact that he had illegal drugs in his body when he committed murder years later certainly lends some substance (pun intended) to the rumors of drugs. Despite this—none of this points to Blackmon being a serial killer any more than Ron Little.

The person that made Ron Little a suspect was Ron Little. He went to the media to brag that he was a suspect—that he had been interviewed by the FBI. In some bizarre way, he must have seen that as a way to drum up business for his security company, though that is impossible to comprehend. His strange behavior certainly helps keep the light of suspicion on Little in the public's eyes.

The person that keeps Ron Little on the lips and minds of Tidewater residents is none other than Fred Atwell. According to one source, "Fred Atwell clearly had an ax to grind—he is the one that is constantly pointing the finger at Blackmon and Little. He always was trying to pin it on them."

Fred Atwell is a highly unreliable source given his track record with the parkway murders.

Was Little tied to the murders of Brian Craig Pettinger or Laura Ann Powell? Both of those cases have solid suspects that the authorities believe may be responsible for their deaths. The connections between these cases and Little's companies are much more tangible, but in the end, the authorities have good suspects identified—they merely lack the evidence to prove their cases conclusively.

Also, if the murders are, indeed, all connected, then Ron Little ceases to be a suspect in that he was deported back to New Zealand by the time of the last pair's killing.

Fred Atwell

It is impossible to *not* consider Fred Atwell as at least a solid person of interest in the parkway murders. This was a convicted felon that inserted himself into the investigation of a serial killing string. Why? He had no tangible connection to the victims or their families. Was it to attempt to wrestle from the families the status of the investigation to protect himself? Or was he merely a friendly neighbor that thought he might be able to help? There is not a lot of middle ground when it comes to Atwell's motivations.

Mike Mather is convinced that Fred had nothing to do with the murders.

"It would be beyond my comprehension for somebody that got away with this crime to do everything he could, twelve to fifteen years later, to bring attention *back* to himself. I never, never thought of that."

The point is well taken. Atwell's machinations only drew more attention to the case, and in some way, positively.

John Morse, who looked into Fred's involvements for the families, has a different feeling.

"My gut tells me that Atwell has something to do with Call-Hailey. Not so much the others, but with Call-Hailey. I think he either was directly involved or was involved with the cover-up [the abandoning of the vehicle]."

Guilt certainly would be a powerful motivator for someone to engage with the families, but Morse is quick to point out that he doesn't have any solid evidence to support his theory.

Joyce Call reflects on Atwell's involvement skeptically.

"I think Fred has issues—no doubt about that. He helped us in one way but hurt us in another. At least he got it back out there. He was really the reason that it got back out there. He started talking about the crime scene photos and all of that. I have to give him credit for that. He was non-stop for a while. I just wish he had been honest about the raffle thing. There was no real reason for that. He was trying real hard. I don't know if it just got the best of him or what."

Karl Knobling's view of Fred Atwell is probably the most pragmatic and blunt.

"That guy was a kook—he wanted to be a cop—that was his deal. Jail is a good place for him."

In a set of cases where quirky people seem drawn to, Fred Atwell is certainly one of the leaders of that pack. He is a man that is many things, right now, an imprisoned felon. That does not make him a serial killer or someone capable of such acts.

The Killer is a Police Officer

Regardless of whether you believe these cases are the work of a serial killer or killers or merely pairs of crimes—one thing can be agreed upon: the killer exerted control. Each of these cases has the hallmark of a person or persons that controlled their intended victims. He was able to separate the victims from their vehicles, restrain them in at least one case, and kill them without being spotted by witnesses.

From an early point, the Colonial Parkway Murders task force said that an authority figure may be involved. That does not necessarily mean a law enforcement officer, but someone that was impersonating someone that could gain physical influence over the victims. Authority could be a badge, flashing lights, or even a stern voice.

Danny Plott of the state police cuts to the chase. "If you have a gun, yes, you're the authority, you can control a group."

Teri Hailey, Cassandra's sister, is one of many that believe a rogue police officer may be the killer.

"I'm *convinced* it is law enforcement. I'm convinced. Back then anybody could buy an old police car. They would leave the spotlight on it. They may remove the wiring, I don't know, but you can put the wiring back in it. You could buy red lights because it was just red lights back then."

There were many sightings of false police in the

Tidewater area, but there's no way to determine if that was a statistical anomaly or if it was a sense of paranoia on the part of the citizens and heightened coverage by the media because of the murders. All the Colonial Parkway Murderer needed was the *impression* that he was a police officer.

If it was a law enforcement official, it would explain how he has not been captured. With inside information on the investigation, a killer-officer might be able to easily cover his tracks.

There are a lot of law enforcement agencies in the Tidewater—nearly twenty if you include the cities, towns, sheriff's departments, state police, NPS, FBI, NCIS, and other law enforcement agencies. A killer-cop could have come from any of these. If it is a police officer, which one?

The Killing Sites Have Nothing in Common so the Cases are Unlikely to be Connected

To the casual observer—with the exception of the two cases tied to the Colonial Parkway—the sites for the murders have nothing in common. Ragged Island is a park on the James River, more swamp than anything else. The murder site in New Kent County was on a deserted logging road. When you compare these to the pair of crimes linked to the parkway, there doesn't seem to be any correlation.

That isn't necessarily the case. Having walked the sites and comparing them with photographs from the period, there are some similarities that could tie to a single killer or pair of murderers. When you look at the Colonial Parkway, it is a narrow strip of road with very few exits and entrances. There were no access points in close proximity to where Keith Call's and Cathy Thomas's cars were found, though Call's car was closest to an entrance—less than a mile. At night, some of the gates are closed and locked, further limiting access.

The parkway is a funnel, a narrow corridor for the killer to operate in. There was no place for his victims to flee if they wanted to. On one side was the York River, the other side was brush and bramble. The victims, if they ever were on the parkway alive, were trapped physically by the characteristics of the terrain. The limited access meant that a killer would have few intrusions or interruptions.

When you go to Ragged Island, even with the changes in recent years, there are still only two ways to get to the water. One is a narrow roadway running parallel to Route 17. On one side is a fence; on the other side is a swamp. The roadway ends at the water. The other is the boardwalk path out to the area where the bodies were found. Three feet on either side of this is swamp. As with the pair of murders on the parkway, Ragged Island provides a physical channel where the killer had complete control of his victims, regardless of which path you choose.

In the New Kent County murder location along the logging road, it is as it was at the time, heavily wooded on either side of the trail. There was only one way in, just like at Ragged Island, and that was where the killer was. The victims had nowhere to run. It was a confining strip of openness in the darkness. To the right and left there were trees and brush and the unknown.

There's also the aspect of the trees themselves. At all of these sites, the trees form a tunnel over the roadway. The parkway, the logging trail, and the trails at Ragged Island are framed by trees both then and now.

Is it possible that the murderer chose these locations subliminally because of this similarity? From a behavioral perspective, that cannot be ruled out. It is possible that the killer was attempting to recreate his experience from the first murders of Cathy Thomas and Rebecca Dowski. Serial killers do that—an attempt to recreate the rush they experienced from previous killings. The psychological effect of the locations chosen for these crimes could very well be linked.

The Calendar Connection

Is there a pattern in the dates of the murders? The Thomas-Dowski murders took place on or about October 9-10, 1986; Knobling-Edwards on September 21, 1987; Call-Hailey on April 10, 1988; and Phelps-Lauer on September 5, 1989.

The following table shows the number of days between the killings:

Dates of Killings	Days Between Killings
October 9, 1986	NA
September 21, 1987	347
April 10, 1988	202
September 5, 1989	513

At first glimpse, this does not offer any sort of discernable pattern. One thing that can be noted is that the killer did not strike in the winter or the summer—only performing the crimes in the spring and autumn. That doesn't mean the killer was not hunting potential prey during those periods of time—only that he did not commit murders during that window. As Larry McCann has pointed out numerous times, these killers, if they are a pair, are very selective in picking their victims. There would be numerous dry runs where potential victims would have been confronted by the killer and let go, never realizing just how close they had come to being slain.

The dates do provide two possible theories. One is that the killer could have been a William and Mary college student. The Thomas-Dowski killings took place right before fall break. The murders of Knobling-Edwards took place on a weekend when classes were not in session; the same with the disappearances of Call-Hailey. The final pair of murders, Phelps-Lauer, took place on Labor Day weekend when classes were not in session. A check of student handbooks shows that these dates align to the campus calendars.

Furthermore all of the murders took place in a four-year period—the same typical length of time that a student attends college. Was the Colonial Parkway Murderer a college student who used his downtime for a thrill-killing? When he graduated, he simply moved on to other cities, or if they were a pair, they split up and the killings subsequently stopped.[20]

Another possible theory is that the killer was a federal employee. The Thomas-Dowski murders took place over a Columbus Day holiday weekend, when it would have been common for a federal employee to take an extra day off. With two of the murders on weekends, a local federal employee could have committed those—Knobling-Edwards and Call-Hailey. Likewise, the Phelps-Lauer case took place on Labor Day weekend, a time when federal employees are off. While Labor Day is a common holiday where people get time off, Columbus Day is not—with banks and the federal government tending to be the largest observers. Adding to this, if the murderer was a federal employee, striking when he did ensured that there would be few employees in the office if they were working—providing him with more freedom of action without detection.

On holidays, law enforcement often changes its patrol patterns to accommodate tourists or those taking the days off. This change of pattern could be something that the murderer took advantage of.

The Tidewater region employs thousands of federal employees even today in the area. The US Navy has a substantial port in Norfolk, employing many civilian and military employees, same with Langley Air Force Base and, at the time, Forts Monroe and Eustis for the army. Is it conceivable that our killer was a federal employee? It most

20   While it is tempting to claim credit for this theory, it was proffered by our researcher, Jean Armstrong—and its validity checked with the help of the College of William and Mary's library team.

certainly is possible. The killer tended to strike when he didn't have to be at work, someone who was conscientious to a fault.

Michael Andrew Nicholaou

Private investigator Lynn-Marie Carty out of St. Petersburg, Florida, believes that the Colonial Parkway Murders were part of a string of unsolved serial killings all related to Michael Andrew Nicholaou.

Separating the facts from the theory is tricky with Michael Nicholaou. He is a murderer; he killed his wife and step-daughter, then turned the gun on himself on New Year's Eve 2005. There is little doubt that he was a violent man, allegedly accused of strafing and killing civilians in Vietnam during his service there in October 1970. According to records that Carty has obtained, it is likely he suffered from post-traumatic stress disorder as well. His first common-law wife, Michelle, disappeared in 1988 from Holyoke, Massachusetts; her fate has yet to be determined. According to Carty he is the likely suspect in her demise. To say that Michael Nicholaou was a dangerous person who was no stranger to violence is safe ground to stand on.

The twist that led him to be considered a serial killer came from a deathbed confession. When Gary Westover made a dying statement to his uncle, Howard Minnon, a retired sheriff's deputy in Grafton County, New Hampshire, he stunned his family. Westover was paralyzed and he told his uncle that three men picked him up for a night of partying years earlier. Westover went on to say that the three men had picked up a young woman, kidnapped her, and killed her—dumping the body off of a back road. Minnon wrote down the names of the three men on a scrap of paper.

There had been a string of serial murders at the time, dubbed by the media as the Connecticut River Valley Murders and the thought was that the three mystery men may have committed one or more of those crimes. Minnon took the names to the police, but they did not appear to take action on them. After Minnon's death, his wife contacted the sister of one of the victims saying that she feared that Westover may have been describing the death of Barbara Agnew, who had been killed on January 10, 1987.

Lynn-Marie Carty's involvement came as she was attempting to investigate a person that Michael Nicholaou may have killed. Carty attempted to determine whether it was possible that one of the names on the list that Howard Minnon provided authorities was that of Nicholaou, but ran into a dead end—common with cold cases. Authorities would not release the information. Howard Minnon's wife said that his name was familiar to one of those named in Westover's confession. He did live in the area at the time, and Carty speculated that he may have met the other accomplices mentioned in the confession at a veteran's hospital. She even speculated that Barbara Agnew might have been lured into pulling into a rest area by the crippled Westover in a wheelchair, human bait for their victim. Her evidence of this was merely a working theory however.

Carty contacted a survivor of a stabbing attack believed to be related to the Connecticut River Valley Murders and said that the person identified Michael Nicholaou as the killer. For authorities, however, it must not have been enough to tie Nicholaou to the crimes.

Lynn-Marie Carty began a one-person crusade to link Nicholaou to other unsolved crimes. For a time he lived in Charlottesville, Virginia, operating a pornography store. There was a pair of rapes in the Blue Ridge Parkway at Big Spy Overlook. The convicted killer, Edward Honaker, was later freed due to DNA testing. Pictures of Nicholaou do appear similar to that of the rapist. Carty contacted the authorities and the press to make her case.

Carty also believes that Nicholaou could be the Colonial Parkway Murderer. According to her, Nicholaou traveled often between Virginia and New England. According to her research, he and his first wife moved back to Virginia in October of 1986. Nicholaou allegedly did not like lesbians and may have reacted in a rage at seeing Cathy Thomas with Rebecca Dowski. Further, she claims that Nicholaou had previously burned a car—and the Colonial Parkway Murderer had tried to set Cathy Thomas's car on fire.

If she is correct, Carty may have uncovered a serial killer that murdered up and down the East Coast.

There are some facts that need to be highlighted. If one examines the Connecticut River Valley Murders, they occurred on the following dates (below). Overlaid are the Colonial Parkway Murders as well.

October 24, 1978   Cathy Millican (stabbed twenty-nine times)

July 25, 1981   Mary Elizabeth Critchley (unable to determine cause of death)

May 30, 1984   Bernice Courtemanche (stabbed to death)

July 20, 1984   Ellen Fried (stabbing wounds and possible sexual assault)

July 10, 1985   Eva Morse (stabbing wounds and possible sexual assault)

April 15, 1986   Lynda Moore (stabbed)

October 9, 1986   **Thomas-Dowski**

January 10, 1987   Barbara Agnew (stabbed)

September 22, 1987   **Knobling-Edwards**

April 9, 1988   **Call-Hailey**

August 6, 1988   Jane Boroski (survived her attack, stabbed twenty-seven times)

September 5, 1989   **Phelps-Lauer**

The days show that it would have been possible for the same killer to have committed these crimes, time-wise, but we have to look at what we know about the Colonial Parkway Murderer—assuming it is one or two men and they are responsible for all of the crimes.

First, why would the pattern of killing in pairs only be in Virginia? Why would geography determine how many people he killed at one time?

Second, the Connecticut River Valley Murderer utilized a knife and excessive overkill. While some elements of that are present with Thomas-Dowski, the same cannot be said of the other victims. Also, the murderer in Knobling-Edwards utilized a gun to commit the crimes—which further does not fit the pattern of the Connecticut River Valley Murderer.

In three cases, the Colonial Parkway Murderer staged the vehicles for apparent easy theft. That trademark signature was not demonstrated in the Connecticut River Valley Murderer's pattern.

Sexual assault was part of the pattern in the Connecticut River Valley killings. We do not know if the killer was responsible for any sexual assaults in the Colonial Parkway cases. We know that Robin Edwards had evidence of intercourse—but we don't know with whom. We have no such evidence in the case of Cassandra Hailey or Annamaria Phelps. None was evident with either Cathy Thomas or Rebecca Dowski.

Finally, the Colonial Parkway Murderer committed his horrific crimes in areas where he had intimate knowledge of the terrain. Carty's own research showed that Michael Nicholaou moved to Virginia in October of 1986. He would have had, at best, nine days to stake out where he would be committing his first crime, assuming he moved in on the first of October 1986. His home in Charlottesville is almost two hours away, depending on traffic. How would he have known about the logging trail for the Phelps-Lauer murder or the isolation of Ragged Island for the Knobling-Edwards crime? The short answer is he wouldn't.

When you research Michael Nicholaou there is a pattern and thread that does connect him to those crimes. That thread is Lynn-Marie Carty. Armed with a potent theory, she is able to put Nicholaou in position to have possibly committed these and other crimes. She has doggedly pursued to test his DNA, and in 2009, under prodding by reporter Mike Mather, the FBI did agree to test Nicholaou's DNA in conjunction with the Colonial Parkway Murders investigation. In every case or article where Nicholaou is implicated in crimes other than the death of his wife and stepdaughter, Carty is identified as the person that drew the link. Either she is a genius that can solve countless unsolved crimes or has little more than a theory based solely on circumstantial hearsay. Only time will tell.

Michael Nicholaou was certainly an unsavory character, a murderer, and doer of other possibly terrible things. He has not been named as the killer in the Connecticut River Valley Murders, the Colonial Parkway Murders, or any additional crimes yet.

The Godsey Tip

During a fundraiser tied to the Colonial Parkway victims, Jennifer Phelps, sister in-law of Annamaria Phelps, was having a meal at a local restaurant and the waitress noticed the posters she had for the parkway murders. This waitress commented that she didn't know that the cases were still unsolved. She commented that she had heard of a rumor that Joe Godsey and a friend named Willy had left the night of the murders, after being dropped off at Godsey's trailer. When they came home they had some feathers with them— identical to those found on the roach clip in Daniel's car. She wasn't sure, but blood might have been involved.

The tip was turned over to the Virginia State Police and was investigated … our own interviews, while off the record, confirmed that. Joe Godsey's location immediately after the murders has never been fully confirmed either—allegedly he disappeared for a few days.

Our own interview with Godsey was short but revealing. When asked about Daniel Lauer's relationship to Christina Sotos, Godsey said, "He did get involved until I intervened and put an end to it. She was a cute little girl. She was turning fifteen, and he was turning nineteen. I told him you don't want to get involved with that—you'll end up in jail. I hold him 'Stay here!' I made him stay at my place. She finally left the county. She was a cute girl."

That is inconsistent with interviews given by the Lauer family at the time of his disappearance and with the scant court records that can be found on the case.[21] As such, what Joe Godsey said was a lie. Why would he lie about something as simple and inconsequential as that?

Our own interview with Joe Godsey was a bit of a confusing jumble. Joe's memories of that night are vague at best.

"All they talked about in the trip home was about Daniel moving in with Anna and Clint. I think Anna was more into Daniel than she was Clinton. ... They dropped us off. They ate some sandwiches. I remember my wife and I making them some sandwiches before they headed off to drop off Anna," Godsey said.

Joe Godsey recalls another aspect that calls his memories into question: "I do remember that Anna called Clinton from my place, said that she was leaving our house and that Daniel was moving in. I remember her making that call right before she left."

If Daniel had only made the decision to move in on the trip back (hence the phone call to Clinton) then why was Annamaria in the car? She would have not had a way back to Virginia Beach if Daniel had not already made up his mind. At best it is a suspicious inconsistency in Joe Godsey's

---

21   The records of Daniel's case were sealed by the court.

account of the night. At worst, it is a lie designed to deceive.

When asked as to whom we should take a look into in regards to the case, his answer is even more bizarre.

"You need to check out his brother. He don't look right—that fella. I never really liked Clint."

The state police long ago removed Clint as a person of interest. He had zero motive and no means to have committed the crime. Clint Lauer is a double victim in this crime—having lost his would-be fiancé and his brother in the same horrific act. For Godsey to implicate Clint Lauer, a collateral *victim*, is eerie and cold, to say the very least.

Joe also admitted that he knew Daniel Lauer was going to be paid that night.

"He was going to get paid for some painting from his dad, Henry."

Was it possible that Joe Godsey and an accomplice arranged to rendezvous with Daniel Lauer and Annamaria Phelps, perhaps under the pretense of a drug deal—then killed them both as the result of a horrible robbery gone astray? Godsey said that Annamaria was a flirt that weekend … was his purpose even more nefarious?

Attempts were made to engage with his former wife, but she did not respond, even to recount what had happened that weekend and what she remembered. This cannot be construed as anything, but one would think someone would be willing to talk about this case after nearly thirty years.

John Morse, who investigated the case extensively, offered this off-the-cuff comment: "I have always thought that guy that rode back with them was responsible for their deaths. There is something in the way he has led his life that points to someone that is struggling with a lot of internal demons."

If Joe Godsey was involved, he refused to admit it. If he was, his last comment on the matter was the most chilling: "Daniel's death is a thorn in my head."

There is No Pattern so These Cases are Not Connected

People want order, structure, and—thanks to television—solid tangible physical evidence, in order to see connections. That is not how behavioral sciences work however. This is about the mind of the murderer, not hard-earned physical evidence linking them.

For those seeking a pattern, here it is in summary form, not repeating some of the other elements already outlined in this chapter:

- The killer always struck at young people, the oldest being twenty-seven-year-old Cathy Thomas. After the first pair of killings, he seemed to concentrate on younger victims, perhaps because we know Thomas resisted.
- The killer struck at night. None of the killings were done in daylight.
- The murderer staked out where the crimes were committed. These locations were not random. Part of the success of this killer was the locales that were chosen. Isolation was the killer's ally.
- The Colonial Parkway Murderer exerted control early on in the encounters with the victims. The removal of shoes, stripping the victims naked, etc., all pointed to someone who sought maximum control of his quarry.
- In three of the four cases, control was lost. Cathleen Thomas had a defensive knife wound on her hand. David Knobling was shot twice, presumably when he tried to get away. Annamaria Phelps had a defensive knife wound on one of her fingers. This means that the victims felt they had a chance to get away, that control was lost. If nothing else, this loss of control points to a single killer rather than a pair. With a pair of killers, it would have been much easier to maintain control of the victims.
- The murderer killed in pairs. There have been other murders of couples, but none that could be linked to the Colonial Parkway Murders either time-wise or pattern-wise.

- The murderer possessed multiple ways to inflict death on his victims. A revolver was used in the Edwards-Knobling case, knives in Thomas-Dowski and Phelps-Lauer. We do not know what was used in Call-Hailey. In Thomas-Dowski, the killer brought accelerant (diesel fuel), matches, and rope. While the original profile for the FBI of the killer indicated that these were implements that were handy, it is also possible that this murderer had a "killing kit" he took with him to commit the crimes. He clearly was prepared for numerous contingencies.
- After the Thomas-Dowski crime, the murderer took measures to separate the victims from their vehicle. The most successful of these was Keith and Cassandra, whose remains have yet to be found. Separating the victims from their vehicles is risky, but it has led to vital evidence not being collected sooner in three of the cases. It is possible that the killer learned his lesson from the first murder and subsequently altered his pattern with the following deaths.
- Killers leave calling cards, and in the Colonial Parkway Murders it is the staging of the vehicle. Except for the first murder, all three subsequent crimes left the vehicles with the keys poised to be stolen. In the case of David Knobling, we know that the vehicle was staged by the killer because the key was turned to Accessories to play the radio—and David and his brother had wired the truck so that was not necessary. The killer didn't know that. David always backed into a parking space—suggesting that the vehicle was driven or repositioned by the killer.

People often try and combine other murders in the area with the four pairs related to the Colonial Parkway cases. There is a reason law enforcement does not lump those murders in. Part of it is those crimes don't fit the pattern. Part of it is that not everyone in law enforcement believes that the cases are connected.

CHAPTER 21:

There are unknowns with almost any murder case, things that don't make sense even with a confession. The Colonial Parkway Murders have more than their share because of the sheer number of victims and the diversity of locations.

It is perfectly natural to want to know what really happened in the victims' final minutes, no matter how frightening and gory those details might be. Our imaginations give us far worse than the reality … at least that is the hope. We want David Knobling to be brave right up to the end. We hope that Annamaria Phelps fought back hard and hurt her assailant. In our minds we can picture these things, and they are best left there, in the dark places where such thoughts reside.

Beyond the basics of each crime, the who-done-it, there are a few things that stand out as unresolved. They are the mysteries of the Colonial Parkway Murders.

Where were Cathy Thomas and Becky Dowski Killed?

While there is no disagreement as to where their bodies were found, the mystery as to where Cathy Thomas and Rebecca Dowski were murdered is unknown. On Thursday, October 9, 1986, the night of their disappearance, there was a brief light rainstorm which might have served to obscure the murder site. The assumption most law enforcement has is that they were killed somewhere on the parkway, not at the pull-out where they were found.

The murderer would have needed a site where he could have tied up the victims and cut their throats then loaded their bodies into Cathy's Honda to dispose of them. All of this would have taken time—time a killer would want to have with some degree of isolation.

The Ringold Plantation site is the nearest parking area

that was open at the time, where someone could have pulled off for an extended period of time without line of sight to the road. Now long closed and overgrown with the remnants of picnic tables and trash containers poking through the brush, this site was off of the parkway by some fifty feet, obscured from passing traffic by trees and brush. There are other such places, but Ringold is less than a mile from where their bodies were discovered.

Of course, it is entirely possible they were killed off of the parkway and merely brought there to be disposed of.

In the last decade or so, local man David Cordle has proffered an alternative. Cordle claims he was working at the Defense Mapping Agency, returning from a meeting in Northern Virginia on Friday, October 10, 1986, driving through a line of thunderstorms in Manassas, Virginia, along the way. He was at the other end of the parkway, along the James River, when he pulled off to urinate at kilometer post 27 at a parking area that is no longer on the maps. He claims to have seen an early model white Honda. There were two people inside, both unmoving. The driver was a woman with dirty blonde—dishwater blonde—hair. It was twilight, and Cordle never got a look at the face of the driver.

If true, Cordle's sighting means that the killer murdered Becky and Cathy where he saw the bodies, then came back during that weekend, *before* Sunday, and moved them most of the length of the parkway to try and dispose of them on, presumably, Saturday night. It also means that Mr. Cordle may very well have inadvertently discovered where Becky and Cathy had been killed.

There are some issues with Mr. Cordle's recollection that are not easy to resolve. Checks of weather history sites and of local newspapers do not report a thunderstorm in Manassas that weekend—but on the Friday before, October 3. Neither victim had hair that could be described as blonde. Cathy Thomas, who would have been in the driver's seat, had bright red hair—not easily confused, even in twilight, with blonde hair.

Then there's the issue of blood. There were no concentrations of blood in the driver's seat area. The only place where that exists for either victim is in the back seat, (Becky) and in the hatchback (Cathy). If they were killed and left in the front seat, in their condition, there would have been more blood in the front of the car than in the back.

Finally there's rigor mortis. If the bodies had been left there for an extended period of time, rigor mortis would have set in, usually eight to twelve hours. If they were moved after that, they likely would have remained rigid. That wasn't the case when they were found. The fact that they were laid in the car the way they were long enough for rigor mortis to set in means they were likely in the car in those positions many hours prior to being discovered on Sunday, October 12.

Unfortunately Mr. Cordle's observation does not add to the narrative. The presumption has always been that the pair was killed elsewhere. Where that was is useful if evidence can be recovered from there, or, if confirmed, other observations can be made—such as the killer handling the bodies or the vehicle the murderer drove was identified.

It is possible that Mr. Cordle got the weekend wrong, and that the women in the car were not dead. If it was, indeed, Cathy Thomas's car, it could be where she and Becky parked a week later when they met their fate. That would be useful, because it would tell investigators that the killer then drove them almost the entire length of the parkway to dispose of his victim's remains. In that respect, Cordle's observations may be of use.

The time window for the Thomas-Dowski murders is disturbing and a mystery all of itself, tied into where they were killed. They were last seen on Thursday evening, October 9. They were not found until Sunday evening, October 12. Was the Honda there that entire time, nose down the embankment hovering over the York River precariously? Why wasn't it seen earlier?

First, it was not a weekend for recreational boating so sightings from the river would have been limited. Also it was a slow period for the Colonial Parkway from a tourist perspective. The cold night air and chill would have limited people from pulling into that pull-out. And there very well may have been sightings of the car earlier that went unreported.

Chris Call, Keith's brother years later recalls, "Ironically I had some friends at William and Mary—actually the Virginia Institute of Marine Science at Gloucester Point which is part of William and Mary. They were out on the boat that day, and they saw their car almost in the water. … It had been pushed down the ledge like they were trying to get it into the water. They remember seeing that car that day. It is so ironic. It came up in conversation, and it was kind of weird. I didn't know the family at the time, but we knew all about that case."

It is entirely likely that people saw the car poised over the river and simply never bothered to call it in.

Do Any of These Crimes or Victims Stand Out More than Another?

The two victims at the extremes of this stand out the most. When you look at all of the victims, Cathy Thomas was the oldest. She had graduated college and was well on her way in life. Most of the other victims were much younger. Being twenty-seven years old, she seems to stand out, not because of importance but because she doesn't fit the mold of the other victims.

Her seniority and being one of the first pair of victims is enough to merit some attention. Was she a target for some reason with the killer? That can only be resolved when the killer is apprehended.

Robin Edwards's death stands out because of her youth— she was only fourteen years old. While Robin physically was young, she was much older from a maturity standpoint.

The killer may not have realized her true age until the press covered the case.

In terms of crimes that stand out, Call-Hailey is one that merits the most attention because of what is missing—the mortal remains of the victims. The lack of bodies severely cut the amount of evidence that could be gathered from that crime scene. We do not know how they met their fate, nor do we know where they were murdered. We do know that neither of them would have gone to the parkway, regardless of what investigators believe. Their first date was not passionate but more social.

Where Keith and Cassandra were intercepted by their killer is a tangent of this. If they were not confronted by their killers on the parkway, it had to be somewhere else. Where that took place is a critical piece of missing evidence. It might tell us what the killer's vehicle looks like, and it might tell us where their remains are located.

With the other murders, there is a possible reason for them to be where they were. Stopping at a rest area on I-64 could have been nothing more than answering the call of nature. Parking at Ragged Island was not out of the norm ... David Knobling knew that location well. Cathy and Becky parking along the Colonial Parkway was not something that was out of the norm. In Keith and Cassandra's case, however, many of the known facts don't fit their personalities or their relationship. Until the killer is caught, their names are intertwined forever.

Have the Police Mishandled the Cases?

Mistakes have been made on every murder case ever investigated. Usually the things that were done right were greater than those done wrong, allowing the scales of justice to tip to a conviction. That does not imply that police mishandling led to a lack of prosecution in these cases.

The National Park Service's mishandling of Keith Call's vehicle and the evidence inside of it stands out as a large blunder. In their defense, the rangers had no idea that this was anything more than an abandoned vehicle. At the same time they should have been more suspicious given the distance from where Cathy Thomas's vehicle was discovered. The rangers simply lacked experience in murder cases and made what now appears as substantial mistakes. The rangers further compounded matters when they failed to call in the FBI—the bureau found out about the crime on the radio and responded on their own accord.

The handling of the deaths of Knobling and Edwards was a debacle. First was the police turning the vehicle and evidence over to Karl Knobling. Then was the loss of the fingerprint cards in the Knoblings' yard. The search of Ragged Island was poorly handled.

"I will be the first to admit that the whole investigation was a comedy of errors at first by all the agencies involved, including Virginia State Police," said Danny Plott. "The bodies were not located for three days I believe, even though 'part' of the area was searched on the first or second day."

This was capped off by how the families were informed of the discovery of their children's remains.

When Daniel Lauer's car was found abandoned at the rest area on I-64, going the opposite direction it should have been traveling, it should have triggered a more coordinated search. The fact their bodies were only one to two miles away from the vehicle is an embarrassment. Finding them even forty-eight hours after their disappearance would have provided vital evidence to the authorities. If nothing else, we would have known how Daniel met his fate. The failure to execute a grid-search centered on the vehicle has cost investigators vital clues and evidence such as the specific cause of death.

The most egregious mistakes made overall in the cases, at a tactical level, was the mishandling of the rape kits from the Thomas-Dowski case and the horrible lack of control of the crime scene photographs for all of the murders. It is difficult to instill confidence in the community and with the victims' families with such public blunders. It is a credit to the local media community that they have not released many of the graphic images of the victims from these photos—or that none of them have ended up on the internet over the years. It makes one wonder how well the FBI has controlled the remainder of the evidence.

Stepping back from the details of the cases, the biggest mistake that law enforcement did was twofold: 1) They did not get on the same page as to whether the cases were connected; 2) They did not form a true task force and include all of the other law enforcement agencies in the region.

Not aligning on the links between the cases has sent a steady stream of mixed messages over the years to both the public and the families of the victims. They needed to coordinate their communications and act in a single voice on the matter. Even to this date, it is not clear that the Virginia State Police and the FBI both believe that the crimes are connected. Certainly from what Bill Thomas has conveyed, the FBI believes that to be the case. Our interviews with former state police investigators indicate a strong thinking that both of their cases are *not* related. Only an arrest in any one of these cases will shatter this long-standing issue.

On the second point, the failure to bring together all of the local law enforcement agencies in the region to assist in the investigations is a mistake that cannot be overstressed. County sheriffs, city police, etc., often have a better feeling for their criminal community than the state police or the FBI. These agencies were kept at arm's length during the investigation of these crimes. In doing so, we have lost many possible opportunities to coordinate or gather useful information or leads.

Why were Robin and David at Ragged Island?

Robin Edwards and David Knobling spent only twenty minutes together on the evening of their disappearance before they met up for their fateful journey. Apparently they established enough of a connection with each other to arrange a rendezvous later that night. The purpose and destination of that early morning meeting could potentially resolve a number of issues.

David Knobling had a long-term girlfriend who was recently pregnant with their child. This seems to negate Robin and David getting together purely for intercourse—though that cannot be entirely eliminated. Robin was physically young but was much more mature in her actions and appearance. Perhaps this was nothing more than two young people getting together to do the kind of things that young people do.

Was it a drug deal gone wrong? This makes some sense on the surface. David had been paid earlier in the week but had not had a chance to cash his first paycheck. Neither victim was a heavy drug user though; both were what could be considered casual in their use of illegal drugs—if that. Robin did not have a sum of money that would have warranted a transaction of any size. What remains is one burning question with this theory: How could a simple drug deal for a small quantity of drugs have gone so horribly wrong? A drug dealer didn't have to kill them to rob them—the killer clearly had a pistol and had control of both victims.

Perhaps it is what the Edwards family likes to believe: Robin liked helping others. Maybe she and David went there simply to talk. Robin's mother believes that Robin may have wanted to talk with David.

"She was a helper—she liked talking to people, she was always trying to help them," Bonnie said.

With David facing the challenges of a pregnant girlfriend, it is just as likely Robin offered to sit and talk with him about it.

"Robin may have known his girlfriend was pregnant and she was a counselor. She thought she could fix anybody's problems."

To her, the age difference would have meant nothing. It is certainly the most palatable scenario.

Ragged Island has to this day a nefarious reputation and both of the victims would have known that. Teri Hailey, who was a law enforcement officer, recalls one of her experiences there.

"Me and Freddie White, a police officer from Newport News—he now works for York County—were stomping around the woods out there and somebody shot in our direction while we were out there. We hit the deck then we were out of there. It's dark. I've ridden back there at night, and it is dark out there—and scary. I wouldn't have gone back there."

The reason that Robin and David were at Ragged Island might tell us a great deal about their killer ... or it could be a dead end. Either way, it remains subject to speculation.

Where are the Bodies of Keith and Cassandra?

With all of the development along Route 17, J. Clyde Morris Boulevard, in the past three decades, one would think that if they were killed near that route, their remains would have turned up. Yet despite the growth in York County, there has been no recovery of the remains of either of these people.

There are myths and legends that circulate, mostly on the internet, as to where their bodies might be. The most widely posted is one dealing with a former Ralston Purina farm in Gloucester County, Virginia. An urban legend says that the two of them were buried in an abandoned silo on the farm site. This myth had spurred many people to go to the site with flashlights and shovels and play amateur archeologists looking for the bodies.

The authorities have looked into this legend and have found it to be unsubstantiated and without merit, but that does not prevent people from taking matters into their own hands.

According to Joyce Call, "I am familiar with the Purina

plant legend. It is actually not too far from me. The dentist that lives there has had to put up no trespassing signs and call the police from time to time because of people snooping around wanting to be the ones to discover the remains. The owner, Dr. Dodd, told me one time that when the stories were highlighted in the media, he could expect people snooping around his property."

Teri Hall is firm in her beliefs. "I'm convinced they are somewhere on J. Clyde. There's a lot of woods there. All of the way up 17 there's a lot of woods."

Her sister Paula Hailey Meehan offers another widely accepted theory.

"Or Crawford Road. Everybody's always talking about Crawford Road—the Dumping Grounds. Over the years there's been a whole lot of things found out at Crawford Road. I ran into a friend at a reunion and it came up.

"I said something about my sister, and he said, 'I heard about that with Crawford Road' as to where my sister might be. He said, 'I didn't bring it up! I didn't bring it up, but now we can talk about it.'

"It's known as the Dumping Grounds because … that's where the Calls always believed they were, they wanted to search there. Several people have been found there." As evidence of this, on May 20, 2017, skeletal remains were located off of Crawford Road, though they were not related to Keith and Cassandra.

Crawford Road seems to be one of those places that is tied to missing persons and even has two ghost stories related to it. On some internet lists, it tops them as being one of Virginia's most haunted locations. It is eerie and certainly has some connections to past crimes. The police have been informed of Crawford Road, but without something specific, the rumors of the remains being there stays in the realm of urban legend, not fact.

Why did the Killer Stop?

In the 1980s and '90s the standing thinking with criminal behavioral experts was that serial killers did not stop until they died, went to prison, or, if they had a partner, one of the partners died or went to prison. That was the accepted thinking during most of the Colonial Parkway Murders.

Irvin Wells of the FBI sums up his thinking on the cases: "If our theory that there were four double murders, lovers' lane situations—even pulling over at the rest area—which doesn't quite fit that … there were eight people killed and it was the same person, why did they stop? Why did they stop doing it?"

Time has advanced and with it our understanding about serial killers. There are some serial killers that *do* stop without dying. Gary Ridgeway, the Green River Killer, stopped when he got married. Another factor that can cause serial killers to stop all together are close calls with law enforcement—that realization that they were lucky to have gotten away with their crime sprees so far. Life changing events in the lives of serial killers can cause them to shatter their patterns.

The FBI's own guidebook to these kind patterned killings, *Serial Murders, Multi-Disciplinary Perspectives for Investigators*, points out that it is now accepted as a myth that serial killers cannot stop killing:

It has been widely believed that once serial killers start killing, they cannot stop. There are, however, some serial killers who stop murdering altogether before being caught. In these instances, there are events or circumstances in offenders' lives that inhibit them from pursuing more victims. These can include increased participation in family activities, sexual substitution, and other diversions.

- *BTK Killer Dennis Rader murdered ten victims from 1974 to 1991. He did not kill any other victims prior to being captured in 2005. During interviews conducted by law enforcement, Rader admitted to engaging in auto-erotic activities as a substitute for his killings.*

- *Jeffrey Gorton killed his first victim in 1986 and his next victim in 1991. He did not kill another victim and was captured in 2002. Gorton engaged in cross-dressing and masturbatory activities, as well as consensual sex with his wife in the interim."[22]*

With this change of thinking, it is entirely possible that this murderer or murderers simply stopped rather than dying or going to prison. If that is the case, he may very well still be out there, posing as a functional member of society.

Will the Murders be Solved?

After three decades, people—including the killer—may think that prosecution is impossible. We wouldn't have undertaken this book for the last year-plus of our lives if we thought that an arrest wasn't a realistic outcome. Cold cases are being solved all of the time from this period.

Technology advances allow for better testing of the evidence, and there are ample amounts of evidence available that can be tested from all of the crime scenes. Each new set of eyes that peruses the case files opens up the opportunity that something will jump out that has been overlooked for decades.

If the crimes are unconnected, that means four to eight murderers got away with killing eight young victims with rich lives and prospects ahead of them. If that doesn't galvanize a community to action, nothing will. Each of these crimes deserves resolution, either individually or jointly. No, deserves is not strong enough—*demands* fits better. We are all lesser people because of the actions of one to eight killers out there who have gone free at the expense of others' most precious possession, their lives.

As authors, we know we were not destined to solve this case. Our purpose was to tell the story of the Colonial Parkway Murders and the lives of the victims. That was our

---

22   https://www.fbi.gov/stats-services/publications/serial-murder

intention. It is our hope that in reading this book, you may have a tip or lead that helps authorities to solve the case.

As Jennifer Phelps put it, "Even resolution to one of these crimes, even if they prove to be unconnected, is a victory for all of us."

In this one sentiment, the families of the victims are solidly aligned.

The people that will solve the cases are you and the investigators. We've given you all of the facts and details we have been able to gather and have tried to present them in a logical and useful manner. We are empowering you, the reader, to dig deeper. Someone out there knows something—they may not even know what value that nugget of information is worth. Someone will come forward, and in doing so, the locked-up wheels of justice can once more churn. We, as authors, are putting the matter in your hands.

The answer is out there ... someone always knows the truth.

EPILOGUE

So much has been made about the debate as to whether the Colonial Parkway Murders are connected or not, that people lose sight of what really matters—the human loss. You don't have to believe that these murders are connected to understand their impact. You do not have to agree that a serial killer killed eight people and got away with it. You don't have to believe that law enforcement thus far has failed and made mistakes along the way. You can deny the theories and experts and draw your own conclusions. As authors, we invite you to do so. Now that you've read this book, the stories are yours, part of our collective conscience.

What you cannot do is ignore the impact of these crimes. Consider this:

- The victims have missed a total of 231 celebrations of their own birthdays.
- Likewise there have been 684 Christmases, Easters, and Fourth of Julys that they did not get to spend with families and friends.
- Six parents or stepparents have died that may not have if they didn't suffer with the grief of their lost or missing child—seven funerals where an empty chair was there to comfort loved ones.
- Two families have been denied a final resting place of their loved ones, Cassandra Hailey and Keith Call.
- One child was born and raised never knowing her father. (Tara Cook gave birth to David's daughter after his death.)
- Assuming average family sizes and that the victims would marry and have children, nineteen children were never born or raised in the world.
- Dozens of nieces and nephews never got to know their

aunts and uncles.

- Eight families still grieve to this day.
- Eight families are left behind without answers.
- Eight human beings were taken away from this world. With not a single person held accountable. Thus far justice is denied. Thus far …

The world is a lesser place because these wonderful people are not in it. In that respect, we are all victims of their killer. We have all been robbed of the millions of impacts their lives would have had on countless other people over the decades. Their deaths stole from their communities and scarred our own innocence. Their deaths and the mysteries that surround them should haunt us, should keep us up at night. At the very least, we should be demanding answers.

We asked the FBI and the Virginia State Police both to grant us interviews, to get answers to these thirty-year-old crimes, so that we could get as much information out as possible to the public. Our hope was to generate new tips, new leads. Both organizations denied us interviews.

These crimes, whether committed by one person or eight; connected or not; remains an open wound for the families and friends. They too are victims, weary of the media, tired of the lack of progress, and drained emotionally by their losses. They demand that we remember. Forgetting even one of these victims would be a crime. Moreover … they demand justice, in whatever form that may come.

We turn the responsibility for their justice over to you. As best we could as storytellers, we have tried to gather the facts. Our own personal theories and beliefs about suspects are unimportant. We sent out over 120 interview requests, conducted dozens of hours of interviews, made trips all over Virginia, scoured libraries, and pursued even the most trivial tidbit related to the story of the victims. Short of the authorities opening the files to us—which they refused— you have a relatively complete story of what transpired with these crimes.

Our role was to tell you the story as best we could. That is what good storytellers do. Now this story is in your hands. Your tips or memories could still lead to an arrest, conviction or the closing of one or more of these cases.

As Jennifer Phelps said, "Even solving one of these crimes is a victory for all of the families."

Should you have that vital tip or rekindled memory that might help, you can contact the FBI at (757) 455-0100 or the Virginia State Police at (804) 674-2000. If you reach out to us, we can pass it on as well, if you are not comfortable talking with the authorities. We can be reached at: Bpardoe870@ aol.com and victoriahester09@gmail.com.

The last words are not ours but go to the friends and family members of those that have been taken from us. This was never about us as writers. It is not about law enforcement or the media. It is about Cathy, Becky, Robin, David, Cassandra, Keith, Annamaria, and Daniel. It has been, and always will be, about them:

Christina Mallery for Daniel Lauer: "He was an incredible human being."

Ginny Minerick for Rebecca Dowski: "She had grown into being a wonderful young woman, and we were looking forward to getting to know her … really know her as an adult. And it just never happened."

Joyce Call-Canada for Keith Call: "His future was stolen. He had a really bright future and was really trying to make something of himself. We don't have anything but him in our hearts. One day we will."

Will Phelps for Annamaria Phelps: "She was truly a happy-go-lucky person who loved her family and friends unconditionally. She would have fought tooth and nail—and that is what I intend to do for her."

Paula Meehan for Cassandra Hailey: "It's so sad that her life is now down to a Rubbermaid container. We have nowhere to visit her. My sister has an angel statue in the front of her house. … That's for our angel, our Missy. She was kind and had the biggest heart. She never had a bad day."

Michael Knobling for David Knobling: "He was going in the right direction in life. He was a good guy; he did what he could to help people. Everything was taken away from him. He was one heck of a great brother."

Bonnie Edwards for Robin Edwards: "She was a free spirit and almost fearless. She always made us laugh."

Lynne Jordan for Cathy Thomas: "Back then we didn't have cell phones, we didn't have email and all of that. If you wanted to see somebody you just most likely dropped by. The best of times is when I went to Virginia Beach, and she would drop by, and we'd get in that little Honda of hers, listening to the same song over and over again, maybe being bad girls and having a hit on a marijuana cigarette, and giggling and laughing. To me, I looked up to her like I looked up to my sister. She was just infectious. You wanted to be around her. You wanted to be her friend. And if you were lucky enough to be her friend, you really were lucky. I loved her."

From Law Enforcement:

"I often hear through television shows or books, old police officers say, 'I don't sleep at night thinking about that crime' or 'That always haunts me.' I don't know if mine is to that degree. But if I had to know one thing before I pass from this world, I would love to know who or whom, or what group or what person or group of people committed those murders. Mine is more or less a professional want. The real victims of this is the victims themselves and the victim's families—especially Keith Call and Cassandra Hailey—who didn't even have remains to bury." — **Danny Plott of the Virginia State Police**

"I would say that the case is still possible. I think it's a mystery. It's a *frustrating* thing. There's not a hell of a lot of cases of that magnitude that aren't solved, but I've got to say, that's one. You know, there's eight people involved that were killed. It's been a long time. We're coming up on the thirtieth anniversary right? It's hard to believe that somebody would be able to kill them ... and get them away ... " — **Irvin Wells of the FBI**

And to the Killer ...

"I have an ongoing picture of everything he has turning to sand. I hope he has a beautiful house, a beautiful wife, I hope his kids are in college, and I hope that everything he has turns to sand. That he is revealed to be the evil that he is. When that happens—I'll be satisfied." — **Deb Hill, friend of Cathy Thomas**

ABOUT THE AUTHORS:

Blaine Pardoe is a New York Times Bestselling and award-winning author of numerous books in the science fiction, military non-fiction, true crime, paranormal, and business management genres. Born in Newport News, Virginia, he has appeared on a number of national television and radio shows to speak about his books. Mr. Pardoe has been a featured speaker at the US National Archives, the United States Navy Museum, and the New York Military Affairs Symposium. He was awarded the State History Award in 2011 by the Historical Society of Michigan and is a two-time silver medal and one time gold winner from the Military Writers Society of America. In 2013 Mr. Pardoe won the Harriet Quimby Award from the Michigan Aviation Hall of Fame for his contributions to aviation history.

His books have even been mentioned on the floor of the US Congress. His works have been printed in six languages and he is recognized worldwide for his historical and true crime works. Mr. Pardoe lives in Culpeper, Virginia.

Victoria Hester became a New York Times Best Selling Author in 2014 for her first true crime work in *The Murder of Maggie Hume*, the first collaboration with her father, Blaine Pardoe. She is a two-time winner of the Michael Carr Award for her work in nonfiction.

Ms. Hester works at Fauquier Hospital as a Registered Nurse. Wife, mother, nurse, and author—Victoria enjoys researching true crimes as much as writing about them. She specializes in cold cases, "Because that is where I feel I can do the most good—generating tips for the authorities and making sure these victims are not forgotten."

*For More News About Blaine L. Pardoe and
Victoria R. Hester Signup For Our Newsletter:*

http://wbp.bz/newsletter

*Word-of-mouth is critical to an author's long-
term success. If you appreciated
this book please leave a review on the Amazon sales page:*

http://wbp.bz/aspecialkindofevila

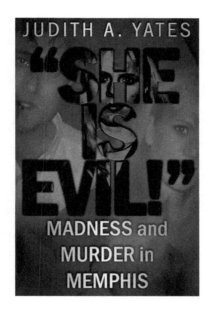

WILDBLUE
PRESS

Another Great True Crime
Read From WildBlue Press

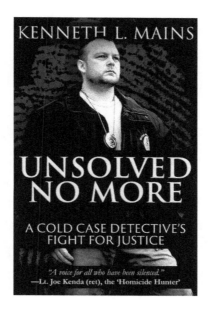

As a law enforcement officer for over fifteen years, Detective Kenneth L. Mains has investigated thousands of cases. Although he has been called "a modern day success story", it wasn't without failure. This book will take you on a journey from a struggling kid who barely graduated High School to a teenager who joined the Marine Corps and finally to a man who put himself through college in order to accomplish his lifelong goal of being a Detective.

Read More: **http://wbp.bz/unsolvednomore**

More True Crime You'll Love From WildBlue Press

BOGEYMAN: He Was Every Parent's Nightmare by Steve Jackson
"A master class in true crime reporting. He writes with both muscle and heart." (Gregg Olsen, New York Time bestselling author). A national true crime bestseller about the efforts of tenacious Texas lawmen to solve the cold case murders of three little girls and hold their killer accountable for his horrific crimes by New York Times bestselling author Steve Jackson. *"Absorbing and haunting!"* (Ron Franscell, national bestselling author and journalist)

wbp.bz/bogeyman

REPEAT OFFENDER by Bradley Nickell
"Best True Crime Book of 2015" (Suspense Magazine) A "Sin City" cop recounts his efforts to catch one of the most prolific criminals to ever walk the neon-lit streets of Las Vegas. *"If you like mayhem, madness, and suspense, Repeat Offender is the book to read."* (Aphrodite Jones, New York Times bestselling author)

wbp.bz/ro

DADDY'S LITTLE SECRET by Denise Wallace
"An engrossing true story." (John Ferak, bestselling author of Failure Of Justice, Body Of Proof, and Dixie's Last Stand) Daddy's Little Secret is the poignant true crime story about a daughter who, upon her father's murder, learns of his secret double-life. She had looked the other way about other hidden facets of his life - deadly secrets that could help his killer escape the death penalty, should she come forward.

wbp.bz/dls

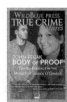

BODY OF PROOF by John Ferak
"A superbly crafted tale of murder and mystery."– (Jim Hollock, author of award-winning BORN TO LOSE) When Jessica O'Grady, a tall, starry-eyed Omaha co-ed, disappeared in May 2006, leaving behind only a blood-stained mattress, her "Mr. Right," Christopher Edwards, became the suspect. Forensic evidence gathered by CSI stalwart Dave Kofoed, a man driven to solve high-profile murders, was used to convict Edwards. But was the evidence tainted? A true crime thriller written by bestselling author and award-winning journalist John Ferak.

wbp.bz/bop

CPSIA information can be obtained
at www.ICGtesting.com
Printed in the USA
BVHW04s2250290618
520506BV00019B/596/P

9 781947 290044